Women's Inheritance Law in the Old Testament

Biblical Hermeneutics Rediscovered

The Series as the name suggests will focus on Biblical Hermeneutics, i.e., literary works concerned with methods of interpreting the Old and New Testaments of the Bible via different stream of topics like Literature and Poetry, Indigenous Philosophizing, Ethical response towards Ecology, Health and Healing, Science and Technology, Feminist Theology, Sociological approach towards Human Rights, Law and Politics, Arts, History of Ideas, Ancient Civilizations, Cultural Contiguity, Religious Cosmologies and Mysticism, Appraisal of various Theologians, World Peace and Harmony, Global Capitalism, Network Marketing, Cybertheology, Population and Demographics, Epigraphic Studies, Contextualized Education, and many others. We welcome a Mss. on any topic/s mentioned, whether they are original works, scholarly monographs, collections of conference papers, revised dissertations, or translations of historical documents. Through the Series we, the Publishers, are striving to put forward published works that may help Institutions, Academic Bodies, Researchers, Scholars and the World at large in furthering their respective knowledge and understanding on the concerned subject. We welcome your comments on our efforts and further suggestions on how we can enshrine new ray of analysing and explaining the written Texts through our upcoming books.

Biblical Hermeneutics Rediscovered - 28

Women's Inheritance Law in the Old Testament

Nyimangyang Chang

Christian World Imprints

First Published in 2020 by

Christian World Imprints
Christian Publishing & Books from India
C-3, Wazirpur Industrial Area
Delhi-110052
cwidelhi2017@gmail.com
www.ChristianWorldImprints.com
Phone: +91 11 41526079

ISBN: 978-93-5148-439-4 (HB)
ISBN: 978-93-5148-440-0 (PB)

Printed in India.

DEDICATION

This book is dedicated to my husband and children who have always stood by me and dealt with all of my absence from many family occasions with a smile.

The book in its original form is the dissertation submitted to the Senate of Serampore College (University), for the Doctor of Theology degree and is published with written permission. The Candidate is responsible for the title, contents and the opinions expressed in it.

Contents

Acknowledgment

It is, first of all, with the greatest of pleasure that I thank God for the provision, protection and guidance throughout my studies under the Senate of Serampore.

This book is based on my doctoral dissertation and I am indebted to so many people in bringing it thus far to completion. I wish to express my gratitude to all who supported me in this research through their concern, financial support, prayer and encouragement. I owe a particular debt of gratitude to my supervisor Professor Paulson Pulikottil, who provided me with the tools and skills necessary to focus and shape my thinking with his encyclopaedic knowledge. He has guided me by his scholarly wisdom, insightful remarks, and the challenge to be creative. His critical observations have helped me to improve the quality of this research. I also wish to thank Dr. Leslene, Moa and Naong, women and man of wisdom and warmth, for their help in myriad details.

I would also like to thank the library staff at Union Biblical Seminary, Pune; Nagaland State library under the department of Art and Culture, Government of Nagaland, Kohima; Ura Academy, College of Teacher Education, Kohima; District Museum, Tuensang; Papal Seminary, Pune; United Theological College, Bangalore; Eastern Theological College, Jorhat; without whose help and services my library research would not have been easy. I sincerely thank various individuals for providing the research materials.

I would also like to express my sincere thanks to all the women and men of my survey towns and villages for their answers to my queries during interviews. I thank all of those who took time to answer and return the questionnaire and the focus group members for their active participation in the discussion.

In a special way, I am deeply grateful to my husband Dr. L. Bimol for his monumental assistance in ways too numerous to list. He has sustained and encouraged me unfailingly over the years. I thank my children Manna and Yensen for their support, sacrifice and encouragement. I also thank my loving parents, brothers, sisters and friends for their constant support and encouragement. Each of them has contributed and offered support in numerous ways.

Thank you all!

Foreword

The various movements for women's rights have impacted the institutions worldwide—the legislatures, law-enforcement systems, the judiciary, religious customs, etc. However, the speed and the spread of these changes in favour of women were never equal. There are many societies tucked away from the main streams of these changes. They remain untouched by the changes these movements have effected. The Chang women mainly in Nagaland and scattered in the neighbouring states of India are one of them.

This work is by a Chang woman. She has endeavoured to explore the property rights of women in the Bible and in her own community. She underscores the fact that Chang women are still not treated equal to their male counterparts when it comes to property rights. So, she turns to the biblical witness regarding the women's right to ancestral property.

Nyimang Chang offers a detailed study of the case of the daughters of Zelophehad found in Numbers 27:1-11. This provides the biblical basis for her exploration. In this narrative, we find a highly patriarchal society allowing women equal right with men to their ancestral property. This is a crucial development in Israelite legal system where the legislators make an exemption in favour of women.

This study is remarkable in many ways. First of all its breadth is remarkable. The author explores the legal systems in the Ancient West Asian cultures and in the various traditions of the Old Testament. Secondly, the author's locus contributes to its comprehensiveness. The author is positioned to offer a 360 degree view of the case. She is a Chang-Naga woman, thus an insider. She is treated as a woman without any legal right to her ancestral property like all other Chang women. However, she is an outsider as well. She is married outside her own community and thus subject to another legal system. As an insider, she has a more empathetic knowledge of the situation. At the same time, as an outsider and as an academic, her study is more objective using tools that are not usually available to ordinary Chang women.

Though the study is limited to the inheritance laws of the Chang community, we need to realize that the situation is not limited to the Chang women. The universal application of the Biblical truth in this particular regard contributes valuable insights for the liberation of women in our times.

Paulson Pulikottil M.A. (Psy), PhD
The Director, iCore Consultancy Services
Pune, India

Abbreviations

abr.	abridged
AB	Anchor Bible
ABD	*Anchor Bible Dictionary*. Edited by D.N. Freedman et al. 6 vols. New York: Doubleday, 1992.
ACLS	Angami Christian Literature Service
ATJ	*Allahabad Theological Journal*
Anbib	*Analectabiblica*
ANE	Ancient Near East
ANET	*Ancient Near Eastern Texts Relating to the Old Testament.* Edited by J.B. Pritchard. Princeton, New Jersey: Princeton University Press, 1969.
ASCE	*Annual of the Society of Christian Ethics*
AWA	Ancient West Asia
BBR	*Bulletin for Biblical Research*
BCE	before the Common Era
BDB	Brown, S.R. Driver, and C.A. Briggs. *A Hebrew and English Lexicon of the Old Testament.* Oxford: Clarendon Press, 1907.
BHS	Biblia Hebraica Stuttgartensia. Edited by K. Ellinger and W. Rudolph, Stuttgart. Deutsche Bibelgesellschaft, 1997.
BibInt	*Biblical Interpretation*
BR	*Biblical Research*
BTESSC	Board of Theological Education of the Senate of Serampore College
C	*Circa* (Latin), approximately
CBLT	Chang Baptist Lashuong Thangyen (Chang Baptist Church Association)
CBTS	Chang Baptist Thangyen Sao (Chang Baptist Women Association)
CC	Covenant Code
CCA	Christian Conference of Asia

CE	Common Era
CEDAW	Convention on the Elimination of all forms of Discrimination against Women
cf.	Compare
Chap/s.	Chapter/s
C–KLR	*Chicago–Kent Law Review*
COS	Context of Scripture
CTC	Clark Theological College
CTM	*Currents in Theology and Mission*
D	Deuteronomic
DC	Deuteronomic Code
DCH	*Dictionary of Classical Hebrew*. Edited by David J.A. Clines et al. Sheffield: Sheffield Phoenix Press, 2007.
DOTP	*Dictionary of the Old Testament: Pentateuch*. Edited by T. Desmond Alexander and David W. Baker. Illinois: IVP Academic, 2003.
DOTHB	*Dictionary of the Old Testament: Historical Books*. Edited by Bill T. Arnold and H. G. M. Williamson. Downers Grove: InterVarsity Press USA, 2005.
ed/s.	Editor/s, edition/s
e.g.	*Exempli gratia*, for example
f.	Feminine
FGD	Focus Group Discussion
G	The Septuagint
GKC	Gesenius, Kautzsch, and Cowley. Edited by *Hebrew Grammar*. Oxford: Clarendon Press, 1970.
HL	Hittite Law
HSS	*Harvard Semitic Series* (miscellaneous texts from Nuzi)
HTS	*Hervormde Teologiese Studies*
HUCA	Hebrew Union College Annual
ICC	International Critical Commentary
IJT	*Indian Journal of Theology*
Int	*Interpretation*
IRM	*International Review of Mission*
ISPCK	Indian Society for Promoting Christian Knowledge
IVP	InterVarsity Press
JAAR	*Journal of the American Academy of Religion*
JAOS	*Journal of the American Oriental Society*
JBL	*Journal of Biblical Literature*
JBQ	*Jewish Bible Quarterly*
JBS	*Journal of Black Studies*
JES	*Journal of Ecumenical Studies*

JETS	*Journal of the Evangelical Theological Society*
JIS	*Journal for Islamic Studies*
JJWS & GS	*Journal of Jewish Women's Studies & Gender Issues*
JSOT	*Journal for the Study of the Old Testament*
JSP	Journal for the Study of the Pseudepigrapha
JSOTSup.	*Journal for the Study of the Old Testament* Supplement Series
KJV	Kings James Version
LE	Law of Eshnunna
LH	Law of Hammurabi
LL	Law of Lipit-Ishtar
LU	Law of Ur-Namma
LXX	Septuagint
mas.	Masculine
MAL	Middle Assyrian Law
Mes	Inscription of Mes
MJT	*Master's Journal of Theology*
MS/MSS	Manuscript/Manuscripts
MSJ	*Master's Seminary Journal*
MT	The Massoretic Text (vocalized text of the Hebrew Bible)
NBDB	New Brown–Driver–Briggs
NBL	Neo-Babylonian Law
NEA	Near Eastern Archaeology
NIDP	*New Interpreter's Dictionary of the Bible*
NIDOTTE	*New International Dictionary of Old Testament Theology and Exegesis*
NIV	New International Version
NP	Nagaland Post (Newspaper)
NRSV	New Revised Standard Version
NSCW	Nagaland State Commission for Women
NT	New Testament
OBC	Oxford Bible Commentary
OM	Operation Mobilization
OT	Old Testament
P	Priestly source
pf.	Perfect
pl.	Plural
PRS	*Perspectives in Religious Studies*
PSB	*Princeton Seminary Bulletin*
PT	*Political Theology*
PTI	Theological Publications of India
QBC	*Catholic Biblical Quarterly*
R & E	*Review & Expositor*

RSR	*Religious Studies Reviews*
RTR	*Reformed Theological Review*
SAIACS	South Asia Institute of Advanced Christian Studies
Sam.	The Samaritan Pentateuch
SAT	Social Action Trust
SATHRI	South Asia Theological Research Institute
SBL	*Society of Biblical Literature*
SBLABS	Society of Biblical Literature Archaeology and Biblical Studies
SCM	Student Christian Movement
Sing:	Singular
SWC	Studies in World Christianity
Syr.	Syriac
TB	*Tyndale Bulletin*
TDCC	Tribal Development and Communication Centre
TDOT	*Theological Dictionary of the Old Testament.*
Tg.	The Talgum
Trans.	Translated by
TSC	*Tribal Study Centre*
TT	*Theology Today*
UDHR	Universal Declaration of Human Rights
UN	United Nations
USQR	*Union Seminary Quarterly Review*
Vg.	The Vulgate
v, vv.	Verse/s
Viz.	Namely
vol.	Volume
VT	*Vetus Testamentum*
WBC	Women's Bible Commentary
WBC	Word Biblical Commentary
W&W	*Word & World*
YHWH	Yahweh
ZAW	*Zeitschriftfür die Alttestamentliche Wissenschaft* Abbreviation for Books of the Bible
Gen.	Genesis
Exod.	Exodus
Lev.	Leviticus
Num.	Numbers
Deut.	Deuteronomy
Josh.	Joshua
Judg.	Judges
Sam.	Samuel

Kgs.	Kings
Chr.	Chronicles
Neh.	Nehemiah
Ps.	Psalm
Prov.	Proverbs
Isa.	Isaiah
Jer.	Jeremiah
Ezek.	Ezekiel
Mic.	Micah
Zech.	Zechariah
Col.	Colossians

NOTE: Abbreviations for Old Testament and New Testament books follow Hunter P. Mabry, *A Manual for Researchers and Writers,* 2013.

Other Ancient Sources

Akkadian
Ancient Near Eastern Text
Assyrian LawTablet A, Law 46.
Law of Hammurabi
Cuneiform
Gudea Statue B
Law of Eshnuna
Law of Lipit–Ishtar paragraph B
MAL
Nuzi
Old Assyrian, 19th century BCE Text (*Inscriptions Cuneiformes du Kult'p'*)
Ostracon
Sumerian

General Introduction

INTRODUCTION

As I grew up as a Chang woman, I realized that I don't have any right on my father's property as my brothers have. My only disqualification is being a Chang Naga woman. This is besides all other injustice that I had to face in the family, the society and the church for just being a woman. This research is inspired by my own experience of injustice.

My casual reading of the act of the daughters of Zelophehad gave me a glimmer of hope. I grew up with a hope that, divine rights sanctioned by God can be reclaimed. There is a message of liberation and hope entrenched in this text. This personal experience has, quite naturally, extended to my academic work.

Here, I speak on behalf of the suppressed voices of Chang women, and in general, Naga women who are the victims of the patriarchal culture. It is an attempt to propose ways of reading the biblical texts to achieve full humanity. Therefore, this research is not just an academic research but it is part of my experience as a woman in a patriarchal society. It is undertaken with a hope to strengthen Chang women in their struggle to reclaim their rights as a rightful citizen of the land.

1. Issues Encountered

The proposed research aims at investigating the consequences of the action of the daughters of Zelophehad in seeking to inherit their father's land as described in Numbers 27:1–11, and its implications for Chang Naga women.[1] The daughters of Zelophehad presented a distinctive case before Moses and the elders of the people so that they could inherit their father's land. They petitioned the court that, since their father died without leaving any male issue they should be accorded the legal status of heirs and be entitled to inherit their deceased father's property. This case created an important legal precedent that paved the way for the enactment of new law on land inheritance for women. This story has been interpreted as the

[1] The terms like the daughters, five daughters, daughters of Zelophehad and Zelophehad's daughters are used interchangeably.

preservation of their father's name and as a result the daughters' contribution to establishing the right of women to inherit land and in the long term to claim a more equal standing with the men of their tribe has been overlooked.

2. An Elaboration

The customary law of the ancient Israelite society is that, each of the twelve tribes of Israel was to own a specific region of land. All the families in each tribe would be allotted some portion of the tribe's lands. Since only men from the age of twenty were counted in the census (Num. 1, 26), the original scheme allowed only male members of the family to inherit the land. But, what happened when a father died without having male heirs? Could his daughters inherit the land instead? It would seem that the answer to this latter question was "No." So, the challenge by the five daughters of Zelophehad whose names were Mahlah, Noah, Hoglah, Milcah, and Tirzah represented a bold and unprecedented attempt to not only change the law of land inheritance, but also to declare that women had the same rights that the men of the tribe had.

The proposed research work focuses upon evaluating the neglected roles and actions of the daughters. It is the contention of the present studies that land inheritance from the feminist perspective in the context of these five daughters has not been dealt with sufficiently. Yael Shemesh, examines the story of Zelophehad's daughters from a gender perspective, and she concludes that the story is set in a patriarchal and androcentric context with "preservation of father's name" as the main theme.[2] Gilad Gevaryahu studies the root word גרע, and claims that the Zelophehad's daughters sought to keep the family's name intact. He further claims that the second case in Numbers 36:1–12 aims to keep the tribe intact.[3]

Numbers 27:1–11 needs further attention to appraise more fully the daughters' act—women who took such a bold step in a context where all social pressures were against woman inheriting property. They were ordinary women who had the strength and courage to challenge the unjust status quo of land inheritance, and by doing so, established that women had rights like men. Women tend to be depicted in the Old Testament in a marginal state however, proper examination of the biblical texts is important to see whether such argument is justified.

---

[2] For further reference see, Yael Shemesh, "A Gender Perspective on the Daughters of Zelophehad: Bible, Talmudic Midrash, and Modern Feminist Midrash," in *BibInt* 15/1 (2007): 80, 84, 93, 108; Dora Rudo Mbuwayesango, argues that the account of the five daughters serves male family, clan or tribal interests where the main concern is to keep land in the original tribal territory. Cf. Dora Rudo Mbuwayesango, "Can Daughters be Sons? The Daughters of Zelophehad in Patriarchal and Imperial Society," in *Relating to the Text: Interdisciplinary and Form-Critical Insights on the Bible* eds. Timothy J. Sandoval and Carleen Mandolfo, (London: T&T Clark International, 2003), 258.

[3] Gilad J. Gevaryahu, "The Root גרע in the Bible: The Case of the Daughters of Zelophehad and beyond," in *JBQ* 41/2 (April 1, 2013): 110–2.

The larger story of the Zelophehad's daughters, representing the new generation, is told in four separate places in the Hebrew Bible.[4] With their accomplishment recorded in the Old Testament, they hold a place of honour in the chronicles of early Israel. The Promised Land, which is perhaps the most important gift of *YHWH* to Israel, is to be apportioned according to the number of names of the second generation counted in the census record in Numbers 26. The daughters of Zelophehad knew that they would be left without an inheritance, so they presented their case before the whole assembly at the entrance to the tent of meeting. They specifically brought their case to inherit their father's share in the Promised Land to the attention of the tribes' chieftains, high priest Eleazar and to Moses. Their individual case served to change the Israelite inheritance law to include women.

It is clear that they were the first women to petition a court of law in the Old Testament. Their legal challenge received God's unreserved approval, thereby becoming instrumental in establishing a law which the men including Moses had overlooked—a law that recognized the dispossessed and disconnected women in their community.

Being single women in a patriarchal society meant having to live without any adequate securities for existence or survival. This research focuses on the role and status of women in the ancient Israelite society in order to see what prompted them to take such a bold step in presenting their case before the assembly.

The daughters of Zelophehad pose the rhetorical question, "Why should the name of our father be withdrawn from the midst of his clan because he had no sons?" (Num. 27:4). The assumption inherent in this statement is that, a name exists as long as it is attached to land. It is because in the agrarian structure, land bestowed on people economic success and provided them with a sense of identity and rootedness in society. It assures them a sense of belongingness to be part of the community. With this injustice brought to the attention of the people in power, the entire system shifted to protect those whom it had initially neglected.

The story of the five daughters also reminds us to recognize the consequences of structural and systemic injustice, and the importance of changing those structures and systems to meet the needs of those whose rights in society are denied. The story demonstrates the unfairness they suffered in the wilderness. They decided to contest the androcentric argument by citing the reason as "preserving their father's name" as it was the only means that men can understand and identify with. In fact, their act is more than preserving their father's name.

---

[4] Num. 26:33; 27:1, 36:11 and in Josh. 17:3. *YHWH* has made it clear that only the new generation will enter the Promised Land, Num. 14:20–35.

The five daughters referred to Korah's assembly to dissociate him from a movement which is considered to be against divinely established order.[5] They present their case that their father died in the wilderness for his own sin.

Nine chapters further on in the Book of Numbers (36:1–11), we read that the family heads of Zelophehad's clan assembled and brought a complaint. The tribe of Manasseh, to which Zelophehad belonged, worried that they might lose part of their inheritance if the inherited women marry to other tribes. Moses consulted *YHWH* and decreed that the inherited women should marry within their father's tribe in order to prevent family's land from transferring to another tribe. Biblical law clearly mentioned that land is not to be transferred outside the family's ownership.

In the Nuzian document, it is said that all citizens in Arraphe, including slaves, were able to seek redress in court, including litigation concerning property ownership and other civil and criminal matters.[6] There is said to be certain similarities between Nuzi and Old Testament laws, therefore, this research attempts to bring out the parallel practices found in Ancient West Asia (hereafter, AWA) and the Old Testament texts, especially in regard to the tribal control of land.[7]

So much for the detail and broad background of the story of the daughters of Zelophehad, now compare this narrative to the Chang tribe where patriarchy is particularly strong.[8] For example, there are only two ordained women in the church. Even from the moment of birth, the life of a boy is celebrated as an event of great joy. It is also important to note that Chang women in most cases lose their identity once they get married. The family surname is discarded and she must take her husband's name, indicating that she no longer belongs to her paternal family.

In the inheritance law of Chang women are not given any share. In the church and society she is denied the leadership status, and she is not a part of any decision making body. That a woman should be able to reclaim her individual identity so completely taken away by such a traditional patriarchal structure is more than just important. What is at stake here is the restoration of basic human rights. In the light of this, the present research has taken the biblical account

[5] Ankie Sterring, "The Will of the Daughters," in *A Feminist Companion to Exodus to Deuteronomy*, series No. 6, ed. Athalya Brenner, (Sheffield: Sheffield Academic Press, 1994), 90.

[6] Martha A. Morrison, "Nuzi," in *ABD,* vol. 4, eds. David Noel Freedman et al., (New York: Doubleday, 1992), 1156.

[7] Alberto Soggin, mentions one the similarities found both in ancient Israel and Nuzi. In Exod. 21:2–6; Deut. 15:12–18; and Jer. 34:9–14 it, mention about an individual who in need of particular protection had entered into slavery, thus guaranteed shelter and food. Legal texts which have been unearthed from the North-eastern Mesopotamian city state of Nuzi contain the parallel story of people who goes into slavery. See, J. Alberto Soggin, *An Introduction to the History of Israel and Judah*, trans. John Bowdon, (London: SCM Press, 1999), 112.

[8] Chang is one of the tribes in Nagaland. The tribe lives in the Tuensang district of Nagaland, India.

concerning the five daughters of Zelophehad. They voiced the injustice prevalent in their society, and they were publicly and legally allotted land in the Promised Land according to God's decree. This story ultimately presents as a powerful theological and social paradigm for the empowerment of Chang women, not only to claim property inheritance rights, but to reclaim her lost identify in the society. Status of Chang Women, her role in the family, society and church will be dealt in detail along with the root cause of all these restrictions made on them. The research further elaborates on the daughters' act as an important paradigm for Chang women to be liberated from unjust practices in the society.

Hypothesis

The assumption here is that the five daughters played an important role, initiating changes in the Israelites legal system. This research will empower women as to point out the injustice prevalent in the present structure and to show that the biblical text has a story where women were granted land inheritance rights. A careful and systematic study of this story can correct the present social system and practices which excludes women especially in sharing power.

3. Background of the Book of Numbers

The Book of Numbers acquired its English title from the Latin *Numeri*, itself derived from the Greek *Arithmoi*. The Hebrew title is בְּמִדְבַּר "In the Wilderness," the fifth word in the first verse.[9] Many Old Testament scholars agree that the diverse materials in Numbers were shaped and developed throughout many different periods and social situations ranging from the earliest to the latest times in Israel's history.[10] It is a mixture of both old traditions and later elements, mostly in Priestly tradition with the holy land as the books' unifying theme.

In spite of its diverse materials and long period in its composition, it has a basic threefold structure with three different geographical references: the wilderness of Sinai, the wilderness of Paran and the plains of Moab. The forty years embrace two generations and both the accounts begin with the census (Num. 1, 26). The present event took place in the plains of Moab.

---

[9] Elmer E. Flack, "Flashes of New Knowledge: Recent Study and the Book of Numbers," in *Int* 13/1 (January 1959): 3; Dennis T. Olson, "Book of Numbers," in *DOTP*, eds. Desmond Alexander and David W. Baker (Illinois: InterVarsity Press, 2003), 611.

[10] Several scholars agree that the Book of Numbers is a mixture of many sources, see B. A. Levine, *Numbers 1–20: A New Translation with Introduction and Commentary* (New York, 1993), 45; See also, Ada Taggar-Cohen, "Law and Family in the Book of Numbers: The Levites and the Tidennutu Documents from Nuzi," in *VT* 48/1 (January 1998): 74–5; Adriane Leveen, *Memory and Tradition in the Book of Numbers* (Cambridge: Cambridge University Press, 2008), 22; Horst Seebass, "'Holy' Land in the Old Testament: Numbers and Joshua," in *VT* 56/1 (2006), 92.

3.1. The Literary Formation of the Book

Many biblical scholars agree that the Book of Numbers was composed of Priestly material because perspective of the priestly tradition dominates the book.[11] There are also some Jewish and Christian scholars who argue for Mosiac period, before the rise of Israel kingship.[12] No doubt the book is a product of fairly lengthy history of literary development that deals with the liberated community with the possession of land as the goal of the journey. This leads to the study of some key verses in 27:1–11.

3.2. Important Key Verses in Numbers 27:1–11

The narrative spans eleven verses, set in three episodes that is,

a) The daughters present their case (chap. 27:1)
b) *YHWH* pronounces judgment (chap. 27:2–5) and
c) *YHWH* instructs future generations (chap. 6–11).

Daughters of Zelophehad 27:1

This first verse introduces the five daughters by names that are to present the case before Moses, Eleazar, chieftains and the congregation. The Hebrew root word קרב, literal meaning, "coming close or bringing close," plays an important role in this story. The story begins with "the daughters approached close," and ends with "Moses brought the case before *YHWH*."[13]

Zelophehad's daughters are introduced by recounting their patrimony back to the most significant ancestors, tracing back to the seven generations. It was done in order to establish their connections to the Israelite community. The author signals that they are significant family that had a complaint rather than just the accidental family.[14]

"Why should the name of our father be taken . . ." (27:4). In this verse they used the expression לָמָּה יִגָּרַע שֵׁם־אָבִינוּ מִתּוֹךְ מִשְׁפַּחְתּוֹ כִּי אֵין לוֹ בֵּן meaning,

[11] Louis Ska talks about how the Book of Numbers functions as a linchpin between Priestly composition present mainly in Genesis–Leviticus, and Deuteronomy and the Deuteronomistic work. Cf. Jean Louis Ska, "Old and New in the Book of Numbers," in *Biblica* 95/1 (2014): 106–7; Rainer Albertz, "A Pentateuchal Redaction in the Book of Numbers? The Late Priestly Layers of Numbers 25–36," in *ZAW* 125/2 (2013), 221.

[12] Herbert Livingston has compiled good materials for background study of the Pentateuch. The book has three distinct part, namely, historical setting, literary parallel with AWA, and critical procedures applicable to the Pentateuch. He has clearly mentioned how Jewish and Christian scholars believed that Moses was the author of the Pentateuch, and how this view continued in Judaism and in Christianity until the 9th century AD. Cf. George Herbert Livingston, *The Pentateuch in its Cultural Environment* (Grand Rapids: Baker Book House, 1977), 218–9.

[13] Yonatan Grossman, "Divine Command and Human Initiative: A Literary view on Numbers 25–31," in *BibInt* 15/1 (2007), 64–5.

[14] John D. Litke, "The Daughters of Zelophehad," in *CTM* 29/3 (June 2002), 210.

"Why should the name of our father be taken away from his clan because he had no son?"[15] Their appeal clearly testifies that there had been no provision for the acknowledgement of daughters as lawful heirs in the existing Israelite law of inheritance.

As the narration unfolds, it revealed about Korah and the Levites who joined with Dathan and Abiram (all from the southern region) and protested against the leadership of Moses in appointing Aaron to the post of high priest. The fact is that, the Lord had assigned each tribe and family to a particular place in his economy. Some were assigned places of great honour in the service, while others had lesser roles. Hence, to rebel against that structure was to rebel against YHWH.[16] It is clear that the rebellion in Numbers 16 was a direct assault on the order established by God. This angered Moses, and upon his specific urging, a wide gap opens on the ground and Korah, Dathan, Abiram and their families are swallowed up.[17] Zelophehad's daughters strongly assert that their father did not belong to this (Korah's assembly), stressing that their father has never belonged to the wrong assembly.[18]

Moses Took Their Case Before YHWH 27:5

An appeal was made to divine legislative authority. Moses brought their case before YHWH to the tent of meeting, a place where Moses met with YHWH (Exod. 33:7–11). This research will further investigate as to why Moses had to inquire from God regarding this specific case.

Verdict issued by YHWH 27:6–11

In these verses, precedent-setting decision was issued. God's verdict was issued indeed to give them their father's share of the inheritance. This decision was accompanied by a general law regarding such a case for the future generation of Israel.

4. Significance of the Research

The society that we live in today is marked by differences, injustices, and gender inequalities. It is painful to see especially Chang women, who continue to suffer under the dominance of men both in church and society. This research is significant, because the Bible has the answer to solve the injustices prevalent in the society, especially in relation to women's inheritance rights. It will enable the women to draw inspiration to move forward to claim their rights. This research

---

[15] Translated from *BHS*.

[16] Iain M. Duguid, *Numbers: God's Presence in the Wilderness*, ed. R. Kent Hughes (Wheaton, Illinois: Crossway Books, 2006), 199–202.

[17] Ronald M. Green, "The Korah Episode: A Rationalistic Reappraisal of Rabbinic Anti-Rationalism," in *ASCE*, (1981), 103.

[18] Further discussion on this issue is made in chapter four.

is also significent because it discusses how women are represented in the Bible, especially in the Old Testament. In fact, Old Testament does not represent the experiences of the entire Israelite society of which the commoners comprised the vast majority of the population.[19] It has silenced the voice of women and it tends to be used as the basis for delineating women as only suitable for submissive roles assigned by the patriarchal ideology. Therefore, there is a need to uncover the different roles and contributions women have made in the Old Testament in order to empower women in the struggle against the oppression of a patriarchy culture, wherever it occurs.

It is important to understand the story of Zelophehad's daughters in a fresh light by exploring the contribution they made in the society of their own times. Close reading suggests that the daughters wanted to change or modify the patriarchal norm that only sons can provide the link between generations. The daughters also struck a blow for family loyalty, because they were also fighting to ensure their father's name should not be forgotten in the pages of Israelite history. Their boldness resulted in bringing changes to the legal system of Israel, which changes continued from that day. This research attempts to let the ancient texts speak meaningfully to a new context.

This research is important to the situation which still exists in many cultures today, like the Chang community, which still adheres to the out-dated customary laws of a patriarchal society which denies equal participation and justice for all genders. It will give awareness to the Chang women about their denied rights and will set before them the example of the Zelophehad's daughters, who fought in their own ways the injustice of their time and achieved their goal.

5. Definition

5.1. Zelophehad

Zelophehad is part of the generation of Israelites who departed from Egypt under Moses' leadership and died during the forty years in the wilderness. He was a member of the tribe of Manasseh. According to the biblical narrative, he died in the wilderness leaving behind five daughters but no son.

5.2. Ancient Israel

The proposed research focuses on the ancient Israelite society during the settlement period within the Pentateuchal narratives. In the Pentateuch, the people of Israel are known as בְּנֵי יִשְׂרָאֵל literally translated as "sons of Israel." This generally refers to the members of the twelve tribes of Israel as an ethnic designation for the

[19] R. L. Hnuni, *Vision for Women in India: Perspectives from the Bible, Church and Society*, (Bangalore: Asian Trading Corporation, 2009), 244; Cf. Susan Ackerman, "Digging up Deborah: Recent Hebrew Bible Scholarship on Gender and the Contribution of Archaeology," in *NEA* 66/4 (December 2003), 174.

descendent of Jacob.[20] The people of Israel slowly came in contact with various other groups of people and nations into a more complex and more urban-based community. Today the scholars have realized that the biblical history took place in social as well as in political context, and recognized the importance of the awareness of the ancient social structures.

5.3. AWA

Through the explorations and excavations carried on in Egypt, Mesopotamia, Asia Minor and Syria, a wealth of new information has become available. These extra biblical sources help in understanding the content of the biblical texts. Old Testament scholarship without acquaintances with the culture of AWA is incomplete.[21] The Mesopotamian evidence shows many parallels to Old Testament customs and ideas, as John Walton claims that the genuine conclusion for Old Testament text was human, not divine.[22] This comparative approach seeks to find some similarities in the social practices to represent the biblical text against its wider literary and cultural environment.

5.4. Biblical and Ancient West Asian Law

Law plays a very prominent role in the Old Testament. There are many terms for law in the Hebrew Bible, such as חק (statute), מִשְׁפָּט (judgment, decision), תּוֹרָה (law).[23] The proposed research work will concentrate on תּוֹרָה which has been translated as law or instruction. It is also surmised that תּוֹרָה is a loan word from Akkadian *tertu(m)*, meaning "directive, instruction."[24] There are about 220 occurrences of תּוֹרָה throughout the Old Testament revealing three main aspects which involves firstly, teaching or instruction to be learned, secondly, commands to be obeyed and thirdly, guidance about how to live in specific situations.[25]

Narrowing down to the Pentateuch, this particular word is mentioned fifty-five times which is used in five different ways, firstly, an individual pronouncement, secondly, a group of laws on a single subject, thirdly, a particular collection of laws, fourthly, a general description for God's laws and fifthly, a combination of

---

20 R. J. D. Knauth, "Israelite," in *DOTP*, 452.

21 Hermann Gunkel, William R. Scott, and John J. Scullion, *The Stories of Genesis*, trans. John J. Scullion (Vallejo: D & F Scott Publication Inclusive, 1994), xv; Cf. M. J. Selman, "Law," in *DOTP*, 505.

22 John H. Walton, *Ancient Near Eastern Thought and the Old Testament: Introducing the Conceptual world of the Hebrew Bible* (Grand Rapids: Baker Academic, 2006), 16.

23 J. M. Sprinkle, "Law," in *DOTHB*, eds. Bill T. Arnold and H. G. M. Williamson (Downers Grove: InterVarsity Press USA, 2005), 643.

24 L. Koehler and Walter Baumgartner, *The Hebrew And Aramaic Lexicon of the Old Testament*, vol. 4, (Leiden: Brill Academic Publication, 1999), 1710.

25 Selman, "Law," in *DOTP*, 498.

narrative and laws.[26] Since the present study is about the law of inheritance, the proposed research makes comparative research on the parallel practices found in the AWA and Egypt with the biblical evidences.

5.5. Inheritance

There are two basic roots for the concept of inheritance in the Old Testament: נחל literal meaning "have or get as a possession or inheritance," and ירש which is translated as "to take or gain possession of," depending upon the grammatical form and the context. It is from the root ירש.[27] In each case, the emphasis was more generally upon possession than upon the process of succession. These two words occur frequently in Books of Numbers and Deuteronomy which look forward for the allotment of land in Canaan and in the Book of Joshua how it was put into effect. This research deals with how the inheritance law was practiced both in ancient Israel and in AWA.

5.6. Allotment of Land

The allocation of land to each tribe was made not by Moses, nor by a council of elders but by lot (Num. 26:55–56). The lot was regarded as a technique by which God in His authority directed the choices. Therefore, in the minds of the Israelites, the distribution of the land was divinely ordained. This is an indication that there was a special relationship between the tribe and its land. The initial division of the land in Israel was explicitly to the households within the tribes. This allocation by lot completed the divine charge given to Joshua in bringing the Israelites into their inheritance (Josh. 1:6). The territory assigned by God through the lot became a tribe's inheritance and possession.[28]

5.7. Zelophehad's Daughters' Act

The daughters' act resulted in making a new law in Israel and they were added to the chain of succession. This story creates a contrast between the census of the heirs to the land conducted by divine command, and the amendment to the law of inheritance, that comes in the wake of human initiative. The narrator highlights the fact that these women are not hesitant to make a move unprecedented in the history of Israel. Because of their courageous act, they are given the status of name bearers of their father's family symbolized by the transference of inheritance to them.

---

[26] Selman, "Law," in *DOTP*, 498.

[27] H. H. Schmid, "ירש," in *Theological Lexicon of the Old Testament,* vol. 2, eds. Ernst Jenni and Claus Westermann, trans. Mark E. Biddle (Peabody, Massachusetts: Hendrickson Publishers, 1997), 579.

[28] L. Daniel Hawk, "Allotment of Land," in *New Interpreter's Dictionary of the Bible,* vol. 1 (A–C), eds. Katharine Doob Sakenfeld et at., (Nashville: Abingdon Press, 2006), 103.

5.8. Chang Tribe

Chang is one of the recognized scheduled tribes in Nagaland, India. According to oral tradition, the people of Chang emerged from a place called *Changsangmongko*, and later settled in a place called *Changsang*. There are two theories for its derivation. Firstly, it is said to have derived from the word "*Chongnyu*" (banyan tree). Second theory says that the people of Chang migrated to the present day Nagaland from the East, and therefore called themselves Chang (Eastern in Chang dialect).[29]

The Chang society is patrilineal, so the male members inherit the land and the position of authority. Their religion was originally Animism, but with the advent of Christianity their indigenous religion was abandoned. Christianity has impacted widely among the people of Chang. The proposed research work studies in detail the status and the role of Chang women in every aspect.

6. Limitations

The present proposed research is limited to the Zelophehad's daughters' act in Numbers 27:1–11 and the reaction of the tribal elders in Numbers 36:1–13. This research focuses on the sources of biblical and the AWA. Mesopotamia and Egypt are given particular attention in an attempt to establish the literary and cultural background of the Zelophehad's narrative.

As it is beyond the scope of this research to cover the entire ancient period, therefore, the study limits to the ancient Israelite period of Iron Age I which is considered as the Israelite formational period.[30] The study is limited to the Biblical law codes that are directly related to the inheritance rights. This research will study Chang society, its customary and cultural practices. Changs are scattered all over Nagaland but for the purpose of this research, the empirical studies will be carried out limited to the selected Chang villages along with Tuensang town.[31] Some important places from each range will be selected.[32]

7. Literary Review

The subject of women in the Old Testament is a fascinating one and substantial work has been done from various feminist perspectives. Lately, feminist scholars are beginning to recognize the important role played by Zelophehad's daughters. Some of the works done by various scholars from different perspectives are highlighted below.

---

[29] H. M. Bareh, *Encyclopaedia of North-East India*, vol. 6 (Nagaland, 2001), 188.

[30] The Iron Age is divided into three periods that is, I, II, and III that starts with the Philistine invasion about 1200 BCE to the Greek invasion in 333 BCE. Iron Age I period falls approximately around 1200–900 BCE, for further reading, see, Livingston, *Pentateuch in Its Cultural*, 17.

[31] There are fifty-three villages.

[32] Chang region is divided into five ranges, further elaboration on these ranges is found in chapter five.

Katharine Doob Sakenfeld analyses the story of the daughters of Zelophehad in Numbers 27 and 36 using literary, literary-cultural, and historical methods.[33] She claims that the Book of Numbers was finalized after the Deuteronomy. According to her Numbers chapter 36 was added after the book was completed as an individual scroll.[34] She claims that the two chapters focus on two different things that is, preservation of the father's name (chap. 27), and property inheritance rights (chap. 36), that concentrate on the economic matter of family property.[35] She affirms that the purpose of preserving the stories in the canon was to address an essential question in a patriarchal culture as to "how will a man's name be preserved if he has no sons, and who is eligible to marry a woman who has inherited land."[36] She states that, daughters' acts enabled them to move two steps forward that is, challenge the existing power structure, achieved a measure of justice and one step back that is, new rule for their marriage which is a step forward for those in authority. She claims that their act has resulted in placing specific restrictions upon any women who inherit under this right.

Sakenfeld in her second article presents three interpretations.[37] Firstly, gynocentric, and here she defines the story of five daughters as a story of great celebration of women who inherit the Promise Land. Yet the story has a sad ending as their marriage was limited within their tribes.[38] Secondly, androcentric, which according to her the five daughters are little more than pawns in a potential land dispute where YHWH has been presented as a decision maker, but is culturally attached to the male power figures of the community.[39] Thirdly, socio-historical, she asserts that the present story functions mainly to support certain case-laws concerning inheritance for Jews in the post-exilic period.[40] In this third interpretation, she points out four things: women's direct access to male authority; women during this period enjoyed the rights to land ownership; the inheriting daughters' obligation to keep the property within the family circle, and

[33] She has written number of articles on the daughters of Zelophehad. For the present study two articles have been reviewed; Sakenfeld, "Zelophehad's Daughters," in *PRS* 15/4 (Winter 1988); Katharine Doob Sakenfeld, "Feminist Biblical Interpretation," in *TT* 46/2 (July 1989). One of the articles which is not included in the review is, "In the Wilderness, Awaiting the Land: The Daughters of Zelophehad and Feminist Interpretation," in *PSB* 9/3 (1988), 179–96.

[34] Her claim is based on the content of Deuteronomy which is concerned about the land distribution and the construction of the Israelite society. Cf. Sakenfeld, "Zelophehad's Daughters," 39.

[35] Sakenfeld, "Zelophehad's Daughters," 40.

[36] Sakenfeld, "Zelophehad's Daughters," 46.

[37] Sakenfeld, "Feminist Biblical Interpretation."

[38] Sakenfeld, "Feminist Biblical Interpretation," 155–7.

[39] Sakenfeld, "Feminist Biblical Interpretation," 157–8.

[40] Sakenfeld, "Feminist Biblical Interpretation," 158.

finally, the marriage customs, which according to her, marriage outside the tribe was permitted not that marriage within the tribes was prohibited.[41]

Ankie Sterring claims that, Zelophehad's daughters refer to Korah's assembly (Num. 16) in order to dissociate themselves from the latter as a matter of strategy, an appropriate example of indirect female strategy that yielded divine legitimation.[42] To her, the second part of the story (Num. 36) introduces confused androcentric objections. She claims that this new rule for the daughters to marry within their tribe is typical of a patriarchal society. She studies the root word דבק literal meaning "to cleave."[43] She argues that the relationship between a male and his land becomes the primary relationship and his relationship with his wife is in effect subordinated to that primary relationship.[44] She acknowledges the daughters' great achievement. She concludes that the story is a source of inspiration for women, albeit with a patriarchal sting.[45]

John D. Litke places the book in an exilic period with post exilic additions.[46] Possession of land for the people Israel was a major part of the covenantal promise. So, having a land possession within Israel became tightly related to keeping the name of a family within the lists of the people of God as land was considered to belong to YHWH. He states that the narrative challenges the divine instructions of who should be counted as belonging to the nation of Israel.[47] His argument is based on the way the case was presented which he feels is not in a proper procedure. Therefore, he claims that Moses, Eleazar and the whole congregation of Israel are witnesses between two groups, namely, "those that are not" and "YHWH." His close reading affirms that they do not claim an inheritance but the land grant that is, אֲחֻזָּה of the Sovereign, so that they and their family can be counted Israelites.[48] He asserts that, since it is a challenge to YHWH, Moses is correct in passing the issue to YHWH and their argument is approved as correct. He finds gender issue as the key point of the text. He maintains that it is the only narrative in the Hebrew Scriptures where God implicitly acknowledges an error and fixes it.[49] He even claims that their names are symbol rather than literal.

---

[41] Sakenfeld, "Feminist Biblical Interpretation," 159–60.

[42] Sterring, "Will of the Daughters," 90–1.

[43] This particular word is used twice in connection with the inherited land which also appears in Genesis 2:22.

[44] Sterring, "Will of the Daughters," 94.

[45] Sterring, "Will of the Daughters," 97–8.

[46] Litke, "Daughters of Zelophehad."

[47] Litke, "Daughters of Zelophehad," 209.

[48] Litke, "Daughters of Zelophehad," 214.

[49] Litke, "Daughters of Zelophehad," 218.

Dean R. Ulrich, notes that the issue raised here addresses the problem regarding the property inheritance in the post-exilic period.[50] He critiques the scholars for emphasizing so much on redaction criticism resulting in overlooking the literary and thematic integrity of the Books' final form. He recognizes the inclusion of Numbers chapter 36 as a literary and theological purpose to frame the unfinished story of the second generation.[51] He claims that the daughters fill the requirement of pedigree and faithfulness in the sight of God by presenting their case before Moses and elders. He stresses that it was important for the daughters to marry within their tribe in order to retain their father Zelophehad's name.

Amadi Amiamadu, reads the story from the Nigerian perspective and emphasizes that this text needs proper interpretation for the emancipation of women today in their struggle to achieve land inheritance rights. He states that this text is often glossed over in church and Christian circles due to lack of interpretive insights. He maintains that the use of functional equivalence approach helps in interpreting and translating the text in a responsible way.[52]

All the above noted scholars have contributed to the story in various ways with different perspectives and interpretive insights from different context. The present work will draw on their contributions; however, it will argue that it was necessary for the elders from the tribe of Manasseh to raise the issue of marriage of women who own landed property. The proposed research aims to depart from previous studies in many ways. It connects the story with the Israelite's understanding of land and its inalienability. As in the agrarian structure to keep the land within their tribe was important as it was dispensed according to the tribe. Moreover, it was not private but tribal property. This is a study from feminist socio-cultural anthropological and rhetorical perspective. The study attempts to achieve empowerment of the Chang women in Nagaland. This research further investigates in length the property inheritance rights of women in the Old Testament.

8. Methodology Adopted

The study undertakes selective approaches. In the wider spectrum it is a research from a feminist perspective and it makes use of social-scientific tools such as

---

[50] Dean R. Ulrich, "The Framing Function of the Narratives About Zelophehad's Daughters," in *JETS* 41/4 (1998): 535.

[51] Ulrich, "Framing Function," 538. Other scholars who take this view are Burke O. Long, "Framing Repetitions in Biblical Historiography," in *JBL* 106 (1987): 385–7; J. S. Talmon, "The Presentation of Synchronicity and Simultaneity," in *Studies in Hebrew Narrative Art throughout the Ages*, Scripta Hierosolymitana eds. Joseph Heinemann and Shmuel Werses (Jerusalem: Magnes Press, 1978), 12–4.

[52] Amadi Amiamadu, "A Functional Equivalence Translation of the Zelophehad Narrative in Numbers 27:1–11," in *Scriptura*, 93 (2006), 293–304.

sociology, archaeological, and anthropology, to throw light on the position of women in ancient Israel.[53]

This study employs literary approach to bring out the full import of the texts as also to ensure careful analysis and study of the biblical texts.[54] The study considers the development and background of the texts. The rhetorical criticism which is also a branch of literary criticism will be employed here to examine the power of language engaged in the texts.

Ancient Israel as an emerging nation did not exist in isolation but shared certain social and religious values with other AWA communities in their social and cultural structure.[55] This study undertakes comparative study of ancient Israelite society with the AWA, as there are many common elements in their cultural practices.[56] Many areas in which they shared commonality with one another are not similar to our modern culture; therefore, this comparative approach is taken to support the biblical view.

This research also employs historical criticism to discover the potential impact of a text in the historical setting.[57] Historical criticism refers to the study of the world behind the biblical texts.[58]

---

[53] Feminist theologies around the globe are united by a common theme seeking to give voice to the voiceless, oppressed and marginalized. For this Peacore claims that, feminist theology has been influenced by liberation theology. She further states that feminist theology is an approach to constructing theological doctrine that upholds the experience of women, their voices included as an equal partner with male voice in theological reflection. Cf. Linda Peacore, "Feminist Theologies," in *Global Dictionary of Theology: A Resource for the Worldwide Church* eds. William A. Dyrness et al., (Downers Grove: InterVarsity Press, 2008), 318.

[54] In other words, it is "the world within the text. The task is to read the texts as a whole and analysed according to their various inter-textual aspects. The focus is on the artistic composition and intention of the final text. For further reading, see, Terence E. Fretheim, *The Pentateuch: Interpreting Biblical Texts*, eds. Gene M. Tucker et al., (Nashville: Abingdon Press, 1996), 32–4; Walter Dietrich, *The Early Monarchy in Israel: The Tenth Century B.C.E.*, trans. Joachim Vette, vol. 3, Biblical Encyclopaedia, (Atlanta: SBL, 2007), 331–2; Victor H. Matthews, *Studying the Ancient Israelite: A Guide to Source and Method* (Michigan: Baker Academic, 2007), 91–122.

[55] Maynard Paul Maidman, *Nuzi Texts and their uses as Historical Evidence* (Atlanta: SBL, 2010), ix.

[56] Walton defines comparative studies as a branch of cultural studies with an aim to draw data from different segments of the broader culture to enhance the understanding of one another. Cf. Walton, *Ancient Near Eastern Thought*, 18.

[57] In the words of James Barr, historical criticism is not strictly a method, but a loose umbrella that covers a range of methods such source, form, and sociological criticisms. These methods are united in interpreting the texts in their historical contexts. Cf. James Barr, *History and Ideology in the Old Testament: Biblical Studies at the End of a Millennium* (Oxford, England: Oxford University Press, 2000), 32–3; See also, John Joseph Collins, *The Bible after Babel: Historical Criticism in a Postmodern Age* (Grand Rapids, Michigan: William B. Eerdmans Publishing Company, 2005), 4.

[58] This approach has been a dominant approach to the Pentateuch beginning from the late 18th century. It is an author-centred approach where the focus is on the production of the texts.

The present research also involves an empirical study to analyse the role and status of Chang women and the tribe's practice of land ownership. The present study dwells on the practice of customary law and customs related to women's inheritance rights. It is an attempt to gain equity for women within the existing structure of customary law in inheritance rights. Further comparative study with other tribes in Nagaland is also incorporated. The data for empirical study includes questionnaires, personal interviews and focus groups discussions.[59]

8.1. Socio-cultural Anthropological Approach in Biblical Studies

Socio-cultural anthropological approach plays an important role in the study of the Old Testament. It is the study of ways and thoughts of human that arise out of studies of one or more cultural groups and domains.[60] George Mendenhall, in the early 1960's uses sociological methods to reconstruct the history of the conquest of Canaan by the Israelites.[61] Norman Gottwald's monumental work is also on the origins of Israel and of Israel's religion which he frames on the pioneering work of Mendenhall.[62] Another prominent scholar Anthony R. Ceresko claims that, Bible contains evidence of similar political, economic and societal processes at work throughout the long history of the Bible's creation, and that the sociological approach helps in gaining some insight into these processes.[63]

Simultaneously, the term culture refers to material substance, norms of behaviours, values, beliefs, and expressive symbols or representations.[64] David Gunn defines culture as a language or set of codes, through which people share values beliefs, behave in certain approved ways, helping them relate to each other, and that these codes are transmitted through generations.[65] Carol Meyers states that, the cultural study focuses on the cultural and social aspects of contemporary or recent populations, recognizing both diversities and similarities among human

---

The intention of the texts can be discovered within the texts. For further information see, Fretheim, *Pentateuch: Interpreting Biblical Texts*, 23–32.

[59] The complete questionnaire is attached in appendix—2.

[60] Paul A. Erickson and Liam D. Murphy, eds., *A History of Anthropological Theory* (Canada: Broadview Press, 2003), 17.

[61] George E. Mendenhall, "Hebrew Conquest of Palestine," in *BA* 25/2 (September 1962), 66–87.

[62] Norman K. Gottwald, *The Tribes of Yahweh: A Sociology of the Religion of Liberated Israel, 1250-1050 B.C.E.* (Maryknoll: Orbis Books, 1981).

[63] Anthony R. Ceresko, *The Old Testament: A Liberation Perspective* (Mumbai: St Paul Press, 1992), 7–8; Cf. Norman K. Gottwald, "Sociology: Ancient Israel," in *ABD,* (Si—Z), vol. 6 eds. David Noel Freedman et al., (New York: Doubleday, 1992), 79.

[64] For further information see, Khiok-Khng Yeo, "Cultural Hermeneutics," in *New Interpreter's Dictionary of the Bible:* (A—C) eds. Katharine Doob Sakenfeld, (Nashville: Abingdon Press, December 2006), 808.

[65] David M. Gunn, "Cultural Criticism," in *Judges and Method: New Approaches in Biblical Studies*, ed. Gale A. Yee (Minneapolis: Fortress Press, 1995), 202.

groups.[66] Cultural studies in Old Testament help to understand the context in which the texts originate so as to evaluate them in relation to the needs, values and beliefs of their own time.

The Old Testament has undergone several rewritings down through the centuries in an attempt to give unifying perspective to the diverse materials contained therein. New themes and stories were added to make the Scriptures come alive and speak meaningfully in a new historical situation. Closer examination of the Old Testament reveals gaps and contradictions; therefore, the application of this method would clarify the relationship between biblical literature and ancient Israel and also help in studying the social organization of Ancient Israel at a given moment.

8.2. Socio-cultural Anthropological Approach in Feminist Studies

Socio-cultural anthropological theory is used to categorize and comprehend the origin and development of ancient Israel as a socially distinct formation in the West Asian world. It continues to provide resources for increasing the visibility of Israelite women. Carol Meyers affirms that, Israelite society should be studied in the context of its own multidimensional environment that includes factors like social, political and economic prehistory.[67] This theory helps in reconstructing the social history of Israel, by utilizing data from cross-cultural studies along with archaeological information.

Sociology recognizes that, society is not one thing but consists of interconnections between different levels and processes of individual and group interaction. Sociology emphasizes how societies conceptualize and organize patterns of social behaviour, whereas anthropology emphasizes comparative cultural phenomena.[68] Sociology studies the patterns of social behaviour described in the biblical text and it also includes archaeological findings as it reflects the social world in and behind the text.[69] By using feminist socio-cultural anthropological tools this research studies the ancient Israelite society especially the kinship structure which is important in order to know the women's role in ancient Israel.[70] An attempt will be made to study the society, including its economic, political

---

[66] Carol Meyers, "Anthropology: Old Testament Cultural," in *New Interpreter's Dictionary*, 170. Meyers has done the sociological, ethnological and archeological studies of ancient Israelite society with gender issues in mind. Cf. Carol L. Meyers, *Discovering Eve: Ancient Israelite Women in Context* (New York: Oxford University Press, 1988).

[67] Meyers, *Discovering Eve*, 9.

[68] Naomi Steinberg, "Sociological Approaches: Toward a Sociology of Childhood in the Hebrew Bible," in *Method Matters: Essays on the Interpretation of the Hebrew Bible in Honor of David L. Petersen*, eds. Joel M. LeMon and Kent Harold Richards (Atlanta: SBL, 2009), 251.

[69] Steinberg, "Sociological Approaches," 251.

[70] Wright defines ancient Israel as having three tier pattern of kinship which comprises of tribe, clan and family of which the family which is known as father's house that plays the most important role. It is unlike today's nuclear family which comprises of parents and children. Cf. Christopher

and social dimensions. Both sociology and anthropology address many of the same questions in their investigations and these two disciplines are separated on what they choose to study and how they go about it to achieve its goal.[71]

The feminist critique of anthropology began in the 1970's primarily as an indictment of male bias in anthropological studies.[72] It attempts to study the society as a whole, and it gives emphasis on cross-cultural investigations. It further investigates how gender roles are defined within cultures, because gender is a major factor in all cultures. This approach explores the realities of women's lives in antiquity with an attempt to reconstruct women's lost history drawing on archaeological, anthropological and cultural studies. It aims to discover the role of women in ancient Israelite society and cult, along with feminine sexuality, goddess worship and intermarriage with non-Israelites.[73]

Tatha Wiley, a feminist theologian asserts that, canon is a collection of real writings reflecting their actual historical and social settings, and dominant views of the culture.[74] She further claims that a literary text is understood only when put in relation to its social and cultural settings. It makes the readers become aware of the differences between the present culture and the biblical world, including differences in horizons, interests and values.[75]

It is an important task to make the Bible relevant to a contemporary female audience as women today look at biblical women's stories for guidance in their lives. Therefore, socio-cultural and anthropology method can contribute towards a better understanding of the aspects of the biblical text.

8.3. Rhetorical Criticism

The rhetorical criticism had its origin with James Muilenburg, who in his celebrated presidential address in 1968, meeting of the SBL, laid out the method.[76]

J. H. Wright, "Year of Jubilee," in *ABD* vol. 3, eds. Freedman et al., (New York, Doubleday: Doubleday, 1992), 1025.

[71] Mary Ann Tolbert, "Social, Sociological, and Anthropological Methods," in *Searching the Scriptures,* vol. 1, ed. Elisabeth Schussler Fiorenza (New York: Crossroad, 1993), 256–7.

[72] Tolbert, "Social, Sociological," 265.

[73] Phyllis A. Bird, "Women in the Ancient Mediterranean World: Ancient Israel," in *BR* 39 (1994), 33.

[74] Tatha Wiley, "Canon and Conscience: A Feminist Perspective," in *W&W* 29/4 (fall 2009): 365.

[75] Wiley, "Canon and Conscience," 362.

[76] Fiorenza has clearly brought out four forms of rhetoric: Firstly, academic communication studies that teaches the art of public speech, secondly, ancient rhetoric that aims at recovering classical handbooks and theories, thirdly, critical literary rhetorical studies that seek to understand the arguments and persuasive power of texts in their context and finally, rhetoric of scholarship that investigates the rhetoricity of knowledge and its institutions. Cf. Elizabeth Schüssler Fiorenza, "Rhetorical-Hermeneutical Criticism," in *The Oxford Encyclopedia of the Bible and Gender Studies:* vol. 2, eds. Julia M. O'Brien et al., (Oxford University Press, 2014), 248. Muilenburg was the key

According to Muilenburg, it takes into account the articulation of the words in their linguistic patterns and formulations.[77] According to Hauser, rhetorical criticism is:

> A form of literary criticism which uses our knowledge of the conventions of literary composition practiced in ancient Israel and its environment to discover and analyse the particular literary artistry found in a specific unit of Old Testament text. This analysis then provides a basis for discussing the message of the text and the impact it had in it audience.[78]

This definition denotes that rhetorical critic attempts to read the literary text of the Old Testament without using the modern literary standard because Old Testament text came from a different literary context. It prefers to examine units of the text to prove that the texts are artfully composed, designed to convey particular messages to the audiences.

Basing on Muilenburg's work, Phyllis Trible is one of the feminist scholars using this method.[79] She states that rhetorical criticism focuses on the totality of the text, stressing and discovering its organic unity.[80] She further states that the rhetoric of the text awakens the imagination, allowing the interpreter to enter into its space and time.[81] The stress is on the literary work itself and not the mind of the audience and the understanding of the original listeners. Rhetorical criticism reads the text in its present state as an intentional composition reflecting the interests and challenges facing the community at the time of composition.

Today it has been recognized that the power of language has played key role where in large measures men have dominated the naming process. It is essential to approach the biblical texts through a variety of literary methods to discover the rhetorical, historical and social features of texts.[82] The two most dominant orientations in rhetorical criticism in biblical studies are "the art of

---

person in launching the current interest in literary analysis among the Old Testament scholars. Cf. Jack R. Lundbom, "Methodological Issues in the Study of the Old Testament: Rhetorical Criticism," in, *Interweaving Methodology and Praxis: Exploring Disciplinary Options in Today's World,* ed. Indukuri John Mohan Razu, (Bangalore: BTESSC/SATHRI, 2007), 148.

[77] James Muilenburg, "Form Criticism and Beyond," in *JBL* 88/1 (March 1969), 8.

[78] Duane F. Watson and Alan J. Hauser, *Rhetorical Criticism of the Bible: A Comprehensive Bibliography with Notes on History and Method* vol. 4 (Leiden, New York: E. J. Brill, 1994), 4.

[79] Her book is the best example where she uses this method to interpret the Book of Jonah; Phyllis Trible, *Rhetorical Criticism: Context Method and the Book of Jonah* (Minneapolis: Augsburg Fortress Press, 1994), 5.

[80] Cited by Leo G. Perdue, *Reconstructing Old Testament Theology: After the Collapse of History* (Minneapolis: Augsburg Fortress Press, 2005), 163.

[81] Cited by Perdue, *Reconstructing Old Testament,* 163.

[82] Perdue, *Reconstructing Old Testament*, 105, 147.

composition" and the "art of persuasion."[83] The art of persuasion approach belong to the classical Aristotelian tradition. Aristotle's definition of rhetoric is "the art of discovering the best possible means of persuasion in regard to any subject whatever."[84] Aristotle was mainly concerned with spoken discourse.

Rhetorical criticism has born much exegetical fruit, and provided new set of lenses for the determination of literary units within a text. The rhetorical critic looks primarily for those appeals that the author finally selected for inclusion rather than the larger range of possibilities. It invites detailed attention to the text in the final form as thoughtfully crafted composition. Therefore, this approach in the present study would contribute in uncovering the richness and dynamic insights hidden in the texts that are studied in relation to the act of the daughters of Zelophehad.

[83] The art of composition approach is associated with James Muilenburgh and those following in his footsteps. His conception of rhetorical criticism is an attempt to overcome the short comings of form criticism. Here emphasis is given to the text's unique stylistic or aesthetic qualities. Cf. David A. deSilva, "Rhetorical Criticism," in *The Oxford Encyclopedia of Biblical Interpretation*, vol. 2, eds. Steven L. Mckenzie et al., (New York: Oxford University Press, 2013), 274–5.

[84] Alan J. Hauser, David J. A. Clines, and David M. Gunn, eds., *Art and Meaning: Rhetoric in Biblical Literature,* JSOTSup series 19, (Sheffield: JSOT Press, 1982), 2.

Chapter 1

Status of Women in Ancient Israel

INTRODUCTION

The Old Testament records the events that assist in reconstructing the history of Israel from the perspectives of those who had power over the composition of the written text.[1] Reading the biblical texts alone clearly expose men assuming the dominant role in the family as fathers, husbands and in the wider society as kings, priests, military leaders, judges. Role and status of women in ancient Israel remained imperfectly defined. Women are generally examined from the perspective of fertility and home maker, thus defining their social roles as wives, mothers and daughters who derived their status from their male associations. Few women are mentioned by name, most of those who came from privileged families and so they are either elite in their wealth or learning. Therefore, the biblical stories about women cannot be taken at its face value.

This section will examine the representation of women in the Hebrew Bible along with its interpretation. In this chapter, attempt is made to identify areas of family life in ancient Israel. The investigation will focus on kinship structure as it is crucial for understanding women's lives in ancient society. It is also crucial for interpreting the meaning of gender as seen through the text. Extra biblical sources such as archaeological and epigraphical evidences will be employed. The role of women in religion, legal system and in household economy will be highlighted. Finally, the status of daughter will be analysed as this research is on the act of the daughters of Zelophehad. This section is very important for the current research because it will have bearing on further discovering the women's act especially that of the daughter.

[1] The terms Hebrew Bible and Old Testament will be used interchangeably.

1. Representation of Women in the Old Testament

The Hebrew Bible has considerably less information about women and their contributions. It is male oriented in authorship, subject matters and perspectives. Beginning from late 1960s and 1970s significant attempts have been made to address the issues of gender in the Bible with an attempt to reinterpret and reconstruct the role of women in the scriptures by critiquing the legacy of patriarchy and by emphasizing a more egalitarian, inclusive and non-sexist approach.

Carol Meyers argues that the Bible is the product of priestly, scribal elite, "an all-man" hereditary group based in the premises of the royal palace in Jerusalem.[2] It is also a theological document that achieved its final form long after the events are reported. Philip King, a biblical scholar and Lawrence Stager, an archaeologist, whose recent field project is in Israel, together have written a book on "Life in Biblical Israel."[3] The book blends relevant passages from the Hebrew Bible with archaeological data with occasional infusion of ethnographic material with its focus on Iron Age I Israel. Over all the book lacks in treatment of gender issues as women were only considered when the focus is on the household, as the bearer of children, educators of girls, preparing food and clothing. King and Stager also comment that the androcentric biases make it weak resource for reconstructing gendered life.[4] The androcentric nature is also seen in a count of personal names that appeared in the Hebrew Bible. There are about 1,426 personal names of which only 111 are women's names, only nine percent of the total.[5] Of the women mentioned, they are mostly from privileged families, elite in their wealth and learning. The impoverished women of all categories are less documented. Therefore, it is far more difficult to discover gender issues from the biblical source alone.

There are gender biases in the representation of privileged male where stories about women are told from the male point of view.[6] For instance in reading the Book of Esther, Vashti as a character, the narrator does not provide any reason as to why she refused to appear before the king. As claimed by

---

[2] Carol L. Meyers, *Discovering Eve: Ancient Israelite Women in Context* (New York: Oxford University Press, 1988), 11–2.

[3] Philip J. King and Lawrence E. Stager, *Life in Biblical Israel*, Library of Ancient Israel, (Louisville: Westminster John Knox, 2002).

[4] King and Stager, *Life in Biblical Israel*, 49.

[5] Carol L. Meyers, "Everyday Life: Women in the Period of the Hebrew Bible," in *WBC*, expanded ed. with Apocrypha, eds. Carol A. Newsom, and Sharon H. Ringe (Louisville: Westminster John Knox Press, 1998), 251–2.

[6] Gerlinde Baumann, "Hermeneutical Perspective on Violence Against Women and on Divine Violence in German-Speaking Old Testament Exegesis," in *Global Hermeneutics? Reflections and Consequences* eds. Knut Holter and Louis C. Jonker (Atlanta: SBL, 2010), 17.

Madipoune Masenya, the omission of such important information is a proof that it informs the reader about the biblical narrator's patriarchal orientation.[7]

Prophet Jeremiah refers to Israel's unfaithfulness in terms of illicit female activity (Jer. 4:30; 2:33–3:20). Another example is found in Jeremiah 13:20–27 that describes about the Babylonian attack as a "rape." The city is personified as a woman and the attack itself is figured as sexual assault. The soldiers in their military advance are portrayed as rapists.[8] Hosea uses his marriage to Gomer, "a wife of harlotry," to illustrate God's relation to his people Israel. Here Hosea represents God and Gomer an idolatrous Israel. Androcentric interpreters have produced a dominant reading of Hosea as a tale of divine/husbandly suffering and persistent love in the face of human/wifely unfaithfulness and sin. Isaiah too calls Jerusalem "a harlot," a language of sexual humiliation (Isa. 1:21; 3:16–24; 57:3–13) where the sexual abuse is at the women of Zion. She is even said to have taught wicked women her ways (Jer. 2:33). Likewise, prophet Ezekiel presented Jerusalem's disloyalty to God as a wife's disloyalty to her caring husband and provides an implicit warning to all women in general. Here the woman is raped which is symbolized by the throwing down of the mound and breaking of high places, and stripped naked before she was stoned to death. The husband shares none of the blame and deserves sympathy as the wronged party. The woman's point of view is not represented. Scholars like Exum and others call this biblical text "by men for men."[9]

In the biblical narratives mothers are shown interfering actively on behalf of their sons, but they never voice any word on behalf of their daughters. The story of Dinah's rape makes no reference to Leah, there is no mention of Jephthah's mother (Judg. 10:6–12:17).[10] The story of the concubine exploited to death by

[7] Madipoane Masenya, *Their Hermeneutics was Strange! Ours is a Necessity! Rereading Vashti as African-South African Women*, in *Her Master's Tools?: Feminist And Postcolonial Engagements of Historical-Critical Discourse*, eds. Caroline Vander Stichele and Todd Penner (Atlanta: SBL, 2005), 192.

[8] Harold C. Washington, "Lest He Die in the Battle and another Man take her: Violence and the Construction of Gender in the Laws of Deuteronomy 20–22," in *Gender and Law in the Hebrew Bible and the Ancient Near East* eds. Victor H. Matthews, Bernard M. Levinson, and Tikva Simone Frymer-Kensky (New York: T&T Clark International, 1998), 198.

[9] J. Cheryl Exum, *Plotted, Shot, and Painted: Cultural Representations of Biblical Women,* (Sheffield: Sheffield Academic Press, 1996), 11; See also, Esther Fuchs, "The Literary Characterization of Mothers and Sexual Politics in the Hebrew Bible," in *Semeia* No. 46, 1989: 151; Renita J. Weems, "Re-Reading for Liberation: African American Women and the Bible," in *Feminist Interpretation of the Bible and the Hermeneutics of Liberation* eds. Silvia Schroer and Sophia Bietenhard, JSOTSup Series 374, (London: Sheffield Academic Press, 2003), 28–9; Phyllis A. Bird, *Missing Persons and Mistaken Identities: Women and Gender in Ancient Israel* (Minneapolis: Fortress Press, 1997), 249.

[10] This narrative is one of the most gruesome examples who sacrificed his daughter as a burnt-offering to fulfil his vow. Cf. Mikael Sjoberg, "Jephthah's Daughter as Object of Desire or Feminist Icon," in *BibInt* 15/4–5 (2007), 377.

the Benjaminites does not mention her mother either. These are few examples that show mothers' complete silence when daughters were exploited. Esther Fuchs states:

> By expatiating on mothers who protect or interfere on behalf of their sons, the biblical narrative creates maternal role models which promote the interests of the male rather than the female child."[11]

Women in biblical text belong to many classes, both high and low. There was Bathsheba, who with the help of Nathan influences the succession to the Israelite throne (1 Kgs. 1). There are numerous examples of wife advising her husbands.[12] The examples range over a long period indicating that the motif of the advising wife was a stable one in biblical culture, reflecting the social role of the wife as a counsellor behind the scenes. The narratives are exclusively written from the male point of view because of which female contributions are ignored.

2. Interpretation of Women in the Old Testament

Biblical scholars especially male, read the biblical text with their own presuppositions and often presented women in an inferior position.[13] Even feminist biblical scholarship in its initial stages tended to think of women primarily in terms of wife, mother and daughter. The word of God was mediated through the words of human beings, overwhelmingly male and patriarchal in their interpretation. So often, women are described as being of loose moral characters and the audience or the readers are encouraged to identify and sympathize with a male-identified deity because female figures are presented in the biblical text in such a way that no dignity was left to them. This is the position taken almost without exception by biblical commentators re-inscribing the text's harmful ideology upon the readers, reflecting the attitudes and values of male dominated societies. Thus, the context that is generated by human have often been transformed and equated with unchanging, divinely revealed or mandated dogmas and laws.[14]

Why there is no better discussion of women's role in what is traditionally considered the male domain? The women's craft productions have contributed greatly into their economic and commercial financial situation. In the matter of governance, they have contributed in their capacities as elders, queen-mothers,

---

[11] Fuchs, "Literary Characterization of Mothers," 163.

[12] See, Claudia V. Camp, *Wisdom and the Feminine in the Book of Proverbs*, Bible and Literature series 11 (Sheffield: Almond Press, 1985), 86–7.

[13] Philomena Njeri Mwaura, "Feminist Biblical Interpretation and the Hermeneutics of Liberation: An African Womanist Perspective." in *Feminist Interpretation of the Bible and the Hermeneutics of Liberation,* vol. 374, eds. Silvia Schroer and Sophia Bietenhard JSOTSup Series (London: Sheffield Academic Press, 2003), 81.

[14] Bruce K. Waltke and Charles Yu, *An Old Testament Theology: An Exegetical, Canonical, and Thematic Approach* (Grand Rapids, Michigan: Zondervan, 2007), 241–2.

judges, and prophetesses. Even in religious observances, in Jerusalem, in their own homes and villages they participated and made significant impact. Despite all these contributions little attention is given to these important matters. Their tasks are enumerated only when the focus is on the house hold.

Hjamil Martinez-Vazquez has rightly said:

> If we continue to uncover voices and interpretations, but do not challenge traditional ways and methods of interpretation, we become agent of oppression and recovered voices are reduced to the footnote.[15]

It is important to reconstruct new theories and methods that will help with the process of interpretation in the context of our own unique places, an interpretation that acknowledges the inherent goodness and value of all humanity. The biblical texts reflect the language and culture of patriarchal society. It is important to read against, and through the text, asking questions about what the text does not say, and to search for women's supressed history.

3. Important Source

Besides biblical source two other sources are studied here, as they contribute in interpreting the Israel's origin and early history: archaeology and epigraphy. The task is to compare and complement. Although, Hebrew Bible provides one important source of information about the women's lives in ancient Israel, it does not provide information on many of the daily-life activities that occupied women who lived in the early Israelite villages. Indeed, it is crucial to utilize the information from extra biblical sources such as the archaeological remains and other texts from ancient West Asia (hereafter, AWA). Therefore, the following section is an attempt to see the contributions of biblical text, archaeological and epigraphical support in studying the ancient Israelite society with special reference to women's status.

3.1. Biblical Evidence

The main written source of information for this research is the Hebrew Bible. The information is crucial for the understanding of Israelite society even though the sources are problematic due to its patriarchal slant. The biblical writings represent a multi-layering of stories, events and ideologies spanning hundreds of years. The biblical scholars are engaged in untangling the various layers of composition to reconstruct the history of Israel. Genesis to Judges reflect certain historical perspective that were popular during those days, such as relationship with the deities, long life-spans, emphasis on divine involvement in human affairs, origin of the various peoples in the world in terms of simple decent from various ancestors. On the contrary, the modern historians informed by anthropological

---

[15] Hjamil A. Martinez-Vazquez, "Breaking the Established Scaffold: Imagination as a Resource in the Development of Biblical Interpretation," in *Her Master's Tools?,* 89.

studies are sceptical on these issues. They dismiss them as an unreliable source of historical information.[16]

It is also evident that the stories are also built on motive patterns, such as, how one seemingly enjoyed a reversal of fate reflecting a specific wilderness milieu.[17] But, one cannot ignore the fact that folk materials embedded in the Hebrew Bible provide a wealth of evidences about the ancient Israelite society. The author(s) mentioned or alluded to in passing references without much elaboration because it is taken for granted that the audience would be familiar with them. There are ideological biases inherent in the biblical narratives where the authors were selective and imaginative in giving accounts of the ancient history. So, using biblical text alone as reliable witness to the emergence of Israel is problematic.[18] Despite this literary and ideological crafting, several kinds of evidence contained in the Biblical text hints to historical authenticity. Many important events were invariably recorded by the scribes of antiquity, the sources that are available are selective and it is due to availability of the sources to them during the compilation. Scholars generally agree that the wide range of literature that existed in the AWA such as stories, poems, collections of proverbs, etc., are reflected in the Old Testament.[19] Harrison states:

> Indeed the collection of writings mirrors its background with such fidelity that can assert quite safely that the Old Testament compositions are in fact a microcosm of Near Eastern life and literary activity.[20]

3.2. Archaeological Evidence

Archaeological evidences play an important role in studying the ancient society. John Drane, in his brief introduction to archaeology and the Old Testament states that Old Testament study today is dominated by social and cultural considerations informed by archaeological evidences.[21] It allows us to place an Old Testament narrative in its social context, along with offering insights into otherwise obscure aspects of the text. However, the archaeology does not attempt to prove or disprove the biblical record, but it is a science that describes what is found and

---

[16] J. Maxwell Miller and John H. Hayes, *A History of Ancient Israel and Judah* (Louisville: Westminster John Knox Press, 2006), 69.

[17] Miller and Hayes, *A History of Ancient Israel and Judah*, 70–2; Cf. R. K. Harrison, *Old Testament Times* (Michigan: William B. Eerdmans Publishing Company, 1974), 19.

[18] Carol Meyers, "Early Israel and the Rise of the Israelite Monarchy," in *The Blackwell Companion to the Hebrew Bible* ed. Leo G. Perdue (Oxford: Blackwell Publishers Ltd, 2001), 66–7.

[19] Tawny L. Holm "Literature," in *A Companion to the Ancient Near East*, Blackwell Companions to the Ancient World, ed. Daniel C. Snell (Oxford: Blackwell Publishing, 2005), 254–64.

[20] Harrison, *Old Testament Times*, 19.

[21] John W. Drane, *Introducing the Old Testament*, 3rd ed., (Oxford: Lion Hudson, 2011), 31–3.

offers hypotheses to be tasted in scholarly debate.[22] It is also related to historical critical approach as it intends to prove the historicity of a particular period. It studies the ancient objects, aspects of the material culture of the biblical world from the artefacts from buried cities and homes. The material remains consist of two kinds of data: the dwellings and settlements of the Israelites themselves as recovered through excavation and survey epigraphic and; epigraphic (ancient written) and iconographic depictions of events and peoples that sheds light on the ancient Israelite society.[23] Feminist archaeologists specializing in ancient Israelite world have entered the field of gendered analysis and Carol Meyers is one among the earliest in this field.

Archaeological discoveries have increasingly brought to light evidence of women's involvement in the society. The study consists of both pictorial and non-pictorial evidence such as, paintings that decorated the interior of palaces, temples, stratified city ruins, abandoned buildings, broken pieces of pottery, remnant of tools and weapons, seeds, bones, and garbage from the ruins of long buried cultures.[24] They try to figure out from the surviving objects how people lived, working mainly from the remains of bronze bracelets, clay jars, stone walls, and some of the writings. For instance, bracelets inform about the fashion of the day, charred wheat grains give evidence of what people ate. During the last two centuries archaeology has made available a lot of data throwing light on the Hebrew language, biblical laws, customs, cults and religion. It contributes in reconstructing the sociological context of the biblical world. The discovery of the Tell el-Amarna site provided scholars with the first major example of international diplomatic correspondence written in cuneiform. The cuneiform tablets from Mari and Nuzi furnished a great deal of information about life in the period of the Hebrew patriarchs.[25]

In the rural culture of ancient Israel, many households made their own pottery, and this has become the most common artefact found in Middle Eastern excavation.[26] It had to be continually produced to replace the broken ware or to create new styles. These physical objects are mute testimony to the activities of the ancient days. Simple pottery and the lack of luxuries bear testimony that the settlers' lives were hard and poor. Scholars like W. F. Albright and A. Alt

---

[22] Bernhard W. Anderson, Steven Bishop, and Judith Newman, *Understanding the Old Testament*, 5th ed., (Upper Saddle River, New Jersey: Pearson Prentice Hall, 2007), 123.

[23] Meyers, "Early Israel," 69.

[24] Miller and Hayes, *A History of Ancient Israel and Judah*, 43; Cf. Harrison, *Old Testament Times*, 14.

[25] Harrison, *Old Testament Times*, 15.

[26] Victor H. Matthews, *Studying the Ancient Israelite: A Guide to Source and Method* (Michigan: Baker Academic, 2007), 68.

constructed the history of early Israel on the basis of a critical appraisal and synthesis of biblical, archaeological and ancient near eastern studies.[27]

Archaeological excavations enable us to know the kind of crops that the Israelites and their neighbours grew, what they ate, how they built their towns, and with whom they traded. There are also evidences where wide range of laboratory tests have been used to date and analyse the civilizations of the ancient Israelites and their neighbours; through this work inscriptions and signet seals have been discovered connecting with individuals mentioned in the biblical texts.[28]

Systematic archaeological explorations and major excavations throughout Palestine and its neighbouring regions have brought a flood of new information to both biblical exegesis and to the history of Israel making a shift in the traditional understanding of the early history of Israel. The limitation of this approach is that it is prone to lead to different conclusions based on diverse interpretations. The archaeological excavations may not add much to a discussion of life-cycle events other than death and burial. Nevertheless, the evidences have served to illumine the contemporary scene in confirming directly or indirectly, the historicity of many events mentioned in the Old Testament. In fact, during the recent years, one of the most significant advances in biblical study has come through the efforts of the archaeologists in understanding the development of earliest Israel it terms of its social dynamics. It has to be recognized that archaeology by itself cannot and ought not to be expected or required to prove the truth of the Old Testament, but it functions to provide such information about the life and structure of AWA society as to enable the modern readers of Scriptures to see that society in proper cultural and historical perspective.

3.3. Epigraphical Evidence

Epigraphical evidences denote literary records. It refers to discovery of written texts and even extensive archives from ancient time, and the decoding of ancient languages and writing systems such as letters written on papyruses, ostracon, and stamp seals.[29] It is said that the vast majority of the people of AWA were busily engaged in making and writing history. There are many written sources of various kinds that have survived to furnish an interesting and authoritative picture of the

[27] Quoted by Thomas L. Thompson, *Early History of the Israelite People: From the Written and Archaeological Sources* (New York: BRILL, 1992), 11.

[28] Israel Finkelstein and Neil Asher Sinberman, *The Bible Unearthed: Archaeology's New Vision of Ancient Israel and the Origin of its Sacred Texts* (New York: A Touchstone Book, 2002), 5.

[29] Ostracon is archaeological remains, piece of pottery usually broken off from a vase or other earthenware vessel. It contains scratched-in words or other forms of writing which may give clues as to the time when the piece was in use. The languages are Hebrew, Canaanite, Phoenician or Moabite.

ancient past reflecting many different situations, including some which have a bearing upon much wider aspects involving the neighbouring nations.[30]

The Hebrew epigraphic remains from Israel in the 12th to 10th centuries BCE are said to be rare. The widely held theory is the absence of a central administration with no unifying power to maintain the scribal office.[31] It helps in providing first hand evidences with specific dates. It also contributes in a verbal form by communicating detailed information about specific people and events. Hebrew words which had been unintelligible have been now clarified by parallels in other Semitic languages like Ugaritic.[32] The handful of inscriptions from the Iron Age I are all said to be written in the old Canaanite script of the late Bronze Age.

William Dever argues that some of the oldest literature in the Bible, written in an archaic Hebrew script, mainly poems in the Pentateuch and some of the Psalms, are very closely related to Canaanite poetry and mythology. Those Canaanite poetry and mythology texts belong to the 14th and 13th centuries BCE and found at Ugarit on the coast of Syria.[33] The disadvantage is that this literature cannot be fully trusted because sometimes they are given to exaggerations especially the sources that are from the royal courts. Another weakness is that it is uneven in its coverage as some regions and groups are well represented while some are not.[34] Nevertheless it offers a great deal of information about the political and social conditions of that time.

There are epigraphic (written) evidences mentioning women. It is said that most of the documents produced by the people of ancient Israel were written on perishable materials, it means that compared to other neighbouring nations there are relatively few epigraphic remains from ancient Israel. Meyers mentions two kinds of inscribed objects that provide information about women's lives in ancient Israel. They are ostracon and stamp seal.[35] She mentions an ostracon dating to the 7th century BCE which is named "A Widow's Plea to an Official." The inscription reads as follows:

> A woman calling herself "your maidservant" (a polite form of address toward an official) and identifying herself as a childless widow

---

[30] Harrison, *Old Testament Times*, 6.

[31] Alan Millard, "The Ostracon from the Days of David Found at Khirbet Qeiyafa," in *TB* 62/1 (2011): 2.

[32] Rui De Menezes, *The Cultural Context of the Old Testament* (Bangalore: Theological Publications of India, 2005), v.

[33] William G. Dever, *Who were the Early Israelites and Where did they Come From* (Grand Rapids: William B. Eerdmanns Publishing Company, 2000), 200.

[34] Hayes, *History of Ancient Israel*, 30.

[35] Carol Meyers, "Archaeology: A Window to the Lives of Israelite Women," in, *Torah*, The Bible and Woman, an Encyclopedia of Exegesis and Cultural History—Hebrew Bible/Old Testament, eds. Irmtraud Fischer et al., (Atlanta: SBL, 2011), 91.

> addresses an officer about rights to at least some of the property of her deceased husband 'Amasyahu: May YHWH bless you in peace. And now may my lord the official listen to your maidservant. My husband has died (leaving) no sons. (I request politely that the following) happen: (let) your hand (be) with me and entrust to your maidservant the inheritance about which you spoke to 'Amasyahu.[36]

The case is also very similar with the case of Zelophehad's daughters. They claim inheritance rights for women. It is no longer legitimate to study the content of the Old Testament in isolation from other aspects of ancient life in the west Asia because Israel was a people of the AWA.

4. Ancient Israelite Women

An examination of Ancient Israelite women's position is very important in considering the biblical society, especially in its formative period because it is the period in which the biblical community was formed. This period is also said to be one of the major periods in history when transitions occurred in the position and role of women in the ancient world.[37] It has been discovered that there were often considerable alterations in the status of women from one period to another, and for this reason historical investigation of women in various periods of the Israelite society, including its formative period, is significant.

John H. Otwell, in his book *And Sarah Laughed*, argues that in the ancient Israelite society procreation and survival were primary values along with cultic and legal functions and within this context motherhood was most highly valued. He further claims that no higher status could be given to anyone other than mothers. He concludes, "She was co-worker with God in the creating and sustaining of the people of God. She also participated fully and freely in the common life of that people."[38]

In the ancient society every member of the family participated in contributing towards their sustenance. Unfortunately women's roles are considered only when the focus is on the household, as the bearers of children, educators of girl children and preparers of food and clothing. However, feminist scholars are engaged in looking at the past more broadly, that emphasizes on the women's contributions in economics, in governance as elders, queen mothers, judges and prophets, and their roles in religious observances. They also emphasize on the lives of unnamed individuals who have contributed to the formation of their societies.

Among the feminist liberationist scholars Evelyn and Frank Stagg regard the status of women in the Old Testament as oppressed. Their claim is based on the

---

[36] Meyers, "Archaeology: A Window," in *Torah*, 92.

[37] Carol L. Meyers, "The Roots of Restriction: Women in Early Israel," in *BA* 41/3 (September 1, 1978): 92.

[38] John H. Otwell, *And Sarah Laughed: The Status of Women in the Old Testament* (Philadelphia: Westminster Press, 1977), 66, 194.

issue that they had no inheritance rights, could not take vows, initiate divorce, excluded from many cultic activities, virginity requirement only from female, etc.[39] On the other hand, there are other scholars who recognize the positive role played by women in the Old Testament. Phyllis Trible identifies several streams of evidence which argue for female liberation from within the Old Testament. She notes the numerous feminine images of God.[40] She states that the Exodus speaks forcefully to women's liberation. She points out that the Hebrew midwives nurtured revolution that led to Israel's release from bondage by disobeying Pharaoh, including his own daughter and her maiden that thwarted him. She avows that a patriarchal religion which creates and preserves such feminist traditions contain resources for overcoming patriarchy.[41]

The term "ancient" is a vast and vague category ranging over thousands of years, but this study concentrates on Iron Age I. Therefore, the following is a brief survey on it.

4.1. Iron Age I (c. 1200-1000 BCE)

This study concentrates on Iron Age I period.[42] It is the period understood to be the formation of Israelite state in Palestine. It highlights the highland side traditionally associated with the emergence of ancient Israel.[43] This is a community bound in covenant with God through the leadership of Moses.

Archeologically, the Israelite formative period coincides with the closing decades of the Late Bronze Age and the beginning of the centuries of the Iron Age in Palestine. The period is known as Iron Age I, because people used iron to make knives, swords and other tools and weapons. The scholars prefer to name periods, especially in ancient history, after the material used to make tools.[44] The Stele of

---

[39] This book synthesizes much material on women in the Jewish world beginning from the Old Testament to Greek and Roman literature and portrays well the status of Women in the time of Jesus. See, Evelyn and Frank Stagg, *Women in the World of Jesus* (Philadelphia: Westminster Press, 1978), 15–32.

[40] Phyllis Trible, "Depatriarchalizing in Biblical Interpretation," in *JAAR* 41/1 (March 1973): 32–3.

[41] Trible, "Depatriarchalizing in Biblical Interpretation," 34.

[42] It is an archaeological designation that expresses the position of ancient Israelite on the continuum of time.

[43] Ann E. Killebrew, *Biblical Peoples and Ethnicity: An Archaeological Study of Egyptians, Canaanites, Philistines, and Early Israel* (Atlanta: SBL, 2005), 156; Cf. Avraham Faust, *The Archaeology of Israelite Society in Iron Age II*, trans. Ruth Ludlum (Winona Lake, Indiana: Eisenbrauns, 2012), 28; Elizabeth Bloch-Smith and Beth Alpert Nakhai, "A Landscape Comes to Life: The Iron I Period," in *NEA* 62/2 (June 1999): 62.

[44] Marian Broida, *Ancient Israelites and their Neighbours: An Activity Guide* (Illinois: Chicago Review Press, 2003), xiv.

Merneptah described Israel not as a city state, but as a separate ethnic group.[45] It is because the people were said to have scattered across the central Israel hill country of Judah and Samaria and beyond, inhabiting numerous small regions.[46]

The exploration of the central highlands is said to have revealed hundreds of villages constructed during the same period and all dating to the Iron Age I.[47] It refers to a period which lasted during the 12th and 11th centuries BCE in the central Israel hill country where the society was said to be more egalitarian.[48] It was an agrarian society pioneering virgin sites which Meyers has compared to smallholders according to today's context.[49] Many scholars are of the view that during Iron Age I period, men and women played vital roles in their households and communities.[50] This group of people formed a cohesive group of agriculturists by the late 12th century BCE sharing material culture with the neighbouring nations.[51] In studying the formative phases of early Israelite history, archaeology helps by acting as a witness to the events described in the biblical text.[52]

An important characteristic of Iron Age I is that, it was the era in which the people of Israel began to develop their own patterns of life that persisted well into the monarchy. It was a period where they developed their individual identities that would eventually provide the basis for nationhood in the subsequent centuries.

---

[45] The stele of Merneptah is an inscription by the Ancient Egyptian king Merneptah, giving accounts of his victory over the Libyans and their allies. He is said to have reigned from 1212 to 1203 BCE. This tablet was discovered by Flinders Petrie in 1896 at Thebes, the capital of Egypt which now housed the Egyptian Museum in Cairo. Cf. http://en.wikipedia.org/wiki/Merneptah_Stele, 2 February 2013.

[46] William J. Dumbrell, *The Faith of Israel: A Theological Survey of the Old Testament*, 2nd ed., (Leicester: Baker Books, 2002), 74.

[47] Beth Alpert Nakhai, "Daily Life in the Ancient Near East: New Thoughts on an Old Topic," in *RSR* 31/3–4 (July 2005): 147.

[48] Jennie R. Ebeling, *Women's Lives in Biblical Times* (Auckland, New Zealand: T&T Clark International, 2010), 17; Cf. Carolyn S. Leeb, *Away from the Father's House: The Social Location of Na'ar and Na'arah in Ancient Israel* (Sheffield: Sheffield Academic Press Ltd, 2000), 30; Carol L. Meyers, "The Family in Early Israel," in *Families in Ancient Israel* eds. Leo G. Perdue, et al., (Louisville: Westminster/John Knox Press, 1997), 1–47.

[49] It is beyond the purview of this research to discuss in detail about the origin of the population of this period. Cf. Meyers, "Family in Early Israel," 3.

[50] Ebeling, *Women's Lives*, 17; Cf. Susan Ackerman, "Digging up Deborah: Recent Hebrew Bible Scholarship on Gender and the Contribution of Archaeology," in *NEA*, No. 4 (December 2003): 175–7; Carol Meyers, "Having their space and eating there too: Bread Production and Female Power in Ancient Israelite Households," in *Nashim: JJWS&GI* No. 5 (October 1, 2002): 28–33.

[51] Ebeling, *Women's Lives*, 15.

[52] Brain B. Schmidt, "A Summary Assessment for Part 1," in *The Quest for the Historical Israel: Debating Archaeology and the History of Early Israel* eds. Israel Finkelstein and Amihai Mazar (Boston: BRILL, 2007), 6.

4.2. Ancient Israel as an Agrarian Society

Without any doubt, ancient Israelite society was an agrarian society with large expanses of cultivable land. As an agrarian society their religion, ethics, and communal life were permeated by agricultural world-views and concerns. Shunya Bendor describes how the Israelite kinship structure was rooted in the sedentary agricultural society.[53] As an agrarian society, their lives were closely tied to the land, working it by the sweat of their brow, given to hard labour where famine was said to be frequent. It is also important to mention that along with farming, herding was also carried out. This pastoral component, wherein flocks of small animals, principally sheep and goats were also said to have provided support to the society, along with their agricultural enterprise, by the production of milk, manure, fiber, and meat.[54] By combining farming and herding they distributed their labour evenly throughout the season and insured themselves against facing the dry season without having produced any food at all.

5. Israelite Kinship Structure

There are three levels of kinship in Israelite society and this is reflected in the way Israelite names were recorded. For example, when the Israelite lost the battle to Ai, the search for the guilty person narrows down from tribe (מַטֶּה/שֵׁבֶט) to clan (מִשְׁפָּחָה) to the family (בֵּית אָב), and finally to the individual Achan.[55] This same three levels of kinship is also found in other biblical passages like 1 Samuel 9:21; 10:20–21; Judges 6:15.

Israel was a patrilineal society, a segmentary lineage system in which each of its house-holds known as *bet-ab* (בֵּית אָב) belonged to the lineage. Bendo states that, this kinship system of ancient Israelite society continued to exist even during the monarchy in the city, when the economy continued to be autarkic.[56] The following is an examination of the Israelite three tiers kinship structure.

5.1. Family

The family is the institution where human life came into being. The Hebrew word בֵּית אָב literally meaning "father's house," is translated into English as

---

[53] Shunya Bendor, *The Social Structure of Ancient Israel: The Institution of the Family* (בית-אב) from the Settlement to the end of the Monarchy (Jerusalem: Simor, 1996), 262–3.

[54] Leeb, *Away from the Father's House*, 30.

[55] Victor Matthew's book, which focuses on the contibution of archaeology in biblical studies, makes use of modern anthropological research, and he attemps to produce the composite picture of the manners and customs of AW Asian societies. He tries to proof how texts and artifacts can comlpement each other to form a vivid picture of everyday life in biblicl times. He also states in detail the importance of the family as the focus of life. Cf. Victor H. Matthews, *Manners and Customs in the Bible: An Illustrated Guide to Daily Life in Bible Times* (Peabody, Mass: Hendrickson, 2006), 62; See also, C.J.H. Wright, "Family," in *ABD* vol. 2 (D–G) eds. David Noel Freedman et al., (New York, Doubleday: Doubleday, 1992), 761.

[56] Economic independence as a national policy. Cf. Bendor, *Social Structure*, 216–24.

"family." It was the smallest unit of the society but a fairly large group of people. It is composed of blood relatives as well as women connected through marriage, and also includes unmarried children, slaves and servants (Deut. 12:7, 12).[57] The sons' wives and children would be part of the household along with patriarch's unmarried brothers and sisters. As seen in Deuteronomy 16:11, the household also incorporates other members of the community like Levites, sojourners, widows and orphans. Here, every individual felt the strongest sense of inclusion, identity protection and responsibility. The household is patrilocal where wives lived with their husbands' families, and the inheritance was passed through the male line. Therefore, in ancient Israel, the family is composed of people connected by blood, marriage or location.[58] All of these members lived in one four room house or in a complex made of several attached houses that provide the total structure for the family's lifestyle. This included work, worship, teaching, discipline, generosity, hospitality and care for the strangers.

The term בֵּית אָב reflects the fact that marriage does not mean a man leaving his family but even after marriage he continues to stay in his father's house with his wife and children. It is a basic unit based on the patriarchal nature where the father had total authority over his children, even the married ones if they continued living with him.[59] After the father's death, the family may have continued to live together and in this case one of the brothers usually the oldest became the head of the household.[60] It is a place of authority, security and protection. Today it would be called the extended family, which was a sizeable group of related nuclear families descended in the male ancestral line that includes up to three or four generations. Socially, the בֵּית אָב was the most important small unit in the nation, providing social identity for the individual Israelite, and with the authority vested with the family patriarch.

The family is also said to be the basic unit in the ownership of property, cultivation of land, and care of pastoral animals.[61] Each family has its own inheritance (נַחֲלָה) of land and they are economically self-sufficient. A family in Israel is defined corporately not only by its human members but also by its

[57] Oded Borowski, *Daily Life in Biblical Times* (Atlanta: SBL, 2003), 22; Cf. John Goldingay, *Old Testament Theology: Israel's Life* vol. 3 (Downers Grove: IVP Academic, 2009), 384.

[58] Caryn A Reeder, "Wives and Daughters: Women, Sex, and Violence in Biblical Tradition," in *Ex Auditu* 28 (2012): 124.

[59] MacVann has also said that, both father and mother are frequently mentioned together and received uncompromised respect and obedience from all the members within the family, but male dominant is clearly preeminent in this strongly patriarchal society. His observation is true in terms of inheritance, but this is very shallow way of looking at the ancient Israelite family where mothers were preeminent. This further opens the avenue to read the biblical text critically and discover the missing information about women's role in the family. Cf. Pilch, John J. and Bruce J. Malina, eds., *Handbook of Biblical Social Values* (Peabody, Mass: Hendrickson Publishers, 2000), 76.

[60] Faust, *Archaeology of Israelite Society*, 11.

[61] Miller and Hayes, *History of Ancient Israel*, 85.

possessions, which allows it to maintain a social position in society. Members are expected to remain within the family to which an inheritance had been apportioned.

The whole of Old Testament gives us no single example of an Israelite voluntarily selling land outside the family. This had one great advantage that is, the family was economically autonomous, in a sense that it did not owe any of its produce to higher authorities in the form of the payments in kind, but they have obligation to extend aid to another בֵּית אָב in need.[62] Max Weber claims that in Ancient Israelite society's authority was located in the family unit where inter-relationship between religion and society was in balance.[63] According to the Pentateuchal narratives, both male and female in the family contributed equally in the family.

5.2. Clan

Beyond the level of the household, the authority was conferred in the hands of the elders. The clan which in Hebrew is מִשְׁפָּחָה was a larger grouping of a number of families related to one another. The population of a village was said to have comprised of more than one בֵּית אָב, and this unit was known as מִשְׁפָּחָה where a person was identified by his father's lineage going back as far as five generations.

(1 Sam. 9:1).[64] It refers to a regional or political entity consisted of several extended families living in close proximity to one another, interlocked by marriage, and employing communal use of land.

This clan is represented by men from every extended family. They were heads of the households and property owners. They represent the collective wisdom of the community and function in the interest of the village and for the welfare of the entire community.

The clan had important responsibility in the preservation of the land allotted to its constituent household.[65] The land of the various households was owned by the מִשְׁפָּחָה which was also the body responsible for redeeming lands. They are responsible for organizing resources and providing goods and services to their overlords. It is said that the surplus was used mainly for storage as a guarantee against the devastating famines that might strike at any time and which

---

[62] Norman K. Gottwald, *The Tribes of Yahweh: A Sociology of the Religion of Liberated Israel, 1250-1050 B.C.E* (Maryknoll: Orbis Books, 1981), 292.

[63] Cited by Naomi Steinberg, "Sociological Approaches: Toward a Sociology of Childhood in the Hebrew Bible," in *Method Matters: Essays on the Interpretation of the Hebrew Bible in Honor of David L. Petersen,* eds. Joel M. LeMon, and Kent Richards (Atlanta: SBL, 2009), 252–3.

[64] Borowski, *Daily Life*, 22.

[65] Christopher J. H. Wright, "Year of Jubilee," in *ABD,* vol. 3, eds. David Noel Freedman et al., (New York: Doubleday, 1992), 1025; Cf. Jason S. Bray, *Sacred Dan: Religious Tradition And Cultic Practice in Judges 17-18* (London: T&T Clark, 2006), 20.

sometimes even lasted for two to three years in a row. In such a situation the מִשְׁפָּחָה stood by to offer relief.[66]

5.3. Tribe

Israel is divided into a number of units each of which may be called "tribe." The two root words שבט (Ps. 122:4) and מטה are used interchangeably for tribe. The tribes in ancient Israelite society deal with communal exigencies that include territorial boundaries and the development of mutual aid. Meyers suggests that tribes might better be captured by the term "chiefdom," a territorially based unit of society in which hierarchies of leadership is based on kinship.[67] According to Thompson tribes were the product of the social structure of a settled, agrarian population comprised of extended families.[68] The tribe served as a larger and more strictly endogamous unit than the clan, that is, person generally married within the clan rather than within the tribe. It is said to be more territorial than genealogical in nature, because the tribal names probably originated from territorial designations.[69] For example the name "Ephraim" is said to have originated referring to the people living in the vicinity of mount Ephraim. The name "Gilead," refers to the people living in the region called Gilead, and "Judah," for people living near mount Judah, "Benjamin," which means son of the south.[70] Along with the tribes' relationship with the geography of the area in which they were located, its relationship with kinship cannot be dismissed. Therefore, tribal identity developed over time among families and clans living in close proximity to one another.

6. The Role of Women in Ancient Israel

One of the most important social revolutions of the late 20th century has been the rise of modern feminism. This consciousness had enlightened the biblical scholars about how patriarchal culture had constructed and maintained male dominance and female subservience. Reading the biblical text with the support from archaeological and epigraphical evidences provides proof about women's role in the society as well as within the family.

The biblical text shows wife addressing her husband as slaves addressed the master by calling him master or lord (Gen. 18:12; Judg. 19:26; Amos 4:1). In the Decalogue wives are also among the husband's possessions together with house,

[66] Gottwald, *Tribes of Yahweh*, 292.

[67] As quoted by Perdue, *Blackwell Companion*, xiii–xiv.

[68] Thompson, *Early History*, 101.

[69] Bray, *Sacred Dan*, 21.

[70] Miller and Hayes, *History of Ancient Israel*, 84–6.

land, slaves, ox, ass. (Exod. 20:17).[71] This claim "wives as men's property" has been challenged by many scholars citing that wife is not listed here as property but as the first-named member of the household.[72] The parallel passage in Deuteronomy 5:21 also made the distinction clearly by placing the wife in a separate clause. Israelites could sell slaves (Exod. 21:2–11; Deut. 15:12–18) but never his wife even if she was acquired as a captive in war (Deut. 21:14). This is the evidence that wife was not considered as property.

Among the biblical feminist scholars, Meyers has been foremost in discovering the reality of women behind the biblical text in her book "Discovering Eve." She used multidisciplinary methods.[73] She discovered that the biblical text is inadequate to start with because of its overlay of theological interpretation. Therefore, she begins with archaeological evidence and demonstrates the significant interdependence among early Israelite women and men in the village-based agricultural society. She asserts that ancient Israelite society was an egalitarian society characterized by a sexual division of labour in which women's reproductive and productive labour was essential for survival.[74] It is said that the population was threatened by famine, disease, and warfare, and therefore women were desperately needed to breed and to labour alongside men in agriculture. When population later increased during the Israelite monarchy, patriarchy became powerful.[75] The social changes prompting this move towards a patriarchal society were due to a shift from rural to an urban society and the institution of the monarchy. It was in this context that more extreme forms of female restriction and subordination began to surface. This view is also supported by Milgrom. He states that, "one must be careful in describing ancient Israelite as "patriarchal" society."[76] He says that a woman is under her father's control before marriage and under husband's control after marriage. It is because of social norms that she is forced to abide by communal decisions to be dependent.[77]

Contrary to Carol Meyers, Frymer-Kensky acknowledges that the world of ancient Israel was a patriarchal society marked by social cleavage and argues that

[71] J. A. Thompson, *Handbook of Life in Bible Times* (Downers Grove: InterVarsity Press, 1986), 88.

[72] Otwell, *Sarah Laughed*, 76; Cf. Robin Gallaher Branch, "Women in the Old Testament," in *The Eerdmans Companion to the Bible*, eds. Gordon D. Fee and Robert L. Hubbard Jr., (Grand Rapids, Michigan: William B. Eerdmans Publishing Company, 2011), 198.

[73] Meyers, *Discovering Eve.*

[74] Meyers, *Discovering Eve*, 169.

[75] Carol Meyers, "The Roots of Destruction," in *The Bible and Liberation: Political and Social Hermeneutics*, eds. Norman K. Gottwald and Richard A. Horsley (Maryknoll, N.Y.; London: Orbis Books, 1993), 289–306.

[76] Jacob Milgrom, "Leviticus 17–22," in *AB: A New Translation with Introduction and Commentary*, vol. 3A (New Delhi: Doubleday, 2000), 1412–3.

[77] Milgrom, *Leviticus 17–22:* in *AB*, vol. 3A, 1413.

"there is nothing distinctively "female" about the way women are portrayed in the Bible."[78] She insists that the biblical image of women is consistently the same as that of men. Looking through an anthropological lens, Madeline McClenney-Sadler claims that woman in the Iron Age household were the legal heads of the family and that Leviticus 18 provides theological and social equity for women in the family.[79] Women's contributions should not be analysed within the framework of domestic realm but should encompass both public and private sphere, therefore, the following is an attempt to examine the role of women in religion, legal system and domestic economy.

6.1. The Role of Women in Israelite Religion

Ancient Israelite religion was in fact a religion of both men and women. A century ago scholars like Wellhausen, Benzinger, and Stade emphasized the masculine character of YHWH but number of studies in the recent years show that women were full and equal members in the Israelite religion.[80] This study limits itself to considering some prominent features to highlight the women's role in the religious activities.

Study of Israel's religion has come a long way during the past century because of the abundance of data provided by archaeologists in the AWA along with the archaeologists studying primitive cultures. In fact there are references in the biblical texts that point to women's rituals that are parallel to those of men. In Genesis 25:22–23 it is mentioned that Rebecca directly consulted YHWH and her prayer was answered. In the Book of I Samuel the first two chapters mentioned about "Hannah's powerful prayer" which is the evidence of female prayer in ancient Israel.

Priesthood of biblical religion is portrayed as a strictly and absolutely male profession. It was confined only to men and this is the reason most often cited to support the lower status of women in the Hebrew Bible. Phyllis Bird asserts that, one of the restrictions of women to the priesthood was because of their regular menstruation which would prevent their serving in the sanctuary (Lev. 15:19–24) and after childbirth (Lev. 12:1–8).[81] Since women's place in society is determined by their role within the family, they are not normally free to operate for extended

[78] Tikva Frymer-Kensky, *In the Wake of the Goddesses: Women, Culture, and the Biblical Transformation of Pagan Myth* (New York: Free Press, 1992), 120–1.

[79] Madeline McClenney-Sadler, "For God's Sake Mommie, Help! The Mother-Daughter Dyad in Leviticus 18 and the Biblical Directive for equity in the family," in *Mother Goose, Mother Jones, Mommie Dearest: Biblical Mothers and their Children* eds. Cheryl A. Kirk-Duggan and Tina Pippin (Atlanta: SBL, 2009), 9.

[80] Quoted by Phyllis A. Bird, "Women in the Ancient Mediterranean World: Ancient Israel," in *BR* 39 (1994): 42.

[81] Bird, *Missing Persons*, 93.

periods outside the home.[82] While these reasons may have contributed to some extend to the exclusion of women from the priesthood in Israel, they do not seem to establish the main reason. There were women who had servants and other female members in the family to perform the household tasks, and thus this maternal restriction did not apply.

Phyllis A. Bird claims that Israelite cultus is represented as a male constituted or male dominated institution and women's function was depicted as playing marginal.[83] In reality women's participation was broader and more significant than commonly depicted. Marc Zvi Brettler makes a survey on the selected texts from the Book of Psalms concerning women's role in ancient Israel's religion. She claims that the primary cultic distinction in the Bible is between priest and laity rather than between male and female.[84] She points out male centred Psalms like 127 and 128 which depict father of the family as one who upholds the religion. She claims that Israelite women too had rituals and prayers not recorded by the biblical authors.[85] The tribal blessings are put on the lips of prototypical fathers of all Israel but the songs of triumphs are often placed on the lips of women. This practice reflects an ancient custom of female singers as the celebrants of war such as, Miriam (Exod. 15:21), Deborah (Judg. 5:1), Hannah, mother of Samuel (1 Sam. 2:1).[86]

Although, only men worked as priests or Levites, both women as well as men could be prophets. They were holy people who could voice God's wishes and predict events in the future and who spoke out on behalf of the poor and downtrodden. Women prophets in the Bible included Deborah, Huldah, and Miriam. Huldah was so important that King Josiah turned to her for advice when some people in the temple found a mysterious scroll of religious law. According to the Bible, Huldah, inspired by the scroll foretold disaster for the people of Judah.

The wisdom books in the Bible (Proverbs, Job and Ecclesiastes) have many parallels with the texts of AWA, especially the Egyptian. The discovery of the instruction of Amenemope in the early 1920's has highlighted the foreign nature of Israelite wisdom.[87] Especially in the Proverbs texts there are mixing of sentences, instruction forms and subject matters similar to Amenemope. This similarity gave

---

[82] Phyllis A. Bird, "The Place of Women in the Israelite Cultus," in *Ancient Israelite Religion: Essays in Honor of Frank Moore Cross*, eds. Patrick D. Miller, Paul D. Hanson, and S. Dean McBride (Philadelphia: Fortress Press, 1987), 406.

[83] Bird, "Place of Women," in *Women in the Hebrew Bible: A Reader* ed. Alice Bach (New York: Routledge, 1998), 3.

[84] Marc Zvi Bretter, "Women and Psalms: Towards an Understanding of the Role of Women's Prayer in the Israelite Cult," in *Gender and Law*, 44.

[85] Bretter, "Women and Psalms," in *Gender and Law*, 44.

[86] Gottwald, *Tribes of Yahweh*, 119.

[87] Katharine J. Dell, *The Book of Proverbs in Social and Theological Context* (Cambridge: Cambridge University Press, 2006), 65.

rise to the suggestion that there was a class of "the wise" in Israel at the courts of kings, a foreign influence through the mechanisms of international diplomacy.[88] Education is the key link between the Israelites and the foreign nations. In Israel education was not detached from religious concerns. Wisdom is personified as woman, and this personified woman is not just a literary figure but a metaphor.[89]

Wisdom is clearly painted in a female form. No doubt, there are underlying meanings and values associated with women in Israel that exhibit connection attributed to the personified wisdom. When we consider the social roles of women in Israel, the ubiquity of wife and motherhood is readily apparent. The patriarchal society of Israel had made women to some degree second class citizens in terms of power, yet within the domestic realm they enjoyed high status where they could exercise both power and authority. Given the wisdoms books characteristic stress on the correct functioning of society, the implication is educational. The Israelites mothers along with the fathers were responsible in handing down the wisdom to the children. The Book of Proverbs provides the clearest picture of the authority of women and their equality to men in the instruction of children.[90]

In the biblical narratives, wives are depicted as counsellor to her husband (Gen. 27:46; 1 Sam. 25; 1 Kgs. 1:17–21, 21:7). If reflects realistically some of the expected responsibilities and modes of operation of the Israelite wife. The woman who gives advice stands at the centre of the sages' vision. It is clear that the woman figure in the Book of Proverbs gives advice. There are also negative female imageries in wisdom literature, particularly the passage in Proverbs 6:20–35 clearly represents an adulteress.

Although, women's voices were muted in the wisdom literature, yet considering the women's social role and the meaning and values associated with them, they employ wisdom tools that are, patience and soft tongue that persuade even rulers, an artfully asserted authority expressed in counsel. Both in real life and in literary imagination Israel wise women provide a cultural context for the theological appropriation.

Life-cycle rites which relates to birth and death, weaving and sewing of vestments, hangings, and other textiles for cultic use (Exod. 35:25–26), preparation for cultic meals used in the rituals (1 Sam. 2:13–17) are some of the main activities women were actively engaged in. Food preparation plays a central role in celebration of all major holidays, because it is the most important ritual activity. Susan Starr Sered affirms that it is the central symbol of each holiday.[91]

---

[88] Roland E. Murphy and O. Carm, *Wisdom Literature: Job, Proverbs, Ruth, Canticles, Ecclesiastes, Esther* (Grand Rapids, Michigan: William B. Eerdmans Publishing Company, 1981), 50.

[89] Camp, *Wisdom and the Feminine*, 13.

[90] Camp, *Wisdom and the Feminine*, 82.

[91] Susan Starr Sered, *Women as Ritual Experts: The Religious Lives of Elderly Jewish Women in Jerusalem* (New York: Oxford University Press, 1992), 55.

Cleaning of cultic vessels, furniture and quarters are also some of the women cultic services.

The biblical writers especially the Levitical writers portray an androcentric view of Hebrew life. The official cultic activities remain in the hands of man and YHWH never speaks to a woman but only to the sons of Aaron and to the gathering of the sons of Israel (Lev. 19:1–2; 21:1). They are also restricted from wearing priestly robes. Such is the portrait of women preserved by the androcentric Levitical writers.

Kaufman states that out of 613 *mitzvot*[92] in the Torah, 14 of these are not binding upon women because of physical inapplicability namely, causing one's wife to rejoice during the first year of marriage and circumcision.[93] It is observed that women also took the role of teaching the Rabbis who are said to be corrupted in the daily commercial world like market place.[94] The fullest and richest evidence for women's religious activity is said to be found in the pre-monarchic literature, such as, Miriam leading the Israelites in a song of victory (Exod. 15:20–21). There were women ministering at the tent of meeting (Exod. 38:8), Deborah as a judge and prophet and she has been honoured as a "mother of Israel," (Judg. 5:7). She is also depicted as a singer of Israel's victory through YHWH (Judg. 5:1). Micah's mother commissioned an image for the family shrine established by his son (Judg. 17:1–13), and there are many more.[95] Brettler claims that women were the reciters of prayers in ancient Israel, a fact which the Biblical authors due to the book's nature and ideology, have not reflected.[96] All these evidences points to Israelite women playing an active role like men in Israel religion, which was organized, centred in a temple, shrine, or other sacred site. This is so because Israelite religion was, from the above evidence, clearly a religion of both men and women.

6.2. The Role of Women in Legal System

There seems to be no fundamental distinction between the rights of the man and woman in the Jewish civil and criminal law. Women are permitted to initiate a court case and also are subject to the same criminal penalties as man. They are given preference and receive more favourable treatment than men by granting them the privilege of being heard first. However, women are said to be excluded from being court witnesses.[97] The misconception has arisen that because they are considered to be lightheaded, brazen or in some way untrustworthy, they

---

[92] A biblical or rabbinic precept or commandment.

[93] Michael Kaufman, *The Woman in Jewish Law and Tradition* (New Jersey: Jason Aronson, 1993), 208.

[94] Kaufman, *Woman in Jewish*, 209.

[95] Bird, "Place of Women." in *Women in the Hebrew Bible*, 8.

[96] Brettler, "Women and Psalms," in *Gender and Law*, 55–6.

[97] Kaufman, *Woman in Jewish Law*, 197.

are regarded as being of "questionable morality," and these cast doubt on their testimony.[98] Kaufmann has compared this situation of women to other groups of people such as kings; for example neither king David nor Solomon was permitted to testify in court which is said to be divine decree. Similarly high priests were also exempted from testifying.[99] Therefore, it may be assumed that disqualification is not based on credibility or reliability, but on technical ground, that is, a divine decree. In ancient Israelite society morality and law were intertwined. The covenant between God and people was a legal formulation and also the greater part of the Pentateuch consists of legal materials. It is fair to say, therefore, that since the Israelite household was the central unit of an agricultural society women were fully engaged with all the activities and so they exercised considerable power even in the legal system.

6.3. The Role of Women in Domestic Economy

The Hebrew word בֵּית means "household" and the household occupies an important place in economic activities in the Israelite society. It is the basic unit of production and consumption marked by self-sufficiency. During the settlement period the economy was mainly autarky but throughout the period of monarchy barter system based on supply and demand was introduced due to production surpluses. Throughout the Iron Age I, women enjoyed high status and had the ability to exercise their power.[100] The Bible also reflects the viewpoint of the literate elite that comprised only 10 percent of the population. As the remaining 90 percent belonging to the rural agriculturists, their views are not represented.[101]

There are many archaeological, ethnographical, epigraphical and other evidences outside the Bible which support women's contribution to the subsistence economy. Some of the evidences are found in Egyptian art showing women's participation in agricultural work. In this art, women of lower-class were depicted with dark skin because of their exposure to the sun out in the field.[102] This expression is also reflected in Hebrew Bible in Song of Songs 1:6: "Do not look at me because I am dark, because the sun has scorched me."

---

[98] Tal Ilan, *Jewish Women in Greco-Roman Palestine: An Inquiry into Image and Status* (Massachusetts: Hendrickson Publishers, 1996), 163.

[99] Kaufman, *Woman in Jewish Law*, 198.

[100] Susan Ackerman, "Digging up Deborah," in *NEA*, 4 (December 2003): 175; Cf. Bernhard Lang, "Women's Work, Household and Property in Two Mediterranean Societies: A Comparative Essay on Proverbs Xxxi 10–31," in *VT* 54/2 (2004): 201.

[101] The biblical source does not adequately represent the women's contribution due to author's emphasis on religious, political and historical aspects. Cf. Hanoch Reviv, *The Society in the Kingdoms of Israel and Judah*, Biblical Encyclopaedia Library (Jerusalem: Mosad Bialik, 1993), 2; See also, Burton McDonald, *East of the Jordan: Territories and Sites of the Hebrew Scriptures* (USA: American Schools of Oriental Research, 2000), 4; Carol L. Meyers, "Was Ancient Israel a Patriarchal Society?" in *JBL* 133/1 (2014): 19.

[102] Ebeling, *Women's Lives*, 36.

The numerous highland sites assumed to be Israel were situated in underdeveloped areas of the central hill country that were rocky, forested, and under-watered. They are said to have practiced terrace farming because settling on hillsides, the slope of the land was too steep to grow crops. Terrace farming meant turning a hillside into something like a staircase. They planted wheat, barley, fig, almond, olive, bushy pomegranate trees, grapevines, beans, lentils.[103] The demand of such environment involved substantial commitments of labour from both men and women.

This was an era of self-sufficiency. They made soap, brewed beer, processed grain, dried vegetables, wove and sewed clothing (Exod. 35:25–26), manufactured pottery and tools. They transformed raw materials into edible food in a pre-industrial world, and this was a world which was associated largely with women. It was time consuming and energy-demanding tasks. Every meal meant hours of work growing crops, grinding grain, pressing olive oil, milking goats, and so on.[104]

In Proverbs 31 there is a woman who is portrayed as an efficient and successful household manager.[105] She exhibits resourcefulness and insightfulness in economic processes. She keeps a record of how much food is available on site, supervises her workers and children. She even engages in the traditional tasks of spinning and weaving. Her duties also extend to ordering food from the outside world, buying and selling property to increase her family's holdings. In a household setting which is larger and more complex than the norm, women had a large economic role, both productive and reproductive. They actively participated in the agrarian work where bearing and caring children are subsumed into the daily routine in agrarian setting which did not disrupt female subsistence labours. They sustained the household with their work, while undergoing an endless series of pregnancies, many of which were said to have been very dangerous. It is said that as many as half of women eventually died in childbirth.[106] All these studies show that unlike today's nuclear families of parents and children, women in early Israelite society lived in extended families, and indeed played active, diverse, wider and vital roles.

Drawing insights from archaeology and comparative anthropological studies, Meyers disagrees with the prevailing view that patriarchy prevailed in every stratum of ancient Israelite society.[107] She maintains that while monarchy

---

[103] Ebeling, *Women's Lives*, 33.

[104] About five hours a day, cf. Ebeling, *Women's Lives*, 48.

[105] This subject will be dealt in detail in chap. 3 under the topic "Strong Woman." The portrait presented here is that of a "landed" upper-class woman whose household is well off. Cf. Carole Fontaine, *Smooth Words: Women, Proverbs and Performance in Biblical Wisdom,* JSOTSup Series No. 356 (New York: Sheffield Academic Press, 2002), 30.

[106] David M. Carr, *An Introduction to the Old Testament: Sacred Texts and Imperial Contexts of the Hebrew Bible* (West Sussex, UK: Wiley-Blackwell, 2010), 86.

[107] Meyers, "Was Ancient Israel," 19–23.

may be accurately termed androcentric institution, she observes that on the basic level, the economy of the ancient agrarian Israelite society was based in the household where women played significant roles, and that male dominance was not in household life.[108] She has presented a convincing argument that the social, economic, and political life at the rural level is significantly more egalitarian. Her claim holds true as during the formational period it was the household which was the centre of every aspect of life, and this is clearly reflected in the Bible and supported by extra biblical evidences. It was during the period beginning from monarchy with the introduction of social institutions that the role of men began to predominate as society started to move away from a house-hold-centred to a more external orientated one.

Constant wars, famine, plagues and childbearing had intensified the role of women in domestic realm. Of necessity their roles were confined within this circle and in the course of time with the introduction of social institutions, men's roles developed outside the domestic sphere and ultimately this shift in power became the basis for the women's subordination that is reflected in the biblical text. So it is quite clear that, even though women's contributions and concerns do not receive equal treatment in the biblical historical record, nevertheless, in the building of civilization, preservation and transmission of culture from one generation to the next, women have shared equally with men. Their involvements in the economic affairs have not only fulfilled individual needs but also served to support in the maintenance of the larger community.

7. The Status of Daughter

The daughters in the biblical texts are often presented as living in an uncertain space and remaining a suppressed voice that is not quite heard or listened to. The sequence of events in life for her was to grow up within the confines of the family to which she was born until the time of her marriage. Until her marriage she was under the protection of her father. As Mace states:

> Every woman in Israel would normally be under the authority of some men. At first it was her father, but on the marriage she was transferred to her husband, the head of the new household which she was to build up. As long as either was alive, therefore, she had to recognize the authority of her father or her husband.[109]

A daughter was passed from her father to her husband's sphere of authority without being consulted. In Genesis 24:51 we see one of the similar incidents where Rebekah was handed over by her father and brother to be Isaac's wife.

---

[108] For detail study see, Carol L. Meyers, *Rediscovering Eve: Ancient Israelite Women in Context* (New York: Oxford University Press, 2013), 183.

[109] David R. Mace, *Hebrew Marriage: A Sociological Study* (New York: Philosophical Library, 1953), 189.

She changed her family when she was married and she could not be expected to preserve her family's name. It was for this reason the law stated that she was entitled to maintenance rather than inheritance in most cases.

Inheritance was an important issue in the Israelite society. Daughter could not inherit property from their father unless there was no male heir. Thus, they can inherit the household's land only if their parents have no sons. They also receive a sum from the property for their dowry.[110] In general, biblical daughters' marriages are initiated by their fathers including their choice of partners.

There is a law concerning the chastity of daughters in Deuteronomy. According to Deuteronomy 22:28–29 (also found in Exod. 22:16–17), if she is seduced into premarital sex, the seducer had to pay the bride-price to her father and then the father could decide whether to grant her to him in marriage. On the Occasion of marriage, after the consummation of the marriage, if the man charges her by saying that she is not virgin and if the charge is true, she is stoned to death in her father's house (Deut. 22:13–21).[111] If she is found innocent she is not compensated and the penalty is that husband should not divorce her. According to these narratives the daughter's sexual purity belongs not only to her and family but to all Israel. Daughters in this passage are truly marginal, that as daughters they are pawns of their families. This offensive test which is a gross violation of women's rights is still openly practiced today.

Times of India reports about a man from Nashik (Maharashtra) ended his marriage after she failed virginity test. According to the report the couple married on 22nd May 2016. The caste panchayat offered the groom a white bed sheet and asked him to return soon after the consummation of marriage. The groom showed the panchayat without any blood stain in it and that led to the groom to terminate the relationship within 48 hours after they tied the knot.[112] This is one of the reported cases among many. Such type of women's rights violation is rampant in our society.

The laws maintained that unmarried women are supposed to remain virgins until they are married to a man of their father's choosing.[113] Ellen states that the primary concern of the law was a man's right to exclusive use of his wife's sexuality or the father's right to the money and honour from his daughter's chastity.[114]

---

[110] Kaufman, *Woman in Jewish Law,* 202.

[111] For further discussion see, Cheryl B. Anderson, *Women, Ideology, and Violence: Critical Theory and the Construction of Gender in the Book of the Covenant and the Deuteronomic Law* (London: T&T Clark, 2006), 40.

[112] Chittaranjan Tembhekar, "Nashik man ends marriage after wife fails 'virginity test," in *Times of India* (1 June 2016).

[113] Matthews, *Manners and Customs,* 36.

[114] Deborah L. Ellens, *Women in the Sex Texts of Leviticus and Deuteronomy: A Comparative Conceptual Analysis,* Library of Hebrew Bible/Old Testament Studies (New York: T&T Clark, 2008), 213.

It is the hierarchical social structure that demands the daughter's chastity. Since disbursing property through dowry was a common practice in the Mediterranean world, this makes it desirable for parents to guard their daughters' chastity.[115] Therefore, parents control their daughters' sexuality to make the best marriage alliances especially when status concerns are at stake in marriage transactions. It is interesting that in all this, chastity is required only from females.

CONCLUSION

Status and role of ancient Israelite women cannot be acquired from Hebrew Bible alone. Social scientific analysis of the Bible has the potential to recover important aspects of gender in antiquity. Sources from archaeology, epigraphy along with Hebrew Bible inform about women's activities. Cross–cultural anthropological studies of the Hebrew Bible demonstrate the significant interdependence among early Israelite women and men.

Kinship studies revealed that ancient Israelite family was composed of a sizable group of related nuclear families descended from the same lineage that includes up to three generations. This family was the cornerstone of Israelite society that provides social identity for every individual. The clan was a larger grouping of a number of families related to one another. Again, they are divided into many units known as tribe. Each member in this family contributed equally to the household economy. Unlike urban life, rural life in Iron Age I was directed mainly at securing the survival of the family. Every member of the family participated in the endeavour to survive. Although biological limitations determined the level of involvement, yet no one could escape participation.

There is a clear indication that there was no hierarchical domination of female by male during the Iron Age I period. In fact, the space women received in the biblical account is relatively brief, but it does not mean that they contributed very little in the society. Closer reading and reading behind the texts, also informed by extra-biblical sources reveals the dominant contributions made by women. They enjoyed rather high status in the domestic realm exercising both power and authority. The leadership principle was operative in the homes where women played vital role.

Compared to sons, daughters were held in less regard. There was always preference for male child to perpetuate the family line and fortune and to preserve the ancestral inheritance. Her father exerts total authority over her even to the extent of owning her sexuality. A man who rapes or seduces a girl must pay her father a penalty equivalent to bride-price. Father arranges her marriage to a man of his choosing even without her consent. But notwithstanding this attitude, Israelite women in general could, and did, hold important places in society.

[115] John K. Chance, "The Anthropology of Honor and Shame: Culture, Values, and Practice," in *Honor and Shame in the World of the Bible* SEMEIA No. 68, eds. Victor H. Matthews, Don C. Benjamin, and Claudia Camp (Atlanta: Scholars Press, 1996), 140–1.

Israelite society did not demand their total subservience; they were autonomous actors in many aspects of household and community life. Wife was treated by her husband in an egalitarian manner and she exercised an equal power at home. It is clear from all the evidences available that women enjoyed dynamic participation in private family decisions, and this meant that as family was the most important social unit where women exercised significant power.

Chapter 2

Biblical Understanding of Land and Its Relationship to the People of Israel

INTRODUCTION

The promise of land is one of the major elements in the Abrahamic promise.[1] Out of forty-six references to the promise–plan of God from Genesis to Judges, only seven references do not mention the land.[2] The Old Testament story is largely about the peoples' relationship to YHWH through the land. Therefore, this chapter focuses on understanding biblical relationships between YHWH, the chosen people of Israel and the Promised Land. This is done by examining the covenant relationships between these three entities.

This chapter begins with the biblical concept of land and different terms employed for land in the Old Testament. It also discusses divine ownership and the custom associated with the ownership such as Sabbath and jubilee year which has implication for poor. The land which has been given by YHWH as gift and received by Israelites is tied with covenantal responsibilities. There are consequences attached to breaking the laws which will result in punishing the people to the extent of eviction from the land. The theme of blessing and curse which is related to land will be discussed. Finally ancient Israelites' land laws will be explored.

Many advance studies on the subject of land and its ownership has been made in recent years but the present research differs in scope and focus from most previous works. This is through a combination of several factors, the main one

---

[1] Gen. 12:7; 15:7; 18–21; 17:8.

[2] Christopher J. H. Wright, *Old Testament Ethics for the People of God* (Leicester: InterVarsity Press, 2004), 78; See also, Gerhard von Rad, *The Problem of the Hexateuch and Other Essays* trans. E. W. Trueman Dicken (Edinburgh: Oliver & Boyd, 1966), 78–80.

being the general position of land as part of a wider study of land inheritance by women.

1. The Biblical Concept of Land

The Hebrew Bible maintains that when the Israelites appeared on the scene, the land they arrived at was already occupied by certain groups of people (Josh. 11:3). Joshua 13–21 strongly claims that YHWH conquered, possessed and gave the land as a gift to Israel. Israelites' understanding of land is governed by the fundamental assertion that is, "divine ownership." The land was promised through Abraham and renewed to Isaac, Jacob and Moses and finally fulfilled through Joshua. Many passages in the Hebrew Bible testify that YHWH has already fulfilled the promise that was made to the people of Israel.[3]

In Genesis 12:1–3, 7, God promised Abraham "people, land, and the ability to be a source of blessing to all families on the earth." Among all the promises YHWH made in the covenant, the promise of land was the most vital part. This covenant with Abraham plays an important role in the redemptive history of the Old Testament. God brought the people of Israel out of Egypt because God remembered the covenant which He made with Abraham, the promise to give them the land of Canaan. The goal of the exodus is therefore, the migration of the people of Israel to a new land which was promised to the patriarch (Exod. 6:2–8).[4]

In the Israelite culture and religion, the concept of land is so important that different terms are employed in the Old Testament to convey its precise meaning in different situations. Here is a brief survey of the three most frequently used terms for land.

1.1. Terminologies

This section concentrates on three key terms denoting the land of Israel in the Old Testament that is, אֶרֶץ (earth), אֲדָמָה (ground) and שָׂדֶה (field). Although, the terms are used synonymously, each has its own particular emphasis.

1.1.1. Earth (אֶרֶץ)

The term אֶרֶץ (earth) is the most frequently used word in the Old Testament. It generally refers to specific geographical regions, to large stretches of territory, that is, a particular region or country (2 Kgs. 19:37, "the land of Ararat"). It also refers

[3] Josh. 11:23; 21:41–45; Neh. 9:21–25. This issue is still in debate. It is beyond the scope of this research to dig into the issue further. Gregory Harris, in his article has well-articulated about the promise of land and he concludes "it is debatable to conclude that the promise of land was fulfilled by *YHWH*." His conclusion is based on reading beyond Joshua 21 and 1 Kings 4. Cf. Gregory H. Harris, "Did God Fulfill every good Promise? Toward a Biblical Understanding of Joshua 21:43–45 Part 2," in *MSJ* 24/1 (2013): 73–4.

[4] Tim Gorringe, "Political Reading of Scriptures," in *The Cambridge Companion to Biblical Interpretation*, Cambridge Companions to Religion ed. John Barton (Cambridge, England: Cambridge University Press, 1998), 77.

to the territory of human habitation, the territory of a specific people and to the earth as a whole (Gen. 15:19). The word אֶרֶץ also refers to a place possessed by people, nation or representative individual (1 Kgs. 10:13), also plots and estates of land (Gen. 23:15), regions within country (Gen. 47:11) or world (Gen. 10:10).[5] Therefore, it is understood that the word אֶרֶץ is used in a much wider range of situations where sometimes it carries global or cosmological connotations, referring to a type of terrain without emphasis on ownership.

1.1.2. Ground (אֲדָמָה)

The second Hebrew word אֲדָמָה is "land or ground." It is a non-political term used predominantly to designate agricultural land.[6] It denotes the habitable as in "useable" earth (Gen. 12:3). It is generally used in contrast to water especially used as productive soil or clay (Gen. 9:2).[7] It is used in relationship with the cultivated field or soil rather than a geographical or political entity.[8] אֲדָמָה is also used to designate a piece of land owned by an individual, by the head of the household or a group according to the land-owning system in Israel.

1.1.3. Field (שָׂדֶה)

The Hebrew word שָׂדֶה is often translated as "field" and it is used to denote a particular country (Gen. 14:7). More explicitly it refers to cultivated land, to open country, fields, open fields, domains. It is used to refer to cultivated land in contrast to wilderness. This signifies that the land is for raising crops, grazing cattle and sheep.[9] A number of passages describe how the people of Israel should care for the fields that they have received as a gift from God. They are required to provide for the family through the proper use of the land as well as to provide for the poor and orphans. They should also give tithes by bringing offerings to the sanctuary.[10]

While אֶרֶץ signifies "the land of Israel," שָׂדֶה serves as a subset. For Israelites שָׂדֶה serves as a realm in which all aspects of life take place. Its fertile soil provides sustenance for human existence and a refuge. It holds a significant place in their life as part of their inheritance from God. Although, not all the occurrences of

---

[5] David J. A. Clines et al., eds., "ארץ," in *The Dictionary of Classical Hebrew,* vol. 1 (א) (Sheffield: Sheffield Academic Press, 1993), 384.

[6] W. Janzen, "Land", in *ABD*, vol. 4 eds. David Noel Freedman et al., (New York, Doubleday: AB, 1992), 143–4.

[7] Clines eds., "אדמא," in *DCH,* vol. 1, 130.

[8] Francis Brown, S. R. Driver, and Charles A. Briggs, "אדמא," in *The NBDB Hebrew and English Lexicon: With an Appendix Containing Biblical Aramaic* (Peabody, Massachusetts: Hendrickson Publishers, 1979), 9.

[9] Michael A. Grisanti, "שדה," in *NIDOTTE*, vol. 3, eds. VanGemeren, et al., (Cumbria, UK: Paternoster Press, 1997), 1217.

[10] Grisanti, "שדה," in *NIDOTTE*, vol. 3, 1218.

the three key terms refer to the land of Israel, nevertheless it is mostly used in association with Israel and Judah for the greater part of their national history.

2. Divine Ownership

Ancient Israel was a nation of landowners with each family having been apportioned plot of land that was to be maintained by the family in perpetuity. However, YHWH is the ultimate owner of the land. Psalm 24:1 and Leviticus 25:23 are the two key passages in the Hebrew Bible that reflect the two basic principles in the land tenure system in ancient Israel that is, YHWH's ownership of land and the inalienability of land. YHWH is the sole owner of the land and it was a grant to the people of Israel under covenant. In today's terms they would be called "tenant farmers," holding their land from the owner (in this case, YHWH) subject to conditions, which included a wide range of responsibilities. The Israelites' identity as YHWH's tenants is evident in the laws of the tithe, first fruits and the first born (Deut. 14:22–23; 15:19–20; cf. 18:3–5).[11] A percentage of their crops and flocks belonged to the landlord "YHWH." The Book of Deuteronomy made it very clear that the land and its produce belong to YHWH.

The concept of divine ownership rests on the use of possessive word forms and the frequent description of the land as YHWH's inheritance. It is indeed through the gift of the land which God promised to the patriarchs that God manifested Himself as the God of Abraham and his descendants. Therefore, land which is owned by YHWH is a gift to the chosen people of Israel and it should not be treated as an incidental item, but as a part of the very substance of the gift.

Christopher Wright, in his brief explanation concerning "the divine ownership of land," states that the phrase "land of Israel" was never used in the context of Israel as the owner.[12] For instance, the use of the phrase אֶרֶץ יִשְׂרָאֵל (the land of Israel) in 1 Samuel 13:19 was used in the context of the Philistine oppression.[13] It is YHWH who owned the people of Israel as well as the land they occupy. Indeed the concept of divine ownership of land and people occupy a foundational position in the Sabbath and Jubilee legislation, as its existence implied YHWH's ownership of the land. A brief survey of the significance of caring for the poor, Sabbath and jubilee years in relation to YHWH's ownership of land will demonstrate this.

---

[11] Sandra L. Richter, "Environmental Law: Wisdom from the Ancients," in *BBR* 24/3 (2014): 313.

[12] Christopher J. H, Wright, "ארץ," in *NIDOTTE,* vol. 1, 522.

[13] See also, Ezek. 40:2; 47:18 (geographical), 1 Chr. 22:2, 2 Chr. 2:17 (referring to aliens in the country). Cf. Wright, "ארץ," in *NIDOTTE,* vol.1, 522.

2.1. Land and the Poor

Israelite law took a special interest in protecting the poor such as widows, orphans, immigrant aliens, Levites. They reserve a portion of their harvests for the poor and marginalized group of people.

The common people in Iron Age I period lived the fragile existence of a subsistence farmer. Their main economy was agriculture and pastoralism. In spite of their subsistence struggles they are commanded to refrain from harvesting the crops completely. They are to leave a portion of the crop for the poor (Deut. 24:19; Lev. 19:9–10; 23:22).[14] Protection of the vulnerable is repeatedly stressed in the Old Testament.

Deuteronomy 15:4 clearly stated that there shall be no poor people among the Israelites. This issue has been well articulated by Robert Wafawanaka in his article.[15] He argues that the poor will never cease to live among the Israelite community because Israel has disobeyed its divine order.[16] He states that this particular verse explains why the poor are always there when they are not supposed to be. Had the people obeyed the *Torah*, there would not be any poor in the community as the community members would take care of them.[17] According to the biblical text, they disobeyed YHWH and because of which the poor continued to be among them. The implication of such a proposition was to undergird exploitative features of Israel's economic system as well as accommodate economically vulnerable persons in the society. Therefore, Deuteronomy 15:4 should be understood in the context that, if the people of the community follow God's laws, there will be no poverty in the society, God will bless the land, hence, by implication, the society will experience poverty if God's instruction is not followed. The God who saved Israelites from the bondage is the protector of the poor, weak and disinherited. The purpose of Israel's economy was to supply to the needy.

2.2. Land and the Sabbath Year

Just as the people of Israel are to work for six days and rest on the seventh day, so also they are to sow and harvest the land for six years and allow it to rest on the seventh year (Exod. 23:10–11). It was real test of faith for the people of Israel. After six years of cultivation and harvest, land is to be left fallow for a year so that whatever the land produces on its own, the poor in their midst and the animals were to eat. The substance of Exodus 23:10–11 is repeated in Leviticus 25 with some expansions. It is said that the land is to have a Sabbath rest, and a

---

[14] Richter, "Environmental Law," 314.

[15] Robert Wafawanaka, "Is the Biblical Perspective on Poverty that "there shall be no Poor among you" or "You will always have the Poor with you?" in *R&E* 111/2 (May 2014): 107–20.

[16] Wafawanaka, "Is the Biblical Perspective," 112.

[17] Wafawanaka, "Is the Biblical Perspective," 112.

Sabbath to the LORD (Lev. 25:2; 23:10). The law of Sabbath year is also found in Deuteronomy 15:1–18.

This sabbatical year legislation also called for the release of Hebrew slaves (Exod. 21:2; Deut. 15:12–15), and cancellation of debts (Deut. 15:1–3).[18] The laws of Deuteronomy 15 are the product of economically driven processes in ancient Israel.

The land is to cease from its activity every seventh year. It is also said that the interruption of all production every seventh year reminds the inhabitants about the authority of the ultimate ownership of the land.[19] This practice of leaving the land fallow for the purpose of rejuvenation was said to be common among Israel's neighbours, although the reason may be different.[20] For the Israelite it was mandatory to keep the land fallow for the benefit of the poor including wild life. Also the land by being left fallow bears witness to YHWH's ownership.

However, if the land is mortgaged for some pressing need to their creditors, it must be handed back so that it may revert to the tribes and families to whom it belonged as an inheritance.

Failure to observe this statute would result in drastic action by God, that is, removal of people from the land (Lev. 26:32–33, 43: 2 Chr. 36:21). Behind the blessing of the land there is a grave warning that without righteousness the land will vomit them out for defiling it (Lev. 18–28). Therefore, the major obligation on the part of the Israelites is to keep the land Sabbath. In sum, by means of Sabbath law, Israel was instructed in the wisdom of longevity and sustainable soil fertility, and it is done in concert with the nation's understanding that the land belonged to YHWH.

In an agrarian society, one's life is dependent on a successful harvest. During this period there was no modern method of food preservation. Hence, it was previously thought to be difficult to imagine that a single harvest on a subsistence farm would feed the extended family members for two years until new crops are harvested. However, extra biblical sources give evidence that the practice of Sabbatical year was observed.[21]

---

[18] It is beyond the scope of this section to discuss in detail the release of slaves and cancelation of debts but special emphasis is made on cessation from cultivation of farmland, because it is the study of land in the wider context.

[19] Adrian Schenker, "The Biblical Legislation on the Release of Slaves: The Road from Exodus to Leviticus," in *JSOT* No. 78 (June 1998): 25.

[20] Elmer A. Martens, "Land and Lifestyle," in *The Flowering of Old Testament Theology: A Reader in the Twentieth Century Old Testament Theology 1930–1990* eds. Ben C. Ollenburger, Elmer A. Martens, and Gerhard F. Hasel (Indiana: Eisenbrauns, 1992), 315.

[21] Lee W. Casperson, "Sabbatical, Jubilee, and the Temple of Solomon," in *VT* 53/3 (2003): 184.

2.3. Land and the Jubilee Year

The word Jubilee comes from the Hebrew word יוֹבֵל meaning "a ram's horn." A ram's horn was to be sounded throughout the land to give signal to the people that the Jubilee year has begun (Lev. 25:9–10). It comes once after every 49 years. It is a proclamation that informed the people to release all who were in financial bondage so they could return to their family's property and clans. In Leviticus 25:18–22, YHWH gives assurance that if they are faithful to keep the command in giving the land rest, the Israelite will not lack food, because YHWH will bless the crop that will be sufficient for each family for the period of two years.

Jubilee was in essence an economic institution with two main concerns, namely, family and the land.[22] Even the land must be freed from exploitation by neither ploughing nor reaping.

All that was prescribed for the Sabbatical year was applied to the Jubilee year as well, but the Jubilee year has some unique characteristics, that is, restoration of Israelite landless slaves (Exod. 21:1–6; Deut. 15:12–17), and return of the land sold during the previous years (Lev. 25:29–31).

The command to observe jubilee is attached to the set of instructions. The Jubilee instruction includes return of person to their landed property and to their clan. These "persons" refer to those who have been alienated from their families and clans through poverty. If a land-holding Israelite falls into debt, in the first place, it was the responsibility of the clan members to purchase the land or in other words redeem it from an outside buyer and thereby keep the land within the clan. Secondly, sometime in dire poverty, his richer kinsman would take the debtor's entire family members into service as bonded labour, or redeem from an outsider to whom he had sold himself.[23]

In the modern world, the individual is sovereign over the land they own, but for the Israelites the land cannot be alienated from the family and clan, and each individual is a mere tenant. The land has to be retained within the particular family of the clan, otherwise descendants of the unfortunate Israelite would be condemned to be property-less. So, Jubilee was a mechanism for preserving equitable land distribution. The Jubilee year comes as a remedy for this eventuality.[24] The focus is more on the preservation of the household and its land. Without such a provision as a Jubilee, territories of a clan could come into the hands of a few families, and the remaining clans' people would be serfs. Therefore, Jubilee rests upon the assumption that all Israelites were attached to family land allotted to the several families at the time of the conquest of Canaan. Therefore, the theological grounds for the Jubilee measures are: firstly, the land cannot be

[22] Christopher J. H. Wright, *The Mission of God: Unlocking the Bible's Grand Narrative* (Downers Grove: IVP Academic, 2006), 290.

[23] Andrew G. Shead, "An Old Testament Theology of the Sabbath Year and Jubilee," in *RTR* 61/1 (April 2002): 21–2.

[24] Martens, "*Land and Lifestyle,*" 316.

sold as it belongs to God, and secondly, Israelites cannot be cast into perpetual slavery for they are servants of God, who brought them out of slavery in Egypt.

As the people of Israel settled in the new land and developed into a nation, they are obligated to observe the entire laws, such as care for the poor, sabbatical year and the year of Jubilee. The main concern of Leviticus is restoration of land to its original owners, release of persons from debt and slavery. In Exodus 23 and Deuteronomy 15, the emphasis is on liberation of person. The basic principles involved in all these passages is that, YHWH, as the creator is the true owner of the land and the people who occupied are only the tenants. They will be scattered throughout other nations if they fail to observe this law. The assertion of divine possession of the land is the fundamental concern of the Sabbath and jubilee legislations.

3. Land as a Gift of God

The theme of land as gift undergirds the Old Testament narrative. It is a proof of YHWH's faithfulness and dependability, and this gift demands gratitude and worship (Deut. 26:1–11). In Deuteronomy, the land became the special area of focus where sixty-nine times the writer repeated the pledge that Israel would one day possess and inherit the land. Repeatedly, the land was called the gift from YHWH.[25] The word נָתַן which means "to give" occurs 167 times in the Book of Deuteronomy out of which 131 have "YHWH" as subject and "land" as the object.[26] This is the clear indication of YHWH's action in Israel's possession of the land.

Land as a gift is also reflected in Isaiah chapter 5:8–10. Here the prophet critiques rich people who are adding house to house and conjoining field to field. The prophet draws attention to the causes of the exile which includes the continuing practice of social injustice. The prophet laments, because the splendid homes and joining field to field were done at the cost of both the land which is the gift from God and the people who depended on it for sustenance (v. 10).[27] Paulson Pulikottil, in his commentary on the book of Isaiah affirms that the large proportion of the Israelite population was left landless because of the greediness of the ruling elites.[28] Prophet Isaiah in his grief predicts that those buildings are destined to fall. It concludes with an explanation that the result of

---

[25] Walter C. Kaiser, *Toward an Old Testament Theology* (Grand Rapids: Zondervan Publishing House, 1991), 124–5.

[26] J. Gordon McConville, *Law and Theology in Deuteronomy* (Sheffield: JSOT Press, 1984), 12.

[27] This particular text has been well articulated by Thomas in his article, Heath Thomas, "Building House to House (Isaiah 5:8): Theological Reflection on Land Development and Creation Care," in *BBR* 21/2 (2011): 189-212.

[28] Paulson Pulikottil, "Isaiah," in *South Asia Bible Commentary: A One-Volume Commentary on the whole Bible* eds. Brian Wintle et al., (Rajasthan, India: Open Door Publications, 2015), 844.

commercialization of land would be the destruction of the people.[29] It condemned human pride and greed at the expense of the land which is a gift from God. It was granted to the people by YHWH as a fief in which she could cultivate and live on it as long as she served God. The divine gift rather than the occupation of the land as such is what lies at the core of Israel's faith and confession.

Leviticus 25:23 is a passage that comes from the context dealing with the year of Jubilee, declaring God as the owner of the land. The context of this passage was the ancient Israelite concept of family property allotted during the settlement period. Thus, one of the central theological affirmations about the land is that, it is the gift of God to Israel. Christoph Barth comments about the many references to the gift of the land and claims that Israel's possession of the land was never sure or self-evident, as it was always a matter of promise. It was an article of faith which stood in close relation to the election of the patriarch and liberation from Egypt.[30]

The phrase וְהָאָרֶץ נִכְבְּשָׁה לִפְנֵיהֶם "And the land was subdued before them," (Josh. 18:1) is found in the contexts concerning the gift of land by YHWH to the Israelites.[31] Ute Neumann-Gorsolke studies the root word כבש which is translated as "subdue" or "bring into bondage" from two passages that is, Joshua 18:1 (Niphal, "to be subdued"), and Genesis 1:28 (Qal "to subdue"). According to him, Genesis was set in a scene of a just created world without any enemies and in Joshua the scene was set in a cultic situation without any notion of warfare. The only activity is, to set up the tent of meeting, representing the powerful presence of God. The land is imagined to be free and empty before them, and they just have to set foot on it to own for themselves.[32] Here, the role of the Israelite is passive, underlining the fact that the Promised Land is a gift of YHWH. Even in the AW Asian practice, "to set foot on," is a symbolic act that expresses the idea of taking possession of land which corresponds to Joshua 18:1. So, it is significant that the phrase "to subdue" is found in the context concerning the gift of the land by YHWH. According to him it is a late priestly-influenced phrase referring to Genesis 1:28. The creation background emphasizes that the gift of the land is the gift of the creator of the world and the culmination is when the Israelites took possession of the Promised Land and the land gets its theological foundation.[33] The idea of trampling the enemy and territory which is also the practice of AWA strikes a familiar note when we consider Old Testament passages like Joshua 1:3.

---

[29] Joseph Blenkinsopp, *Isaiah 1-39* ed. William Foxwell Albright et al., vol. 19 AB (New York: Doubleday, 2000), 212–3.

[30] Christoph Barth, *God With Us: A Theological Introduction to the Old Testament,* ed. Geoffrey W. Bromiley (Grand Rapids: William B. Eerdmans Publishing Company, 1991), 168.

[31] Ute Neumann-Gorsolke "'And the Land Was Subdued Before Them,'? Some Remarks on the Meaning of כבש in Joshua 18:1 and Related Texts," in *The Land of Israel in Bible, History, and Theology* vol. 124 eds. Jacques van Ruiten and J. Cornelis de Vos (Leiden: BRILL, 2009), 84–5.

[32] Neumann-Gorsolke, "Land Was Subdued," 83–4.

[33] Neumann-Gorsolke, "Land Was Subdued," 84–5.

Walter Brueggemann, in his book "*The Land*," investigates the biblical function of land using socio-economic, political and environmental methods. He claims that the "land is a central theme of biblical faith." To put it in another way, "it is the land that fully permits Israel to be Israel, YHWH to be YHWH, YHWH and Israel to have history together."[34] According to him the land as a gift must be managed properly. He noted two models of land management, that is, the judges and the kings. The judges engaged primarily in crisis intervention at the behest of YHWH.[35] The root word שפט which means "to rule or govern," describes a range of actions that restore or preserve order in society. YHWH delegates to certain individuals the responsibility to administer justice. In the course of time, prior to the monarchic regime, it was the head of the household or representative of the family in the clan to whom were assigned the responsibility to make decision on legal issues.[36]

Kingship is another form of decision-making where the king presided over the organized life of Israel. The Israelites recognized the kingship as an appropriate authority for land management, so they asked for a king like other nations (1 Sam. 8:5, 19–20). But, the speeches at the boundary in Deuteronomy make it clear that Israel is to hold the land in a way different from that of other nations. Israel was granted permission to have a king with a condition that the form may be same but the intent is to be different. This was because the political reality of land settlement in Israel's neighbourhood was, that the kings had primary access to land and control over the land.[37] On the other hand, the king of Israel is to manage the land as a gift entrusted to him but it is never to be possessed by him.[38]

In the Old Testament, the divine gift of land demands Israel's intentional care, that they in return illustrate God's grace to the nations. It is echoed throughout the biblical text as the people of God are continually called to leave the land (Egypt), embrace the wilderness, and receive the land.

---

[34] Walter Brueggemann, *The Land: Place as Gift, Promise, and Challenge in Biblical Faith* (Minneapolis: Fortress, 2002), 133.

[35] Brueggemann, *Land: Place as Gift,* 73.

[36] E. J. Pentiuc, "Judges," in *DOTP,* eds. T. Desmond Alexander and David W. Baker (Illinois: InterVarsity Press, 2003), 484–5.

[37] A Hittite text states that the storm god made the king, the *Labarna,* the governor of the land of Hatti. Quoted by G. W. Ahlstrom, *Royal Administration and National Religion in Ancient Palestine,* Studies in the History of the ANE series (Leiden: E. J. Brill, 1982), 6; In Egypt, the supreme god "Re" entrusted the land to his son, the King. Cf. Ahlstrom, *Royal Administration,* 6; Hammurabi of Babylon describes himself as the caretaker, restorer and organizer of the land and the cult; See, Ahlstrom, *Royal Administration,* 7.

[38] Brueggemann, *Land: Place as Gift,* 73–5.

3.1. Fulfilment of the Promise

The promise made by God to Abraham is found in Genesis 13:14–17.[39] YHWH confirmed to Abraham that the Promised Land would belong to his descendants forever (Gen. 17:4–8). As the Hebrew Bible testifies, the land had been granted to the patriarchs by virtue of the divine word and oath. What the patriarchs had enjoyed solely in the form of promissory words became reality only under Joshua's leadership. In Exodus through Joshua, more than thirty references are made to the fact that YHWH swore, vowed to give the land to the offspring of the patriarchs.

3.2. Allotment of Land

The land is an important theme in the Old Testament. Norman Habel even suggests that the land is such an important factor that it could be ranked next to God.[40] The initial division of land in Israel was explicitly to the households within the tribes, under the general title that each receives land according to size and need.[41] The book of Joshua clearly gives the picture of land distribution by lots during the settlement period (cf. Josh. 15:1; 15:17–18). Joshua chapters 13–21 are often ignored in the reading and application of the Book of Joshua. Indeed, these chapters give the clear picture of land distribution pointing to ideals of equality and justice that emerged from distribution of the land according to God's instruction.[42] This allocation by lot completed the divine charge given to Joshua in bringing the Israelites into their inheritance (Josh. 1:6). The territory assigned by God through the lot system became a tribe's "inheritance" (נַחֲלָה) and "possession" (יְרֻשָּׁה). Among the twelve tribes of Israel, the Levites were not allotted any share of land but they were assigned the key role of camping between YHWH and the people by having charge of the tabernacle. They were assigned to perform all the work associated with the tabernacle.

A critical reading on the issue of allotment of land focuses on God's uncompromising commitment to Israel to have a secure home land. It is divine fidelity, divine resolve, and divine efficacy that delivered the land to those destined to hold it.[43]

Deuteronomy contains a list of communal curses (Deut. 27:15–26). It is interesting that while majority of the offences relate to dealing justly with the

---

[39] In Genesis 15:18–21, *YHWH* gave Abraham a more precise description of the Promised Land's boundaries.

[40] Norman C. Habel, *The Land is Mine: Six Biblical Land Ideologies* (Minneapolis: Fortress Press, 1995), 6.

[41] Wright, "Year of Jubilee," in *ABD,* vol. 3, eds., David Noel Freedman et al., (New York: Doubleday, 1992), 1025.

[42] Jerome F. D. Creach, "Joshua 13–21 and the Politics of Land Division," in *Int* 66/2 (April 2012): 153.

[43] Walter Brueggemann, "The God of Joshua . . . Give or Take the Land," in *Int* 66/2 (2012): 165.

poor and marginalized and with sexual impropriety, the third offence is a curse on anyone who "moves a neighbour's boundary stone." This offence comes even before dealing justly with the poor (Deut. 19:14).[44] The land signifies the place of communion with God, and a place where the people as a "holy nation," can live according to certain specific values prescribed by the laws of the covenant. There is blessing in fulfilling the law and curse in disobeying. To appreciate the importance of this fundamental element of their faith, and its consequences, it is necessary to examine the theme of blessing and curse in brief.

3.3. Blessing and Curse

The possession of land was part of God's covenant with his people. The covenant entailed responsibility. It was after they had been brought out from Egyptian captivity that the law was given. In Deuteronomy 27–28 YHWH narrates Israel's prospects of blessings and curse. There is a greater blessing for the nation if they are obedient to the law.

In the words of Monica Melanchthon, blessings are considered to be positive utterances, a pronouncement made for the good and prosperity of the receiver.[45] She further claims that the biblical account of blessing is depicted as a mark of God's relationship with the chosen people and nation Israel, in that when a person is blessed, it is sign of God's grace and presence upon them.[46]

YHWH allocates the land to the people of Israel, and the occupation of it by any given generation is conditioned on obedience. This obedience to the law was not conceived as a way of earning God's favour but as a response to God's grace in delivering Israel from Egyptian bondage. The tithe which was a dedication of the produce of the land was to be offered to YHWH. The first fruits have to be offered, as in an agricultural society crops were the immediate token of God's goodness, and they were thus an inevitable part of worship. The Sabbath and Jubilee year are to be observed. By being obedient to the law they would be blessed, that they would have good harvests, numerous children, freedom from hunger and disease, victory over their enemies and God's continuous presence in the land. Breaking the law would lead to all sorts of disasters like drought, hunger, disease and ultimately expulsion from the land (Lev. 26 cf. Deut. 28).[47]

---

[44] Raymond Westbrook, *A History of Ancient Near Eastern Law* Handbook of Oriental Studies (Leiden: Brill, 2003), 976.

[45] Monica Jyotsna Melanchthon, "Liberation Hermeneutics and India's Dalits," in *The Bible and the Hermeneutics of Liberation*, 59 eds. Alejandro F. Botta, and Pablo R. Andinach (Atlanta: SBL, 2009), 205.

[46] Melanchthon, "Liberation Hermeneutics," 205–6.

[47] Leland Ryken, James C. Wilhoit, and Tremper Longman III, eds., "Promised Land," in *Dictionary of Biblical Imagery* (Secunderabad: OM-Authentic Books, 1998), 666.

Isaiah 24:5 says: "And the earth lies polluted under its inhabitants; for they have transgressed the laws, violated the statutes, broken the everlasting covenant."[48]

Here, the covenant is portrayed as having been broken. The basic storyline of the Old Testament reveals that the people of Israel failed to keep the law and forsook their God, and God responded by sending them into exile for their disobedience to the law.[49] In Jeremiah 9:2 (*BHS* 9:1) prophet Jeremiah laments as follows: "Oh that I had in the desert a traveller's lodging place, that I might leave my people and go away from them! For they are all adulterers, a band of traitors."[50]

Hilary Marlow, in his article explains that the reason for land being ruined was not natural disaster nor prolonged drought nor military activity but it is because of their failure to keep God's law.[51] As the people of Israel begin to live as a nation, a specially chosen people of God, there were also obligations laid upon them to fulfil. Deuteronomy 28:16–44 clearly indicates about blessing for obedience and curse for disobedience, therefore the people experienced desolation culminating in the abandonment of the land given to them due to their failure to obey the law. It is therefore, evident that the promise of the land and the covenant of YHWH with the people of Israel are central to the land as gift.

4. Land and its Relationship to the People of Israel

Throughout the Hebrew Bible the people of Israel constantly appears in relationship with land and YHWH. In the creation story it is clearly mentioned that God created human beings from the dust of the ground (Gen. 2:7) and that they return to the ground. The earth is the basis on which the people are rooted. Therefore, people are wholly related to land in their origin, life and destination. This implies that they are to care for it.

It is *Torah* that links Israel to the land. This *Torah* is to remind the people about the divine ownership of land. It consists of guidelines for land management focusing on three tasks that is, to have no images other than their God, to keep the Sabbath holy and to honour and care for those who are poor, strangers, sojourners, widows, orphans and the Levites.[52]

Brueggemann investigates the biblical function of land within a social-scientific framework and focuses his argument on the importance of the connection between land possession and *Torah* obedience.[53] The transgression

---

[48] Translated from *BHS*.

[49] G. J. Wenham, "Law," in *New Bible Dictionary*, eds. I. Howard Marshall et al., (Secunderabad: OM-Authentic Books, 2007), 675.

[50] Translated from *BHS*.

[51] Hilary Marlow, "Law and the Ruining of the Land: Deuteronomy and Jeremiah in Dialogue," in *PT* 14/5 (2013): 650–1.

[52] G. J. Volschenk, "The Land: Primary Category of Faith," in *HTS* 60/1 (2004): 631–2.

[53] Brueggemann, *Land: Place as Gift*.

of the *Torah* would lead to landlessness, homelessness and eventually to death. No one has special privilege of ownership, neither it is to be understood as a commodity that can be confiscated or purchased, but as a birth right that is inalienable.[54] The land that is managed outside the covenant will be lost (see Deut. 28:63–68).

Going a step further, G. J. Volschenk recognizes the triangular interrelationship where God is on top and below is land and Israel and in the centre is the *Torah*/covenant.[55] The land belongs to YHWH and therefore, must be organized and governed according to YHWH's will and the consequence for violation is that the people of Israel will not remain YHWH's beloved people. The description of the land as Israel's inheritance underlines the status of Israel as YHWH's first born son (Exod. 4:22), and the loss of land symbolized the broken covenant relationship between YHWH and the recipient Israel.

The biblical descriptions of burial practices also functions as a means of establishing claim to tribal territories. The bones of Joseph which were carried by the people out of Egypt during exodus were buried in a plot of land near Shechem (Josh. 24:32). This land was purchased by his father Jacob from king Hamor (Gen. 33:18–20).[56] Through this action the tribe of Joseph legitimized their claim to that area of land. Joshua was also buried in his own inheritance at Timnath-serah, in the hill country of Ephraim (Josh. 24:30). The graves of the dead also serve as a boundary marker.[57]

Just as there are three key terms used in the Old Testament to denote land, so there are also three terms used in connection with land and its relationship to Israel. The three terms are נַחֲלָה, יְרֻשָּׁה, and אֲחֻזָּה as set out hereunder.

4.1. Biblical Concept of נַחֲלָה

The Hebrew word נַחֲלָה is translated as "have or get as an inheritance."[58] The word נַחֲלָה occurred frequently in the Books of Numbers and Deuteronomy which look forward to the allotment of land in Canaan. The word "inheritance" designates the land as transferred to Israel by God without the right of sale. Only God has the authority to dispose the land. The giving of נַחֲלָה points to a very personal bond between God and Israel.

---

54 Brueggemann, *Land: Place as Gift*, 175.

55 Volschenk, "land: Primary Category," 638.

56 Victor H. Matthews, *Manners and Customs in the Bible: An Illustrated Guide to Daily Life in Bible Times* (Peabody, Mass: Hendrickson, 2006), 69.

57 Joshua is said to have been buried upon the boundary of his ancestral estate, and in 1 Sam 10:2, the boundary of the Benjamin is marked by tomb of the ancestress Rachael. Cf. Francesca Stavrakopoulou, *Land of Our Fathers: The Roles of Ancestor Veneration in Biblical Land Claims*, Library of Hebrew Bible/Old Testament Studies (New York: T&T Clark, 2010), 13.

58 H. H. Schmid, "ירשׁ," in *Theological Lexicon of the Old Testament*, vol. 2 trans. Mark E. Biddle, eds. Ernst Jenni and Claus Westermann (Massachusetts: Hendrickson Publishers, 1997), 579.

According to Wright, נַחֲלָה is used to signify four things:

1) The land as Israel's inheritance, which he elaborates as the land which belonged to the individual and the household, was the נַחֲלָה which was allotted to the family within the tribal division of territory (Deut. 32:18; 19:14);
2) The land as YHWH's inheritance, in the sense that the land possessed by Israelites had once belonged to other nations (Ps. 111:6), but in a deeper sense, it is given by YHWH because it already belonged to him as his נַחֲלָה.[59]
3) Israel as YHWH's inheritance, which means that the land always stood as a kind of testimony in the primary relationship between YHWH and his people. The use of the possessive suffixes such as "his," "my," and "your" נַחֲלָה, refers to Israel in relation to YHWH, and it expresses a strong theological conviction.
4) YHWH as Israel's inheritance signifies that just as Israel is specially bonded to YHWH as his נַחֲלָה, so, YHWH is their God and the most precious possession of the people of Israel.[60]

The emphasis falls on God as the supreme authority to dispose of the land. In fact the word נַחֲלָה has a very wide connotation, so it cannot be interpreted in a single model. It is not simply a property that is handed down from one generation to another, but the entitlement which is legitimized by recognized social custom along with legal process. It points to a very personal bond between the giver, YHWH and the receiver, Israel.

4.2. Biblical Concept of יְרֻשָּׁה

The root word ירשׁ is another term that defines the Israelites' relationship to God. The word is used in connection with possession or inheritance of property. Its verbal root means "take possession of, inherit, dispossess" (depending upon grammatical form and content), suggesting that the land which now Israel possessed had once belonged to the Canaanite.[61] The noun יְרֻשָּׁה is translated as "possession." Therefore, it refers to the land of Canaan given by YHWH to Israel as its possession (יְרֻשָּׁה).

The root word ירשׁ particularly in qal form of the verb is translated in the majority of the cases with "to take into possession," where the object is usually the land.[62] It is also said to have an ordinary secular usage in relation to acquiring possession of something through either family inheritance or leadership, especially

---

[59] Wright, "נחל," in *NIDOTTE*, vol. 3, 79.

[60] Wright, "נחל," in *NIDOTTE*, vol. 3, 80.

[61] Janzen, "Land," in *ABD*, vol. 4, 145.

[62] Schmid, "ירשׁ," in *Theological Lexicon*, vol. 2, 579.

land through conquest (Josh. 19:47; Judg. 3:13).[63] The emphasis was more generally upon possession than upon the process of succession.

Theologically, the word applies to Israel's possession of the land of Canaan by dispossessing the Canaanite nation. This stands in relation to YHWH's promise to the patriarch Abraham to give this land to his offspring (Gen. 12:1–7). As John Goldingay has clearly elaborated, for YHWH to make Abraham's family into nation a land is needed, and he went on to say that the Exodus was freedom from servitude and bringing them to another land (Exod. 3:8).[64] Framed in the theory of conquest, the word יָרַשׁ in Deuteronomy has a moral connotation. The emphasis here is that the Israelites possessed the land not because of their own righteousness, but because of the wickedness of the former inhabitants, the Canaanites (Deut. 9:4–5). So, it was YHWH who made it possible for Israelite to dispossess them and take possession of their land.[65] The land was promised as a gift to Israel's ancestors and to their descendants. Therefore, here the giver is the possessor of the gift and is in a position to give it to someone else. So, the land of other people thus become the possession (יְרֻשָּׁה) of Israel.

Wright states that the original division of land was specifically designed to enable every household to have a possession, the territory to be allotted according to the families where the property was usually owned by father or male member of the family.[66] The term perhaps has this background that each family possessed their נַחֲלָה not by right but as gift.

4.3. Biblical Concept of אֲחֻזָּה

This is another important term that defines Israel's relationship to the land as acquired ownership. Its verbal root אחז which means "to grasp, take hold or take possession" clearly points to the fact that the land which now belongs to Israel was the possession of other people.[67] Although etymologically, the word is related to the concept of grasping, seizing, holding, but in the context of the Old Testament, it is related to the Israel's possession of land as the providential gift of YHWH. So it is not attached to the concept of seize.[68] This particular word occurs most commonly in reference to the Promised Land that was given to Israel, which

---

[63] Wright, "ירשׁ," in *NIDOTTE,* vol. 2, 547.

[64] John Goldingay, *Old Testament Theology Israel's Faith*, vol. 2 (Downers Grove, Ill: InterVarsity; Paternoster, 2006), 211.

[65] See the usage of the root word ירשׁ in Deut. 1:8; 3:18, 20. Cf. Ottosson, "ארץ," in *Theological Dictionary of the Old Testament,* vol. 1 eds. G. Johannes Botterweck and Helmer Ringgren, trans. John T. Willis (Grand Rapids, Michigan: William B. Eerdmans Publishing Company, 1977), 404.

[66] Wright, *Old Testament Ethics*, 342.

[67] Konkel, "אחז," in *NIDOTTE,* vol. 1, 354.

[68] Konkel, "אחז," in *NIDOTTE* vol. 1, 357.

implies a gift of property from YHWH.[69] Many times land is identified as the land to which Israel has a claim.

In Genesis 47:11, Joseph gave a portion of land to his father Jacob and brothers in the land of Egypt to live. Here, it is used in association with יָשַׁב meaning to "dwell," or "to remain." The narration continues as they lived in the land of Goshen and they possessed it (47:27). In this context the noun אֲחֻזָּה is used to designate the actual territory possessed.[70]

God promised to give Abraham eternal possession of the territory of his sojourning (Gen. 17:8). The same promise of land was repeated to Jacob (Gen. 48:4). The people of Israel were landless people, their complete history and life must be understood in terms of the hope for, and in response to the promise of land to the patriarchs. The following is a brief survey of Israel's law concerning the land.

5. Ancient Israelite Land Law

It is not possible to understand Israel's law on land without understanding Israel's relationship to YHWH and land. As studied earlier, it is YHWH who is the ultimate owner of the land and the people of Israel are just a tenant. All the biblical collections of law are set within a covenant framework because it is clear that law formed a personal relationship between God and Israel.

The Hebrew word תּוֹרָה is the word most often used for "law" which is still the subject of debate. In Judaism, this term is used to designate the five books of the Old Testament, the Pentateuch (*Torah*). The various expressions for *Torah* incorporate an extensive series of norms, laws, instructions, guidance, and regulations given to the people of Israel by YHWH through Moses.[71] It embraces a highly complex entity.

The word תּוֹרָה is found 44 times in the prophetical books, and the word appears in parallel with the word "Word," (דָּבָר) as well. The word תּוֹרָה can also be translated as "oracle" for it refers to the message the prophets received from YHWH. Garcia Lopez has said, "*In the Old Testament, then Torah can mean a particular individual instruction embodying a command or decision, communicated in the temple by a priest.*"[72]

The three books in the Old Testament namely, Exodus, Leviticus and Numbers focused largely on YHWH's law, which was given to the people of Israel

---

[69] William T. Koopmans, "אחזה," in *NIDOTTE,* vol. 1, 358.

[70] See also Gen. 24:4, 9, 20; Num. 32:29; Josh. 22:9, 19; Cf. Konkel, "אחז," in *NIDOTTE,* vol. 1, 356–7.

[71] Burton L. Goddard, "Law," in *New International Bible Dictionary*, eds. J. D. Douglas et at., (Grand Rapids, Michigan: Zondervan Publishing House, 1987), 583.

[72] Garcia Lopez, "תורה," in *Theological Dictionary of the Old Testament* vol. 15, eds. G. Johannes Botterweck, Helmer Ringgren, and Heinz-Josef Fabry, trans. David E. Green (Grand Rapids: William B. Eerdmans Publishing Company, 2006), 640.

during their journey to the Promised Land. The law was directly communicated to Moses by YHWH through revelation. The laws expressed God's expectation both for the moral and spiritual conduct of the people of Israel.[73] The entire motifs of the biblical law is that, it comes from God which is intended for human benefit, a reliable guide to living that illuminates one's mind or understanding. It functions as an aspect of God's covenant with his people.

5.1. Law of Succession

In the Israelite society father is the ultimate owner of the family's property. He establishes the rules and accordingly plans how the estate would be divided among the siblings.

It is understood that the culture of ancient Israel was a clan-based and kin-oriented with three-tier pattern of kinship, comprising of the tribe, clan and the family. Clan and family had greater social and economic responsibilities. It is the clan which is a unit of kinship that preserves Israel's system of land tenure. The fundamental principle of Hebrew society was that property belonged to the family and it must therefore remain in the family. Strong warning is given in biblical law that land should not be transferred to other tribes.

Land is perceived in the Bible as the "patrimony," which means family's property. As Joshua chapters 15–22 makes clear that the territory was first allotted according to tribes, then it was distributed according to the clans and finally within the clans each family had its portion or heritage.[74]

The Book of Joshua (chaps. 13–21) systematically gives the tribal lists and the territorial division of land which is the evidence that the original division of land was to be equally distributed throughout the whole kinship system. It was not to be bought and sold but to remain within the extended family or at least within the circles of families in the clan. The clan's on-going concern would be to ensure that the area of land stays among its households.[75] The areas of tribal settlement were determined by lot in order to eliminate human bias as to ensure fair distribution of land to the various families that are listed and it became tribe's inheritance and possession.[76]

The term בֵּית אָב which is translated as "father's house," is the third level of the kinship structure in Israel.[77] Father's house was composed of blood relatives as well as women connected through marriage. It includes three to four generations

[73] Ryken, Wilhoit, and Longman III, eds. "Law," in *Dictionary of Biblical Imagery*, 489.

[74] Wright, *Mission of God*, 291.

[75] For further explanation see, Goldingay, *Old Testament Theology*, 404; Cf. Wright, "Year of Jubilee," in *ABD*, vol. 3 eds. Freedman et al., (New York: Doubleday, 1992), 1025.

[76] L. Daniel Hawk, "Allotment of Land," in *New Interpreter's Dictionary of the Bible:* (A—C) ed. Katharine Doob Sakenfeld (Nashville: Abingdon Press, December 2006), 103.

[77] The other two levels of the kinship structures are tribe and clan.

living together along with slaves and servants.[78] In this structure, an individual felt the strongest sense of inclusion, identity, protection and responsibility.[79] The father's house represents a socio-economic reality in Israelite settlement. When the father dies the property will be transferred to the eldest son in the family.[80] The father's house survives as long as the family property remains intact. The structure will change if they decide to divide the property after the father's death.

If the father had died without a son, then the inheritance went to the daughters.[81] If he has no daughter then it went to his brothers, if no brother then to his father's brothers and to the next of kin (Num. 27:8–11).[82]

Given the importance of the patriarchal line within the family, it is clear why marriage plays such an important role. It was simply the fact that, one of the primary purposes of marriage in biblical times was to produce heir.[83] Failure to produce an heir was considered as major calamity for the family because it meant a disruption in the generational inheritance pattern. The male heir is the person who has authority over the property to be inherited after the death of his father. This law of succession is designed to maintain tribal identification and function.

5.2. Redemptive Rights

Ancient legal norms commonly entitled a person to redeem formerly owned land.[84] It was the responsibility of the גֹּאֵל (kinsman-redeemer) to redeem the land if it is sold by relatives due to poverty. The term גֹּאֵל derives from the realm of Israelite family law. The term גֹּאֵל describes a close relative, a kinsman-redeemer who takes upon himself the duty of redemption or recovery on behalf of needy family members. These redemptive rights were premised on the notion that patrimonial land lost on account of temporary financial crisis should be reclaimable (Lev. 25:24).

---

[78] Ebeling, *Women's Lives*, 27; Cf. Wright, *Mission of God*, 291.

[79] Wright, "Family," in *ABD,* vol. 2, eds. David Noel Freedman et al., (New York: Doubleday, 1992), 762.

[80] Raymond Westbrook, *Property and the Family in Biblical Law* in JSOTSup (Sheffield: JSOT Press, 1991), 14.

[81] The entire focus of this research is how this law, "daughter's inheritance rights" came to be enacted.

[82] R. E. Nixon, "Inheritance," in *NBD,* 505.

[83] V. H. Matthews, "Family Relationships," in *DOTP,* 295.

[84] There are also other obligations for the kinsman-redeemer to perform toward his needy relatives. In Num. 35:16–21, the word is used in the context of avenging the death of a relative known as the "redeemer of blood." He also receives monetary restitution when a deceased relative commits wrong against him (Num. 5:8). He also assists his relatives in obtaining justice in the lawsuit. The present section limits its investigation to redemption related to property rather than person; For other related responsibilities see, Robert L. Hubbard, "The *Go'el* in Ancient Israel: Theological Reflections on an Israelite Institution," in *BBR* No. 1 (1991): 4–5.

This custom and procedure of redemptive rights is well presented in the Book of Ruth. In Ruth 4:3–4 we read of Boaz presenting the importance of the case before the kinsman and the assembled witnesses.[85] He spoke of the duty of redemption. Therefore, redemptive right is derived from the concept of the family holdings in any given generations because the family was attached to the land.

The question arises, "If there is a *goel* institution to redeem the land, what is the implication of the fifty-year jubilee where all the land had to be reverted to the rightful owner?" Jack M. Sasson asserts that the jubilee restoration was a second line of defence.[86] In absence of גֹּאֵל (kinsman-redeemer) to redeem the land, the jubilee law of reverting the land comes to defend the land being transferred. Israelites clung to their ancestral property even in the face of royal pressure which is demonstrated in Naboth's refusal to sell his land to king Ahab. The following is a discussion on Naboth's refusal to surrender his vineyard.

5.3. Ahab's Acquisition of Naboth's Land

The patrimonial plot of land of any size was not supposed to be sold. The incident of Naboth with king Ahab in 1 Kings 21:1–16 best illustrates this practice.[87]

Laws governing transfer of field, orchard, and house appear in LH, where the owner of the property surrendered willingly or unwillingly because he failed to fulfil his feudal obligation. LH 30 reads as follows:

> If either a private soldier or a commissary gave up is field, orchard and house on account of the feudal obligations and has then absented himself, (and) after his (departure) another took over his field, orchard and house and has looked after the feudal obligations for three years—if he has returned and demands his field, orchard and house, they shall not be given to him; the one who has taken over and looked after his feudal obligations shall himself become the feudatory.[88]

In 1 Kings 21:1–4, king Ahab attempts to purchase the vineyard of Jezreelite named Naboth. This is an evidence of Israelite king who tried to exercise his power over land in the manner of surrounding nations.[89] It so happened that, Naboth owned a vineyard in Jezreel where king Ahab and queen Jezebel had a second royal residence. The vineyard got in the way of Ahab's development plans,

---

[85] The case is about Noami's plot of land which she inherited from her late husband Elimelech. Boaz presents about her plan to sell the plot of land. The issue here is about who should redeem it without letting it go out of their tribe. Cf. Jack M. Sasson, "The Issue of *Ge'ullāh* in Ruth," in *JSOT* No. 5 (January 1978): 54.

[86] Sasson, "Issue of *Ge'ullāh*," 60.

[87] This is well illustrated by Russell in his article, Stephen C. Russell, "The Hierarchy of Estates in Land and Naboth's Vineyard," in *JSOT* 38/4 (June 2014): 453–69.

[88] Pritchart, *ANET*, 167.

[89] Matthews, *Manners and Customs*, 122.

so he offered to buy it. Ahab made Naboth an offer which he thought he could hardly refuse. But, surprisingly Naboth refused to sell this plot of land. He had good grounds for refusing it. It was against the Old Testament law of inheritance. Naboth was very clear that the land belonged to YHWH. He was also aware that if he sells the land he cuts off his descendants from their heritage from God.[90]

There is rhetorical force in the speech of Naboth when he connected himself to his ancestor which is an indication that Ahab does not share the same lineage with Naboth.[91] The limitation of royal power over land in ancient Israel is best explained in Naboth's refusal. The fact that vineyard represented an enormous investment of time and effort was also a factor, but the primary reason for the refusal proceeded from well considered theological-ethical reflection that, "The LORD forbids selling of the father's inheritance." It talked about continuity of land ownership. It is unlike the practice of the Canaanite kings who thought all the land belonged to the royal family and is entrusted to their subjects.[92] The conflict between Ahab and Naboth could have been resolved if the king was reminded about the ethical issue related to the land. Jezebel along with the support of corrupted courtiers successfully framed Naboth and stoned him to death along with his son (2 Kgs. 9:26).

After this incident, Ahab went to take possession of Naboth's field. There he met prophet Elijah, who pronounced curse upon his entire family for trying to take possession of the land which does not belong to them (1 Kgs. 21:15–19). The writer of the Kings emphasizes that the king is not above the law.

While talking about inalienability of land, Brueggemann discusses the incident in Meribaal's estate (2 Sam. 18–19). Here, the land which once was considered a paternal inheritance was transferred to royal ownership. He labels this concept as royal/urban because it rests on the power of the monarchy and benefits the urban class.[93] In this concept of land, possession implies legitimacy while the landless people have no rights, and the king has the power to grant or withdraw the possession. In opposition to such a system was a "covenantal/ prophetic" model for property ownership which stresses respect for the poor and restraint on the rich. In this model, no one has special privileges of ownership, and land is not understood as a commodity that can be confiscated or purchased, but as a birth right that is inalienable.[94] In fact, law and custom offer a system of rules that secure the settlement of disputes without recourse to violence.

---

[90] Bruce K. Waltke and Charles Yu, *An Old Testament Theology: An Exegetical, Canonical, and Thematic Approach* (Grand Rapids, Michigan: Zondervan, 2007), 271.

[91] This claim is also made by Russell in his article, "Hierarchy of Estates," 456.

[92] Waltke and Yu, *Old Testament Theology*, 721.

[93] Walter Brueggemann, "Reflections on Biblical Understandings of Property," in *IRM* 64/256 (October 1975): 354.

[94] Brueggemann, "Reflections on Biblical Understandings," 356.

CONCLUSION

Land is YHWH's gift to Israel and it grounds the people and their faith. The fundamental issue is that there is an interrelationship between God, the land, Israel and *Torah*. The land has a theological significance. It is YHWH's personal property and is viewed as a conditional grant to the Israelites.

Central to land is the *Torah* which consists of guidelines for land management. Israel's survival in the land is conditioned on faithfulness to the covenantal responsibilities. The Israelites' as tenants are required to offer first fruits of the harvest, tithe from the income, and other voluntary offerings.[95] They are also obligated to offer first born in the land (Deut. 14:22–23; 15:19–20; Cf. 18:3–5).[96] A percentage of their crops and flocks belonged to the landlord "YHWH." It bears blessings for obedience and curses for disobedience. When the people violate their relationship with God, they pollute the sacred land. Depopulation and desolation is depicted clearly in the biblical account as consequences for breaking the covenantal laws.

The tribe's perpetuation of land plays a significant role. This is premised on the understanding of "YHWH's ownership." Within this framework there is a theological legislation that prohibits permanent sale of land. To sell it permanently is to infringe on YHWH's rights. In any way land which is allotted to each tribe through lot should not be transferred to other tribe. Each family guarded its property carefully and each estate was defined by boundaries which were not to be removed. The land relates to a social rather than economic position.

Of special interest are the land rest laws namely, Sabbath and Jubilee which are unique to Israel. Every seventh and fiftieth year, the Israelites are to allow their land to lie fallow. The fallowing of the land was intended for poor, strangers and animals to eat whatever crop is left. Landless and poor must be provided for and they should not be exploited. We can imagine that life in Israel is ordered by YHWH so that both the strong and the weak may live together peacefully and justly. This prevents accumulation of land in the hands of few rich people, which would result in social division. Redemption requirement seeks to prevent accumulation of property and economic power with few rich people. Whether accomplish by the kinsmen, by self-redemption or by jubilee, YHWH's intention is to maintain social and economic stability in Israel. The Israelites גֹּאֵל institution guarded YHWH's rights to His land.

The law of succession was designed by YHWH to ensure that the people would continue to enjoy their inheritance in the land. Israelites were deeply attached to the land, an example of which was Naboth's refusal to surrender his vineyard to the king. Their relationship with YHWH and their faith have rooted them in the land YHWH gave them.

---

[95] Exod. 34:20; Lev. 22:18; Deut. 12:6.

[96] Sandra L. Richter, "Environmental Law: Wisdom from the Ancients," in *BBR* 24/3 (2014): 313.

Chapter 3

Property Inheritance Rights of Women in the Old Testament in the Light of Ancient West Asia

INTRODUCTION

To study women in antiquity on the basis of Hebrew Bible alone is inadequate because Bible abounds in male imagery and language. In reality, the general status of women in the Old Testament is a complex one and must be discovered by being brought out of the biblical text and by reading between the lines. This is done by reading specific examples of the depiction of women and their circumstances in the Old Testament. The focus of this chapter is to understand the legal status of ancient Israelites women. The method used to gain the insights will be a comparative approach with the AWA.[1] This includes studying the literary world of AWA, their important law codes, and women's property rights law. Important evidences of AWA women with property inheritance rights will be brought out. The present study relies on women in the AWA as a context wider than that of the Old Testament. Further queries will be made whether there were mutual influences.

This leads to the study of inheritance issue of women in the Old Testament. To a large extent it is socio-cultural, anthropological and literary approach. This investigation will stress the importance of the interconnection between the subjects of marriage and ownership of land. The primary aim is to discover the legal status of ancient Israelite women. Some biblical passages will be selected for this study and the selection will be done based on their representation in the Old Testament with property inheritance rights. Four categories of women namely,

[1] The term Ancient Near East (ANE) refers to proximity to Europe, which is Eurocentric, therefore, here in this study, the term AWA or Western Asia is used.

widow, wife, daughter and mother will be emphasized. The final section will be summary and evaluation of women's inheritance rights.

1. Ancient West Asia

The region which the historians roughly called ancient Western civilization does not define specific location but it refers to a series of cultures that have slowly changed and spread until Western civilization has made an impact all over the world today. The discoveries made by archaeologists during the past centuries have clearly demonstrated that the people of the AWA have played crucial roles in forming common human heritage. The world's oldest laws are found in the AWA dating from twenty-sixth century until the fourth century BCE.[2] Archaeology and progress in the AWA studies contribute to a great extent in understanding the Old Testament.

The AWA was a patriarchal society so the subject of the law was adult male. The laws generally protect and reinforce the privilege of the male citizen where the gender roles were strictly divided.

It has been the general consensus among the scholars that there are many similarities between the biblical and AWA law codes.[3] Therefore, a survey of women's inheritance rights in AWA will help towards a better understanding of women's inheritance rights in the Old Testament.

It is beyond the scope of this research to study the entire world of AWA. The following is a brief study of each of the successive dynasties considered in this chapter. The selection was made depending on the subjects undertaken.

1.1. Mesopotamia

The ancient cities in Mesopotamia were individual states, each comprising not only the fortified nucleus but also a rural hinterland of farms and villages. They formed an inter-dependent economic, social and political system. Their texts and images recorded the primacy of the male ruler. Indeed patriarchal power structure sustained Mesopotamian civilization. Even so, women, inclusive of cultural expectations and competing family obligations played vital roles in all levels of society. They contributed to the male-dominated spheres of the arts, economy, religion and government.

Mesopotamia witnessed a long and well-established legal history. Laws concerning inheritance were found in all the major collections. For this reason along with Egypt, ancient Mesopotamia is also known as the birthplace of civilization. It was the home of a succession of glorious civilizations that flourished

---

[2] Julye Bidmead, "Legal Status: Ancient Near East," in *The Oxford Encyclopedia of the Bible and Gender Studies,* vol. 1 eds. Julia M. O'Brien et al., (New York: Oxford University Press, 2013), 403.

[3] Victor H. Matthews and James C. Moyer, *The Old Testament: Text and Context* (Grand Rapids, Michigan: Baker Academic, 2012), 55.

for more than three millennia that is, from 3500 to 500 BCE.[4] The following is a brief look at each succeeding dynasty.

1.1.1. Sumer

Ancient Sumer was the birthplace of many cities and Western civilization. It is said that a distinctive group called "Sumerian" began to emerge from around 3400 BCE. They used unique language of their own that became the common speech of their society.[5] The difference between the Sumerians and predecessors was purely language. The style of script used by the Sumerians is called cuneiform because it was written by pressing a pointed stick into a tablet or soft clay, leaving an impression in the shape of a wedge.[6] The language was spoken more than four thousand years ago in southern Mesopotamia and was popularly in use until the early second millennium. Though the language is no longer spoken, it continued to be used as a language of scholarship and cult until the end of the first millennium BCE.[7] This demonstrates the advanced nature of Sumerian culture.

In terms of land owning system, in the Sumerian city-states, the gods through the temples were the major land owners.[8] So, in the Sumerian South, communal identity found its visible manifestation in the religious institutions of the respective urban settlement. This gave birth to the concept of the temple as the focal point of the entire society.

The tablets that have been unearthed from sites in ancient Sumer show that its culture is found to be extremely advanced for the period. It contains scientific topics such as astronomy, mathematics, geography, pharmacy and medicine. There are parallels between the Hebrew Bible and Sumerian literature.[9] For example, the dual accounts of the creation of man and woman in Genesis 1 and 2 have a parallel in the myth of "Enki and Ninmah."[10] The 120 years limit on a person's

---

[4] Stephen Bertman, *Handbook to Life in Ancient Mesopotamia* (New York: Facts on file, 2003), x.

[5] Tim Harris et al., eds., *Ancient Egypt and the Near East: An Illustrated History* (New York: Marshall Cavendish Reference, 2011), 46.

[6] Harris et al., eds., *Ancient Egypt,* 60.

[7] Abraham Hendrik Jagersma, *A Descriptive Grammar of Sumerian* (Germany: LOT, 2010), 1.

[8] Harris et al., eds. *Ancient Egypt,* 53.

[9] There are similar motifs that occur in both the Bible and Sumerian literature, such as "humankind fashioned out of clay and granted the "breathe of life" creation by both command and "making" or "fashioning," paradise stories, the flood, rivalry motifs like that of Cain and Abel, Tower of Babel, personal god, law and law codes. Cf. Richard E. Everbeck, "Sumer, the Bible, and Comparative Method: Historiography and Temple Building," in *Mesopotamia and the Bible: Comparative Explorations,* eds. Mark W. Chavalas and K. Lawson Younger JSOTSup series No. 341 (New York: T&T Clark International, 2003), 90.

[10] One of the best preserved texts of the Sumerian myths. Cf. J. Klein, "Enki and Ninmah," in *The Context of Scripture: Canonical Compositions from the Biblical World* vol. 1 eds. William W. Hallo and K. Lawson Younger (Leiden: E. J. Brill, 1997), 516–8.

longevity (Gen. 6:3) surfaces also in "Enlil and Namzitara."[11] The combination of the creation of human beings and animals, the antediluvian culture, and the flood story in Genesis 1–9 has its parallel in a single Sumerian composition.[12]

Thus, there are connections between the Hebrew Bible and Sumerians even though they are far removed historically, geographically and linguistically from each other. Sumer and the Sumerian language and literature influenced AWA culture in various ways. It is because their historiography was formative in the cuneiform world of the AWA. Therefore, the underlying common cultural foundations that developed through this influence penetrated into and persisted in many cultures near and far, both geographically and chronologically.

1.1.2. Babylon

Ancient Babylonia was located in southern Mesopotamia.[13] The fall of the third dynasty of Ur in 2004 BCE marked the beginning of new period in Mesopotamia known as the old Babylonian period that lasted till 1595 BCE.[14]

The period of the greatest power came during the reign of Hammurabi, the 6th ruler of Babylonian's first dynasty (1792–1750 BCE).[15] He created the most celebrated Mesopotamian legal code reflecting the social condition of that period.[16] He was popularly known as an energetic young man with an outstanding gift of diplomacy and military strategy.[17] Hammurabi and his lawmakers compiled "the longest and best organized of the law collections from Mesopotamia."[18] It is considered as one of the most complete texts and the only one with monumental dimension.[19] The laws are a collection of common laws that existed for centuries but for various reasons, had never been codified and written down in one document.

---

[11] Enlil is the Patron god of city Nippur, whose temple was the Ekur; consort of the goddess Ninlil. One of the most important deities of the Sumerian pantheon. Cf. Klein "Enki and Ninmah," in *Context of Scripture,* 516–8.

[12] Antediluvian culture refers to the period before the biblical flood. See, T. Jacobsen, "The Eridu Genesis," in *COS,* vol. I, 513–5.

[13] There are numbers of books written on Ancient Babylonian but the book, '*Who Were the Babylonians*' is one of the first in a single group that is handled so briefly and still so ably with overwhelming amounts of information. See, Bill T. Arnold, *Who Were the Babylonians?* (Atlanta: SBL, 2004).

[14] Ur is an ancient city of Mesopotamia.

[15] Harris et al., eds., *Ancient Egypt,* 62.

[16] R. K. Harrison, *Old Testament Times* (Michigan: William B. Eerdmans Publishing Company, 1974), 8.

[17] Dominique Charpin, *Writing, Law, and Kingship in Old Babylonian Mesopotamia,* trans. Jane Marie Todd (Chicago: University Of Chicago Press, 2010), 134, notes No. 11.

[18] John Sassoon, *Ancient Laws and Modern Problems: The Balance between Justice and a Legal System* (Bristol: Intellect Books, 2005).

[19] Charpin, *Writing, Law,* 71.

Unlike his Sumerian predecessors, he was an Amorite, an AWA nomadic group which infiltrated from the desert, an area of Babylonia and established a firm rule in the early 18th century BCE.[20] During his reign, he united a vast expanse of land extending from the southern Sumerian states to the northern Akkadian regions signalling "a unified empire on Mesopotamian soil."

Pattern of land ownership in Babylon was quite distinct as the distribution of land was based on the feudal system. Fief as grants of immovable property was gifted by the king for rendering meritorious services.[21]

The kingdom of Eshnunna is one of several kingdoms which flourished in Babylon between the downfall of the 3rd dynasty of Ur and the rise of the empire established by Hammurabi. Archaeologists have discovered two sets of tablets containing the laws of Eshnunna.[22]

1.1.3. Ugarit

Ugarit is an ancient city presently called the *Ras Shamra* in Arabic. The recovery of textual material, tablets, manuscripts such as Elephantine papyri, Dead Sea Scrolls, have revolutionized our understanding of virtually every aspect of biblical studies. Of the many discoveries during the past century, Ugarit tablets also have had one of the most profound effects in our understanding of ancient Israelite religion and culture. Its archives and ancient texts have added fundamentally to our knowledge of the Old Testament world.

In the spring of 1928, a farm worker while ploughing on the Mediterranean coast of Syria discovered a large human-made flagstone, and beneath it, he saw a short subterranean passageway leading into an ancient tomb. This led to extraordinary discoveries concerning ancient history and civilization to the extent of producing a new appraisal of the nature and contents of the Old Testament.[23]

The Ugaritic language is said to be closely related to Hebrew and it has provided an extraordinary amount of insight into Hebrew grammatical structure

---

[20] Walter A. Fairservis, *Mesopotamia, the Civilization that Rose out of Clay* (New York: The Macmillan Company, 1964), 52.

[21] Bill T. Arnold, *Who Were the Babylonians?* SBLABS (Atlanta: Society of Biblical Literature, 2004), 71.

[22] The Laws of Eshnuna (LE), from a city of that name in northern Mesopotamia, in Akkadian and dating to around 1770. The first tablet was discovered in 1945, an almost complete form of law with its surface badly worn. The second tablet was discovered in 1947. Both tablets are said to have contained approximately the same set of laws, though differing from each other in several minor respects. The events are said to have taken place during the reign of Dadusha, the ruler of the kingdom of Eshnunna during the Old Babylonian period. Cf. Martha Tobi Roth, *Law Collections from Mesopotamia and Asia Minor*, ed. Piotr Michalowski 2nd ed., vol. 6 Writings from the Ancient World, SBL (Atlanta, Georgia: Scholars Press, 1997), 57.

[23] Peter C. Craigie, *Ugarit and the Old Testament* (Grand Rapids: Eerdmans, 1983), 7.

and lexicon.[24] Before the discovery of Ugaritic tablets very little was known about Canaanite gods and goddesses, but the discovery of Ugaritic literary texts have provided primary information concerning the mythology of the gods of Canaan. This information has contributed in our understanding of the Canaanite background of Israelite religions out of which Israel emerged.

A substantial number of biblical scholars have published valuable studies on Ugaritic matters and demonstrated parallels between the religion and culture of Ugarites and the Israelites. The Ugaritic script is said to be similar with Hebrew as they both shared Canaanite background.[25] There is clear evidence that there was correspondence between the cultures of Ugarit and Israel. It is because they both spring out of Canaanite culture. Initially the two cultures shared the Canaanite background and later parted ways, with Ugarit continuing along the line of Polytheism and Israel toward monolatry.[26]

1.1.4. Nuzi

Archaeologists have discovered the most important documents known as the Nuzi tablets from Nuzi in Northern Iraq which date to the fifteenth century BCE.[27] These documents have contributed important insights to the understanding of the biblical narratives. Social and legal practices that are found in biblical narratives have been shown to be similar to those which were practiced in their societies.[28] Thousands of Babylonian clay tablets of the fifteenth century BCE were excavated from Nuzi. Most of them have come from family archives. Several families had

---

[24] Wayne T. Pitard, "Voices from the Dust: The Tablets from Ugarit and the Bible," in *Mesopotamia and the Bible*, eds. Chavalas and Younger, 252; See also, Hennie J. Marsman, *Women in Ugarit and Israel: Their Social and Religious Position in the Context of the Ancient Near East* (Boston: BRILL, 2003), 33.

[25] Peter T. Daniels, "The Decipherment of the Ancient Near East," in *A Companion to the Ancient Near East* Blackwell Companions to the Ancient World ed. Daniel C. Snell (Oxford: Blackwell Publishing, 2005), 424–5; Cf. P.C. Craigie, "The Poetry of Ugarit and Israel," in *TB*, (1971): 7.

[26] Marsman, *Women in Ugarit*, 34.

[27] Nuzi is one of the provincial administrative centres of the land of Arraphe, one of the great ancient nations of the AWA at that time. Nuzi's fame derives from the over 3,000 cuneiforms tablets found there, such as the documents of the administrative activities, social and economic transactions, legal structures and practices at Nuzi and neighbouring cities and towns illustrating vividly the daily life of the mid 2nd millennium BCE community of the AWA. Excavations at this city started in 1925 by the American School of Oriental Research in Baghdad lead by Edward Chiera. Cf. Cyrus Herzl Gordon, "Biblical Customs and the Nuzu Tablets," in *BA* 3/1 (February 1940): 1–2.

[28] The customs and events that have taken place at Haran, the Northern Mesopotamia (Gen. 11:31; 28:10). Cf. Samuel Greengus, "Sisterhood Adoption at Nuzi and the "Wife—Sister" in Genesis," in *HUCA* No. 46 (1975): 5; Israel Finkelstein and Neil Asher Silberman, *The Bible Unearthed: Archaeology's New Vision of Ancient Israel and the Origin of its Sacred Texts* (New York: Simon and Schuster, 2002), 322.

carefully preserved their social and business transaction records, which were stored away in archive rooms. Some of the important family documents that were excavated include adaptation of a male child, marriage contracts, bridal price.[29] When the excavations were completed in 1931 good amount of resources of the life of this ancient city were at hand.

The native population of Nuzi is now shown to have been largely Hurrian in character, the long lost Horites of the Old Testament.[30] Another significant fact is that, the archives of the Horite city of Nuzi reflect ways of living that are similar to the place and time of biblical Patriarchs.[31]

Nuzian was also a patriarchal society. In Patriarchal form of society the first–born son gets the maximum benefit. He gets the double share of the inheritance from his father, and takes over the responsibility of his father in the family and also in the clan. There is closeness between biblical and Nuzian practices of inheritance in regard to illegitimate sons, rights of the adopted son, and slave. All these evidences point to the geographical and cultural provenience of the patriarchs.

1.1.5. Assyria

Assyria was one of the earliest empires to be established in western Asia. It is said that during the 3rd millennium BCE the region came under the influence of the Akkadian civilization. The inhabitants adopted the Akkadian language and cuneiform script. But when the southern empires of Sumer and Akkad collapsed around 2000 BCE, thereafter, a distinct Assyrian culture began to emerge.[32]

Assyrian Empire is generally divided into three periods, that is, the Old Empire (c. 2000–1760 BCE), the Middle Empire (c. 1363–1000 BCE), and the new Empire (c. 1000–612 BCE).[33] The laws of Middle Assyria are a by-product of powerful empire under Tiglath-Pileser I (1115–1077 BCE) after he united Southern Mesopotamia and Northern Anatolia.[34] The law that we are presently aware of is not in a complete form. Archaeologists have yet to discover a single compilation of laws from any of the three periods. What we do have appears to have come from Middle Assyrian period. This is a series of cuneiform tablets from

---

[29] Roger T. O'Callaghan, "Historical Parallels to Patriarchal Social Custom," in *CBQ* 6/4 (October 1944): 396.

[30] O'Callaghan, "Historical Parallels," 395.

[31] According to Gen. 15:2–3 Abraham's heir was a slave by the name of Eliezer. The adoption of slaves is known in the tablets from the archives of Nuzi. It is because it was a custom at Nuzi for childless people to adopt a son to serve them as long as they lived and to bury and mourn for them when they die. The adopted son becomes the heir in exchange of the service he rendered. But if the adopter begets a son after the adoption, the real son becomes the rightful heir. Cf. Gordon, "Biblical Customs," 2–3.

[32] Harris et al., eds., *Ancient Egypt*, 102.

[33] Harris et al., eds., *Ancient Egypt*, 102.

[34] Bertman, *Handbook to Life*, 340–1.

A to O unearthed by archaeologists and assigned by scholars as MAL (Middle Assyrian Laws). This gives us an incomplete but generally comprehensive picture of the legal system of that period.

1.2. Egypt

Egypt was in some ways dissimilar to Mesopotamia. Politically it was a unified country, not a group of city-states.[35] It enjoyed stable agricultural economy because of the annual flooding of the Nile River. Historians divide ancient Egyptian history into dynasties, a line of hereditary rulers. So, change of dynasty would suggest that another ruling family had taken power.[36] Whichever Pharaoh held power had the status of a god and reigned supreme as the son of the god Amon who was the supreme head of a large society of gods. The chief religious preoccupations were the sun and underworld. In the Egyptian cosmos, the sun sailed daily into the underworld and back.[37]

In Egypt, land ownership pattern was unique. As a god, Pharaoh's word was law and he holds the supreme authority. He was considered as their divine being, a god incarnate. He ensures that justice remained in the land. The people were subject to the pharaoh's order. The royal family grew richer from the taxes paid by their subjects.[38] The operation and the use of land were based on two tier system of land tenancy with Pharaoh as the owner of the land and the subject as the cultivators. The subject gave one-fifth of the land produce to the king as remuneration for the use of land (Gen. 47:26).[39]

Egypt has great influence on the institutions of ancient Israelite society.[40] Scholars have pointed out that there are Egyptian loan words in the Hebrew

---

[35] It is theoretically a union of two countries, that is, Upper and Lower Egypt.

[36] For detail background see, Harris et al., eds., *Ancient Egypt,* 12.

[37] Philip R. Davies, "The Ancient World," in *The Blackwell Companion to the Bible and Culture* Blackwell Companions to Religion ed. John F. A. Sawyer (Oxford: Blackwell, 2006), 14.

[38] Robert Ellickson and Charles Thorland, "Ancient Land Law: Mesopotamia, Egypt, Israel," in *C-KLR* No. 71(October 1, 1995): 336.

[39] Ellickson and Thorland, "Ancient Land Law," 336.

[40] Shiju Mathew, in his article points out that the biblical law codes derived strong influence from the neighbouring powerful nations. According to him, each culture is unique, yet the individual cultures of each society were not isolated from each other, so they were subject to mutual influences. Cf. Shiju Mathew, "Deuteronomy and Women's Rights: A Subaltern Reading," in *Journeys into the Deep: Hermeneutical Pattern of M. M. Thomas,* eds. C. I. David Joy and P. Mohan Larbeer (Bangalore: BTESSC, 2016), 55.

Bible.[41] Various names, titles and concepts in the Hebrew Bible have been attributed to Egyptian origins or influence especially in the wisdom literature.[42]

The Egyptian texts had wisdom dialogues, proverbs and creation myths which are similar in form and content to those texts popularly found in Mesopotamia and the literature of the Old Testament. The Book of Proverbs (22:17–24:22) contains sayings identical to those in the Egyptian wisdom of Amenemope.[43] Egyptian model of schools were known to have existed for the training of courtiers. The writing down of these proverbs is attributed to a small group of educated sages that have clustered around the king and his court. It can be assumed that the Book of Proverbs, the literature of the Old Testament partly depends on the Egyptian Proverbs.

2. The Ancient Law Codes

Mesopotamian societies developed sophisticated legal institutions with village council serving as a court of first resort. These legal institutions left a considerable body of writings and modern scholars have published editions translating hundreds of tablets recording legal transactions such as sales, estate decisions, court decisions, with still many left unpublished.[44] These ancient law codes which have come down to us still form the part of the many legal systems today. They have been preserved in a number of different forms like in Stele, clay tablets, cuneiform on stone pillars.[45] Although, all these law codes were published by rulers of distinct countries in different centuries, they all share numerous similar themes and provisions. These abundant corpora of laws from such a wide variety of civilizations throughout AWA history all attest to a long-standing concern regarding legal status and societal issues. Because of the commonalities in the laws of the AWA scholar like Raymond Westbrook, states that the AWA societies belonged to a common legal culture.[46] These laws draw upon earlier legal

[41] Words like "בחן," cf. Benjamin J. Noonan, "Zion's Foundation: The Meaning of בחן in Isaiah 28:16," in *ZAW* 125/2 (2013): 316; See also, אבינ meaning "poor, needy, wretch," in, Thomas O. Lambdin, "Egyptian Loan Words in the Old Testament" in *JAOS* vol. 73/3 (July–September, 1953): 145.

[42] F. V. Greifenhagen, *Egypt on the Pentateuch's Ideological Map: Constructing Biblical Israel's Identity* JSOT (London: Sheffield Academic Press, 2002), 4.

[43] Katherine Dell, "Wisdom," in *Biblical World*, vol. 1 ed. John Barton (New York: Routledge, 2002), 110; For detail study on the link of Prov. 22:17–24:22 with Amenemope see, Katharine J. Dell, *The Book of Proverbs in Social and Theological Context* (Cambridge: Cambridge University Press, 2006), 65–7.

[44] Ellickson and Thorland, "Ancient Land Law," 331.

[45] Stele is a standing stone slab used in the ancient world either to mark the site of a grave or to commemorate historic event.

[46] Raymond Westbrook, *A History of Ancient Near Eastern Law* Handbook of Oriental Studies (Leiden: Brill, 2003), 4.

traditions and established AWA societal norms. The following are some of the ancient prominent law codes:[47]

1. The Law of Ur-Namma (LU) from Ur in Southern Mesopotamia, in Sumerian (c. 2100 BCE).
2. The Law of Lipit-Ishtar (LL) from Isin in Southern Mesopotamia, in Sumerian (c. 1900 BCE).
3. The Law of Eshnunna (LE) from Eshnunna in Nothern Mesopotamia, in Akkadian (c. 1770 BCE) and
4. The Law of Hammurabi (LH) from Babylon in Akkadian (c. 1750 BCE).[48]
5. The Middle Assyrian Law (MAL) from Assur, in Akkadian (c. 13th century BCE).
6. The Neo-Babylonian Law (NBL) from Sippar in Central Mesopotamia, in Akkadian (c. 7th century BCE).
7. The Hittite Law (HL) from Anatolia in Hittite (between 16–12 centuries BCE).[49]

3. Literary World of AWA

One of the important social classes of the AWA was the scribal class. The administration required knowledgeable persons with the skill of reading and writing to record all the information covering topics ranging from royal commands to economic concerns. The competence of the scribal class included diplomacy, hence knowledge of more than one language. The records include myths, annals, prayers, and others. These are recorded permanently on clay, wood and papyrus. By 3000 BCE, before any society could develop the system of writing, the people of Mesopotamia and Egypt had developed systems of writing, capable of living in cities and had begun massive construction projects.[50] This was far in advance of any other civilization of the period.

[47] Westbrook has listed most of the important ancient law codes. For this study, only the law codes that are related to this study are selected. See, Westbrook, *History of Ancient Near Eastern Law*, 8–9.

[48] The above listed 1–4 are the oldest and most complete of the known codes issued under the name of a ruler of an ascendant city-state in Mesopotamia.

[49] The Hittite kingdom lasted for approximately four hundred years (c. 1650 to 1180 BCE).

Two fragments of codes have been identified in Hebrew Bible: The Covenant Code (CC), found in Exod. 21, 22; The Deuteronomic Code (DC), scattered over in Deut. 15–25. The scholars have also associated scattered laws found in Leviticus and Numbers with a similar law code. Cf. Billie Jean Collins, *The Hittites and Their World* Archaeology and Biblical Studies No. 7 ed. Andrew G. Vaughn (Atlanta: SBL, 2007), ix; Westbrook, *History of Ancient Near Eastern Law*, 8–9; Sassoon, *Ancient Laws*, 29–39.

[50] Ellickson and Thorland, "Ancient Land Law," 328.

Philip R. Davies supports the theory that the biblical books have its antecedents in Mesopotamia.[51] It is generally agreed that the Israel scribal work originated with the rise of monarchy as administrative officers.[52] They had record keeping like archives and libraries, records that are engraved on tombs, letters scrawled on pottery, labels stamped on storage jars. There are also histories preserved by telling, writing or communicating stories about particular pasts. These histories serve immeasurably in enlarging the horizon in the knowledge of the AWA world along with sharpening the understanding of the content of the Bible.

Israel is said to have emerged from the West Asian cultures.[53] Clear significant parallels exist between Old Testament and AWA literatures as claimed by many scholars.[54] The Old Testament contains sacred story, history, law and many other subjects which are neither comprehensive in scope nor altogether detailed in their explanation. There are also many questions unanswered, because these texts were written down long after the events had taken place. Therefore, other writings help illuminate the past by using the literary texts and the material remaining.

Law codes, especially early Sumerians (Ur), Hammurabi, MAL, Nuzi documents, are analysed because they represent the dominant cultures of the AWA. The historians that study the ancient Israelite society understand the importance of trade and cultural exchange in the ancient world.

Raymond Westbrook, firmly claims that writing was first invented toward the end of the 4th millennium BCE in the AWA, and that, it is home to the world's oldest law. This has the advantage that the advent of writing has left durable traces to reconstruct what were once living institutions.[55] It will provide some important background and missing information in the study of Old Testament. This is true especially on the subject of inheritance rights of the women where there is shortage of information in the biblical record.

4. Inheritance Rights of AWA Women

The administrative records, contracts, records of legal disputes, letters, edicts, annals, ritual texts, myths, fables, law codes, give glimpses into the life of ancient societies. These records contain types of material and cover areas of life outside the

---

[51] Davies, "Ancient World" in *Blackwell Companion*, 24.

[52] For further reference read, Paulson Pulikottil, *Transmission of Biblical Texts in Qumran: The Case of the Larger Isaiah Scroll 1QIsa[a]*, JSPSup series No. 34 (Sheffield: Sheffield Academic Press, 2001), 32–3.

[53] Carol L. Meyers, "The Roots of Restriction: Women in Early Israel," in *BA* 41/3 (September 1, 1978): 92.

[54] Roland E. Murphy and O. Carm, *Wisdom Literature: Job, Proverbs, Ruth, Canticles, Ecclesiastes, Esther*, Forms of the Old Testament Literature (Grand Rapids, Michigan: William B. Eerdmans Publishing Company, 1981), 9.

[55] Westbrook, *History of Ancient*, 1.

range of the biblical sources. In those glimpses women appear, and even speak in their own voices in their own capacities. However, it varies from period to period and place to place, indicating the existence of distinct cultural groups over the period of more than two millennia.

Beginning with the third millennium Laws of Ur-Namma, Lipit-Ishtar, through the second millennium LH, LE, MAL to the first millennium New Babylonian laws, the successive kingdoms of the Mesopotamia had fully operative laws and legal systems to govern inheritance. Inheritance laws were also found in legal texts such as court cases, and marriage contracts. Much of the code of Hammurabi consists of laws dating back to ancient times, so the section dealing with marriage often describe rules that had been in force in Mesopotamia for centuries.

Egyptian women are said to have equal property rights compared with men. Wife was often the head of the family, with all the rights such a position entailed.[56] They were the independent managers of the property in their own rights.[57] Compared to other societies in AWA, women in ancient Egypt enjoyed higher rights and freedom.

Regarding the women's inheritance rights in Egypt, one of the *Inscriptions of Mes* dated from 1250 BCE, records a long standing land dispute of about nine acres of land within two families, each family claiming ownership.[58] The dispute dragged on for several generations. At one point of time, a delegation of judges travelled to the central archives Piramesse, the capital at that time, to survey the land registers. It was found out that in this particular case women were managing the family holding, contesting claims and acting as witnesses.[59] This is clear evidence that women were exercising equal power in land management along with men in Egypt.

Cyrus Herzl Gordon has produced a series of articles relating to Nuzi custom including "women at Nuzi." In his study of women, he traces the broad picture of women's rights. According to him, women were entitled to own and dispose of property including real estate, enter into contracts, go to court to protect their proprietary rights. They could also become heirs and executors of estates to the extent of declining marriage arrangements.[60] He states that women and men were able to participate equally in the social and economic life of the community.

[56] Roland de Vaux, *Ancient Israel: Its Life and Institutions* trans. John McHugh (London: Darton, Longman & Todd, 1961), 40.

[57] Bernhard Lang, "Women's Work, Household and Property in two Mediterranean Societies: A Comparative Essay on Proverbs xxxi 10–31," in *VT* 54/2 (2004): 201.

[58] The New Egyptian Kingdom "Inscription of Mes," sometimes written as "Mose" is a record of a protracted legal disputes; Cf. Carolyn Graves-Brown, *Dancing for Hathor: Women in Ancient Egypt* (London: Continuum, 2010), 41.

[59] Graves-Brown, *Dancing for Hathor*, 41.

[60] Cyrus Herzl Gordon, "Nuzi Tablets Relating to Women" (1935c), in *Muséon* No. 48, 113-32.

In Assyria society, women are said to have exercised very few rights. They are said to have lived a restricted life and had to wear veils whenever they go out in public places.[61] According to this law no estate was left to their wives. Law 46 states that, in the case of husband's death, the man's sons must provide for her, even if she is their stepmother.[62]

It is fair to say throughout the AWA history, women generally have had as much legal capacity as men but notions of equality cannot be seriously entertained.

5. Inheritance Rights of Ancient Israelite Women

In this section an attempt is made to highlight some scholarly contribution on how women inherited property in Israel.

According to the *Torah*, woman has full rights to the extent of buying, selling, retaining, or mortgaging property. By Rabbinic ordinance, her rights are reduced to some extent in marriage where the husband has the use of the earning of his wife's property for the duration of the marriage.[63] Mariam Peskowitz also states that women owned many kinds of property but according to her, women's legal potential to own and control property changes with marriage. Her relationship to property such as land, animals, metals, money, clothing and other possessions shifts according to her legal relationship with different men. As a wife, a woman may still own some kinds of property but the husband has control over it.[64] From the extra-biblical sources, she explains the categories of property such as new and old property. New property refers to the property gained during the marriage, which she earned through her labour. Old property refers to gifts on occasion of her marriage from family, private holdings, family inheritances before her marriage. It is said that the husband owns the new property and her old property is maintained and titled by her but he still has control over it even to the extent of preventing her from selling.[65] It is further said that a husband may not sell the property, mortgage it or encumber it without his wife's consent, except in certain exceptional cases. In such cases, if he does sell the property then he is obliged to restore with equal value.[66]

The Rabbinic texts have not mentioned anything regarding the marriage law which also includes the issue of inheritance. It is generally believed that the rabbis

---

[61] Harris et al., eds., *Ancient Egypt*, 106.

[62] Tablet A, Law 46.

[63] Markham J. Geller, "*New Sources for the Origins of the Rabbinic Ketubah,*" in *HUCA*, 49 (1978): 228–9; Cf. Michael Kaufman, *The Woman in Jewish Law and Tradition* (New Jersey: Jason Aronson Inc., 1993), 204.

[64] Miriam Peskowitz, "Rabbis, Feminists and Patriarchy's Ordinariness," in *A Feminist Companion to Reading the Bible: Approaches, Methods and Strategies* eds. Athalya Brenner and Carole R. Fontaine (Sheffield: Sheffield Academic Press, 1997), 496.

[65] Peskowitz, "Rabbis, Feminists and Patriarchy's," 496–7.

[66] Kaufman, *Woman in Jewish Law*, 204.

have omitted the marriage issue, and it has also been avoided by the Hebrew writers.[67] However, a wider perspective in looking at the issue of inheritance rights of women can be obtained from a brief study of marriage and its related components.

5.1. Marriage

In Israelite society, a person is expected to be married. The regulations regarding marriage were part of the family law.[68] Marriages within the circle of the family and the extended family were strictly prohibited, but within the larger circle of the clan, marriage was encouraged, especially for daughters with inheritance rights. This endogamy in marriage is preferred because inheritance of land played a major role.[69] There are also several theories on matrilineal and matriarchal forms of marriage, but these are exceptional cases, not the general practice found in the ancient Israelite society.

Marriage in ancient times represented far more than just an alliance between two individuals. It is a symbolic expression of far-reaching alliance between two different families or lineages. It was a common practice that marriage was not made according to sentiments, but something deemed useful and suitable for the welfare of the family. In addition to property concerns in marriage heavy emphasis was placed on procreation.[70]

The betrothal type-scenes in biblical narratives are framed by reference to male initiatives. Women are systematically excluded as the primary initiator of the marriage contract. In marriage arrangement, the two verbs לָקַח meaning "to take," ascribing to groom and נָתַן meaning "to give," ascribing to the father are dominantly found. The daughters' nuptials are routinely depicted as arranged by her father or by her brothers if the father is not alive or otherwise unable to act. In Genesis 24:50–51, we see Laban and Bethuel's response to the servant's bid.[71] Here, the bridegroom's representative takes the woman, and it is her father and brother who give the bride to him, an act which occurs in all the betrothal narratives.[72] Father

[67] This comprises of one of numerous traditions for which the Hebrew Bible was considered as an authoritative and ancestral source.

[68] Investigating Israelite marriage is a frustrating task because Bible contains no systematic laws about marriage. Information about marriage can be gleaned from scattered legal statements that deal with marriage or divorce and other AWA legal writings.

[69] Marsman, *Women in Ugarit*, 61.

[70] Victor P. Hamilton, "Marriage," in *ABD,* vol. 4 eds. David Noel Freedman et al., (New York: Doubleday, 1992), 561; See also, Gordon, "Biblical Customs," 3.

[71] Then Laban and Bethuel answered, "The thing comes from the LORD; we cannot speak to you anything bad or good. Look, Rebekah is before you, "take her and go," and let her be the wife of your master's son, as the LORD has spoken." Translated from *BHS*.

[72] Esther Fuchs, *Sexual Politics in the Biblical Narrative: Reading the Hebrew Bible as a Woman* (Sheffield: Sheffield Academic Press, 2000), 112. Other biblical passages are Gen. 29:15–30 (Laban arranges the marriage of his daughters Rachel and Leah); Exod. 2:21(Reuel arranges the marriage

could choose or break her betrothal agreement. This undoubtedly demonstrates that matrimony was basically organized along patriarchal rules.

The importance of marriage as a social contract between two families rather than between two individuals is shown in the following example of Assyrian marriage contract. The Assyrian marriage contract text reads as follows:

> Laqipum has married Hatala, daughter of Enishru. In the country (that is, Central Anatolia) Laqipum (5) may not marry another (woman)—(but) in the City (that is, Ashur) he may marry a hierodule. If within two years she (that is, Hatala) does not provide him with offspring, (10) she herself will purchase a slave woman, and later on, after she will have produced a child by him, (15) he may then dispose of her by sale wheresoever he pleases. Should Laqipum choose to divorce her (text: "him"), he must pay (her) five minas of silver; (20) and should Hatala choose to divorce him, she must pay (him) five minas of silver. Witnesses: Masa, Ashurishtikal, (25) Talia, Shupianika.[73]

Hatala observed her father and father-in-law making an agreement about her marriage in which both signed date and sealed the marriage contract without her approval. The condition is that, if Hatala's husband Laqipum travelled to another city frequently for business, then he could marry another woman in that city. If Hatala could not provide children after two years of their marriage, she must provide her husband another woman who would bear male child to continue the family line, to take care of them in their old age, and to carry on the family business. The witnesses of both the families read the contract and agreed. There is a sigh of relief for both the fathers because prestige and wealth has been added through this union.

This is one of the legal examples of many of an Old Assyrian marriage contract that clearly reflects women's marital position. It is a legal example of AWA's stipulation against women's autonomy. The young couples have nothing to say in the betrothal process. A woman's security in a marriage depends upon her ability to produce an heir, failing to do would require her to provide him with a concubine as demonstrated in Hatala's marital contract. According to Hammurabi law code she would even suffer divorce.[74]

---

of his daughter Zipporah); Judg. 1:11–15 (Caleb arranges the marriage of his daughter Achsah); 1 Sam. 18:17–29 (Saul arranges the marriage of his daughters Merab and Michal).

[73] Old Assyrian, 19th century BCE Text: B. Hrozn, *Inscriptions Cuneiformes du Kult'p'* (Praha, 1952). Transliteration and translation, Hrozn, in *Symbolae Koschaker* (*Studia et Documenta* II, 1939), 108.

[74] Roth, *Law Collections*, 107 (Law 138).

However, there are few instances where women made their own choice of partner. In the song, "The Wiles of Women," one such example is found.[75] The Sumerian text reads as follows:

> . . . I (Inanna) have come to our mother's gate, I, in joy I walk, I have come to Ningal's (her mother) gate, I in joy I walk. To my mother he will say the word, He will sprinkle cypress oil on the ground, to my mother Ningal he will say the word (Sumerian Sacred Marriage Text lines 5, 10).[76]

In this text, goddess Inanna makes her own choice of a lover that is, Dumuzi, the shepherd.[77] She convinced him to go to her mother Ningal to ask for her hand. The text shows Dumuzi is now following her home to her mother to formally ask for her hand. The same story in another Mesopotamian text places Inanna in a more conventional way by leaving the choice to her older brother, the sun god Utu. As custom dictates, her brother makes the arrangement with the one she loves.[78]

In Egyptian marriage, it has been observed that the obligation to marry a relative did not exist as a general rule, the reason being the bureaucratic state.[79] In regulating the matters of matrimonial property, if in due course, husband wanted to dispose some of this secured property, he needed his wife's consent in a written statement. Therefore, a pledge of security gave a wife a firm, proprietary position.[80]

Walther Eichrodt states that the law of marriage which was an important part of the book of covenant has been lost today. He is of the view that the marriage law existed in ancient Israel at one point of time, but the Bible is silent about it. According to him the marriage law is supposed to appear after Exodus 22:17.[81]

In today's context, marriage is considered as a personal relationship between two people who typically cohabit, share the responsibilities, joys and difficulties of life. However for ancient Israelite people marriage normally was arranged by

[75] Thorkild Jacobsen, *The Treasures of Darkness: A History of Mesopotamian Religion* (New Haven: Yale University Press, 1976), 28.

[76] Dumuzi-Inanna myth is fragmentary, so little can be made of its contents. It seems to begin with an account of a marriage ceremony, and continues with many obscure words and meanings. The text cited above reads that, Dumuzi has come to Inanna's house at her request for admittance.

[77] Inanna was the Sumerian fertility goddess, and she was also the daughter of Anu, (the god of heaven and ruler of the gods). Cf. Harris et al., eds., *Ancient Egypt*, 140.

[78] Jacobsen, *Treasures of Darkness*, 29–31.

[79] Marsman, *Women in Ugaritl*, 57.

[80] P. W. Pestman, *Marriage and Matrimonial Property in Ancient Egypt: A Contribution to Establishing the Legal Position of the Woman* (Leiden: E. J. Brill, 1961), 133–6.

[81] Walther Eichrodt, *Theology of the Old Testament,* vol. 1 trans. J. A. Baker (Philadelphia: Westminster Press, 1961), 80.

parents indicating that the larger kinship context was far more important than the personal relationship between husband and wife. Lineage rather than choice of partner was what mattered. Endogamous marriage is preferred because it contributes to community bonds and relationships within the clan, and that they can support each other in times of need.

5.2. Bride Price (מֹהַר) and Dowry (שִׁלֻּחִים)

Marriage consisted of two important elements, namely, bride price (מֹהַר) and dowry (שִׁלֻּחִים).[82] The bridegroom had to pay bride-price to her family and in return the bride's family gives the daughter a dowry. It was a cycle of economic exchange and above all her personal reputation and that of her family helped set a high bride-price. It has been observed that daughters represented an economic value, because the head of the household was to be paid a marriage deposit called rh;mo as a compensation gift to the bride's father when a daughter is married.[83]

If the woman is young and still under her father's care, the husband or his agents give her father a bride price (מֹהַר).[84] Bride price is then added on the occasion of marriage to the bride's dowry, and therefore returned to the groom's house. Wife has the authority over it, which means that the מֹהַר becomes part of the bride's assets which can be taken with her in case of divorce.

If the groom-to-be was a fugitive or could not claim rights to the paternal property, he could give his father-in-law the equivalent of the marriage deposit in labour as was done by Jacob and Moses (Gen. 29; Exod. 2:21).[85] There are also instances where the groom or his father gave gifts along with מֹהַר. Abraham sent costly gifts to Rebekah through his servants (Gen. 24:53). Ancient Babylonian law mentions as follows:

> . . . The first wife shall take her dowry and the marriage gift which her husband, upon giving (it) to her, wrote down on a tablet for her, and

[82] The term for dowry in Hebrew is שִׁלֻּחִים (m. pl) which is mentioned in 1 Kings. 9:16. It means sending away of (a) wife, (b) daughter, accompanied by marriage present. Cf. "שִׁלֻּחִים," *Gesenius' Hebrew and Chaldee Lexicon to the Old Testament Scriptures*. Trans. Samuel Prideaux Tregelles (Grand Rapids: Baker Book House, 1979), 825.

[83] In Gen. 31:14–16, we see Laban's daughters, Leah and Rachael, lament about their father's refusal to pay their dowries. Cf. Victor H. Matthews, *Manners and Customs in the Bible: An Illustrated Guide to Daily Life in Bible Times* (Peabody, Mass: Hendrickson, 2006), 39; See also, Marsman, *Women in Ugarit*, 69; Meyers, "Roots of Restriction," 98.

[84] Rachel Adler, *Engendering Judaism: An Inclusive Theology and Ethics*, 1st ed. (Illinois, USA: Varda Books, 1999), 170.

[85] Jacob agrees to serve Laban for seven years for his daughter Rachael. But Laban deceived him by replacing Leah instead of Rachael. Jacob was required to make another labour contract with him in order to marry Rachael. This new contract provides Laban with an additional seven years of labour. Such labour contracts are also said to be found among the business documents unearthed in the remains of Nuzi. Cf. Matthews, *Manners and Customs*, 38; Greengus, "Sisterhood Adoption at Nuzi," 5–6; Marsman, *Women in Ugarit*, 103.

> living in the home of her husband, she shall have the usufruct (of it) as long as she lives, without even selling (it), since her heritage belongs to her children (LH 171).

According to this law, wife will have the authority over the property that is, dowry and the marriage settlement as long as she resides in her husband's dwelling. She shall enjoy the use of it but she should not sell it because it will belong only to her children. Here the law gives her only what was hers to begin with and there is no freedom over this inheritance.

There is a mention in LH 162, that after the death of mother, the dowry goes to children. In case, if there is no child, LH 163 prescribed that dowry belongs to the woman's father with a condition that the father returns the bride wealth in order to receive the dowry. Without children the dowry supports no relative from the woman's family and thus the dowry as a family gift returns to the family from where it was originally acquired.

The marriage contract marked the transfer of money or property from the bridegroom to his future father-in-law. After the marriage ceremony, these assets remained the possession of the bride's father. He in turn had to make a payment of a dowry which remained the property of the wife.[86] The LH provides dowry and gifts which her husband had deeded to her during his life passes to a widow who has given birth to children.[87]

In women's rights to divorce, the LH 142 declares that the wife can declare divorce without specific grounds. In this case her statement of personal incompatibility was enough. If she was found innocent by the council, she is permitted to take her dowry and go off to her father's house.[88]

According to the practice in MAL, the woman's dowry and whatever she brings from her father's house, and whatever she received from her father-in-law upon entering the house, the law explicitly allows all these things to go to her sons. However, a husband may overrule this custom at his choosing, so that if he wished to do so, he shall give it to whichever of his sons he wishes.[89]

1 Samuel 25:42 records about dowry carried over by wife when she remarried.[90] Dowry was the private property of the woman which she could take along with her when she remarried.

The son's share was usually larger than that of the daughter, which she receives when she gets married. It is considered as wife's property with a purpose to provide some financial security in case a woman became widowed or was

[86] Harris et al., eds., *Ancient Egypt*, 70.

[87] Isaac Mendelsohn, "The Family in the Ancient Near East," in *BA* 11/2 (May 1, 1948): 34.

[88] Sassoon, *Ancient Laws*, 79–80.

[89] Tablet A, Law 29.

[90] 1 Sam. 25:42, "Abigail got up hurriedly and rode away on a donkey; her five maids attended her; she went after the messengers of David, and became his wife." Translated from *BHS*.

divorced without grounds.[91] Marriage deposit functioned as a surety between the two parties for a wedding to take place. There are certain grounds, for instance if the groom decides not to marry the bride after the engagement, then he is required to return double the amount of the marriage deposit to the father of the bride and vice versa.[92]

Dowry has great social-legal significance despite the fact that, it is not included in the formulation of Biblical law.[93] It is a transaction within a family, regarded as an advance form of daughter's inheritance.[94] It consists of movables items such as cloths, jewellery, kitchen utensils, furniture, clothing, mirrors, beds, money. Some wealthy fathers even include slaves, cattle, land or a house.[95] It has been observed that not all the fathers were that generous to their daughters, but it was customary for daughters to receive dowry.

5.3. Marriage Contract (כְּתוּבָה)

It has been observed that one of the basic instruments for the protection of woman's material security is the כְּתוּבָה, "the marriage contract." It provides protection for the wife after the husband and father's death.[96] This is an obligation by the husband that certain amount is fixed and placed in the name of his wife. In case of his death or divorce, the amount is transferred to his wife. It guarantees complete security for her from the estate which includes all the property she brought into the marriage and the כְּתוּבָה sum, the dowry increment listed in the כְּתוּבָה paid to her.[97] It also mentions that both husband and wife will have equal power over their property.[98]

Marriage contract documents in Egypt have not been found and this has led people to believe that the marriage agreement was an unwritten custom.[99] Some form of binding agreement was necessary to the validity of the marriage. The LH 128 states as follows: "If a man takes a wife but does not draw up a contract for her, that woman is not a wife."

---

[91] Mendelsohn, "Family in the Ancient," 28.

[92] Mendelsohn, "Family in the Ancient," 28.

[93] Joseph Fleishman, "A Daughter's Demand and a Father's Compliance: The Legal Background to Achsah's Claim and Caleb's Agreement (Josh. 15:16–19; Judg. 1:12–15)," in *ZAW* 118/3 (2006): 355.

[94] Marsman, *Women in Ugarit*, 95.

[95] Marsman, *Women in Ugarit*, 95–6.

[96] Kaufman, *Woman in Jewish Law*, 202.

[97] Kaufman, *Woman in Jewish Law*, 202.

[98] Anita Diamant, *The New Jewish Wedding* (New York: Simon and Schuster, 1985), 243.

[99] Gay Robins, *Women in Ancient Egypt* (Cambridge: Harvard University Press, 1993), 60.

Regarding the marriage contract, the LE 27 also states as follows:

> If a man marries the daughter of another man without the consent of her father and mother and moreover does not conclude the nuptial feast and the contract for (?) her father and mother, should she reside in his house for even one full year, she is not a wife.

The law is clear that if the girl marries without the consent of her parents she was not considered a legal wife. The conditions of a nuptial feast and a marriage contract must be fulfilled in order to recognize her as wife.[100]

Marriage contracts were also drawn up at Nuzi. The Nuzi documents that deal with marriage contracts are designed to protect the rights of the bride, groom and their future children, and they are concerned with the disposition of property.[101]

A marriage arrangement made between two families was considered binding, part of it consists of marriage deposit, a sign of binding the groom to his commitment. Once marriage deposits and gifts were exchanged, they are bound to marry. A marriage could be dissolved at this stage, but that would have its financial consequences as mentioned above. A woman's dowry remained her property for her personal use.

Among the sources, marriage document is one of the important sources that provide information about women and their property. It is because matrimonial property constitutes an important part of a woman's assets. The כְּתוּבָּה has served as an enlightened instrument committing the husband to certain fundamental responsibilities and guaranteeing a wife inalienable rights and privileges. The כְּתוּבָּה raises woman's status, placing a substantial measure of control in her hands.[102]

5.4. Levirate Marriage

Another important component of marriage is "Levirate marriage."[103] The purpose of Levirate marriage in Israel was to provide male offspring for the childless widow whose husband had died without leaving a male child. The law is laid forth in Deuteronomy 25:5–10. This practice was carried out in order to give the husband progeny. It served the ends of inheritance by allowing the first-born son of the union to inherit the estate of the deceased husband.[104]

---

[100] Roth, *Law Collections*, 63.

[101] Marsman, *Women in Ugarit*, 92.

[102] Kaufman, *Woman in Jewish Law*, 121–2.

[103] This subject is being considered here because it is also related to the issue of inheritance.

[104] Westbrook is right in arguing that, redemption and levirate marriage goes hand-in-hand. Without the inheritance of landed property there is no basis for the near-kinsman of the deceased to father a child for the widow. See, Raymond Westbrook, *Property and the Family in Biblical Law* JSOTSup No. 113 (Sheffield: JSOT Press, 1991), 58–67.

Levirate marriage was also practiced in other ancient societies. In MAL, the parallel Levirate marriage exists. MAL 33 reads as follows:

> [If] a woman is residing in her own father's house, her husband is dead and she has son's [. . .] she shall dwell in a house belonging to th[em]. [If] she has no [son, her father-in-law shall give her to whichever of his sons] he likes [. . .] [. . .] [. . .] or [if he so pleases], he shall give her a spouse to her father-in-law. If her husband and her father-in-law are (both) dead, and she has no son, she is indeed a widow: she shall go wherever she pleases.[105]

Another parallel law is also found in the LH 193 and it reads:

> If a man has a wife, and the man dies, his brother shall take his widow as a wife. (If the brother dies) his father shall take her. When afterwards his father dies, his (that is, the father's) brother shall take the woman whom he had.[106]

Both MAL and LH discuss practices that resemble the biblical custom of levirate marriage.

Akkadian document excavated from the royal palace of Ugarit in 1952 has similar evidence that has bearing on the Levirate marriage Law. The text reads as follows:

> Thus says Arihalbu, King of Ugarit: "Whoever, after my death, takes (in marriage) my wife, Kubaba, daughter of Takan (?) from my brother–May Baal crush him, May he not make great (his) throne, May he not dwell in a (royal) house, Baal of Mt. Casius crush him."[107]

As revealed in the text about the royal marriage, it is found that the king was succeeded by his son on the throne. Arihalba who succeeded his father Niqmad II did not have a son to take over the throne. He willed that his wife Kubaba after his death should be wedded to her brother-in-law by the name Neqmepa. He warned that, no other man outside the family should marry Kubaba.[108] This is the clear evidence of Levirate marriage law. It is because the property and inheritance should remain within the particular royal lineage.

---

[105] Benjamin Kilchor, "Levirate Marriage in Deuteronomy 25:5–10 and its Precursors in Leviticus and Numbers: A Test Case for the Relationship between P/H and D," in *CBQ* 77/3 (July 2015): 434.

[106] There are variations in translation arising from an imperfect text. This translation is taken from, Kilchor, "Levirate Marriage in Deuteronomy 25," 435; See also, Hamilton, "Marriage," in *ABD*, vol. 4, 560–1; Ziony Zevit, "Dating Ruth: Legal, Linguistic and Historical Observations," in *ZAW* 117/4 (2005): 579.

[107] Donald A. Leggett, *Levirate and Goel Institutions in the Old Testament with Special Attention to the Book of Ruth* (Cherry Hill, New Jersey: Mack Publishing Company, 1974), 25.

[108] Hamilton, "Marriage," in *ABD*, vol. 4, 560.

5.5. Institution of Sisterhood Adoption

Institution of sisterhood adoption is said to be a common practice in Nuzi, Old Babylon and Ur III periods. Brothers are believed to have some authority over their sisters in matters relating to her marriage. It is said that, especially in Nuzi, in the area of marriage, women needed an agent to make the arrangement for them. This need for a guardian appeared to give rise to the institution of "sisterhood" texts. Here a woman was either given or gives herself to a guardian, who usually agreed to arrange for her marriage.[109]

Ephraim Speiser was the first scholar to associate this AWA practice of sisterhood institution with biblical story in Genesis 12:13.[110] Abraham, faced with the thread of death in Egypt, passes Sarah off as his sister. Speiser compares this Abraham's narrative with the narrative found in HSS 5 80.[111] According to this text, the woman Beltakkadiummi was promised by her brother Ana Assati "as a wife" to Hurazzi. In the second text, HSS 5 69, the same woman is given to the same man "as his sister." In the third text, HSS 5 25, she was married to Hurazzi by her own free will.[112] Speiser based his argument on these three Nuzi texts that revolve around the marriage, and suggested that these texts provided an answer behind Abraham's claim in Genesis 12:13. He asserts that, since Abraham had spent part of his life at Haran, he was exposed to this custom.[113] There is enough similarity in the practice to justify his claim.

Another document from the city-state of Nuzi in Mesopotamia mentions the status and economic problems associated with unmarried daughters. It mentions about the father having three options with respect to the disposal of his unmarried daughters: Firstly, to negotiate bride-price and give her in marriage; secondly, to give her in adoptive "daughter-ship" or "daughter-in-law" to another man. It was done with a goal of arranging a marriage of full status for her at a later date. Thirdly, to sell her as slave.[114] Nuzi text mentions the documentation of this institution. The text reads as follows:

> Declaration with Kuni-asu daughter of Hut-tesup, made in front of these witnesses: "in the past, Akam-musni married (me) off and took

[109] Martha A. Morrison, "A Continuing Adventure: Cyrus Gordon and Mesopotamia," in *BA* (March 1, 1996): 32.

[110] Ephraim A. Speiser, "The Wife-Sister Motif in the Patriarchal Narratives," in *Biblical and Other Studies*, ed. Alexander Altmann (Cambridge: Harvard University Press, 1963).

[111] *Harvard Semitic Series.* It comprises of miscellaneous texts from Nuzi.

[112] Greengus, "Sisterhood Adoption at Nuzi," 7.

[113] Speiser, "The Wife-Sister Motif, 15–25.

[114] B. L. Eichler, "Another Look at the Nuzi Sistership Contracts," in *Essays on the Ancient Near East in Memory of Jacob Joel Finkelstein*, memoirs of the Connecticut Academy of Arts and Sciences, eds. Maria de Jong Ellis, Hamden (Connecticut: Archon Books, 1977), 45–59; Cf. Carole Fontaine, *Smooth Words: Women, Proverbs and Performance in Biblical Wisdom,* JSOTSup Series 356 (New York: Sheffield Academic Press, 2002), 22–3.

> 40 shekels of silver from me from my husband, but now Akam-musni and my husband are (both) dead, and now (as to) myself, Akkiya, son of Hut-tesup, seized me in the street as his sister and took the authority (of brother) over a sister for me. He will marry me off and take 10 shekels of surampashu silver from my (future) husband."[115]

This is also an evidence of sisterhood adoption. Even after her husband's death, she was taken by force by another man and adopted as sister with a prospect to fetch bride-price from the future husband. It can be presumed that as an adopted sister, the woman must have given him a considerable economic advantage in domestic work in exchange for room and board.

Marriage customs and practices that we see are mainly based on those practiced by people of power and influence in society. The literature of antiquity highlights royalty more than commoners. In Egypt there is no evidence of formal marriage ceremonies nor were there contracts binding together two parties. It is possible that, like in ancient Israelite society, in Egypt as well, marriage agreement was an unwritten custom. The evidence for written documents in Egypt starts only from 9th century.

The following study considers different categories of women in ancient Israel who are presented in the Hebrew Bible with the property rights. To do this, firstly, inheritance rights of widow will be studied.

6. Inheritance Rights of the Widow

The Hebrew word for widow is אַלְמָנָה which occurs fifty-five times in the Old Testament.[116] In the DC, the widows are grouped with the poor, orphans and aliens (Deut. 14:28–29; 24:19). Corneluis Van Leeuven explains that, initially the lot of widow was not a problem at all as she could return to her parental home and would be cared for and protected by the clan and other members of the family. He further explains that, after the settlement in Canaan, the tribalism gave way to the life in cities and villages, because of which the widows became victims of the development of growing social contrasts.[117]

Naomi Steinberg, in her article expresses her disagreement on the depiction of widow in the Old Testament based on the word אַלְמָנָה for widow.[118] She has identified three different terms for widow in the Old Testament. Firstly, אלְמָנָה is a widow who may have had other male members and relative, but they are either too poor or unwilling to support her. Secondly, אִשָּׁה־אלְמָנָה is a widow with

[115] Hamilton, "Marriage," in *ABD*, vol. 4, 562.

[116] Corneluis Van Leeuwen, "אלמנה," in *NIDOTTE*, vol. 1, eds. VanGemeren et al., (Cumbria, UK: Paternoster Press, 1997), 413.

[117] Leeuwen, "אלמנה," in *NIDOTTE,* vol. 1, 413.

[118] Naomi Steinberg, *Romancing the Widow: The Economic Distinctions Between The almana, The issa-almana and the eset-Hammet*, (2004), 1, in https://www.google.co.in/ pdf, 19 June 2016.

redemption rights in her husband's ancestral estate which she exercised through her son, and thirdly, אֵשֶׁת־הַמֵּת refers to a widow whose husband has died before fathering a son to inherit the property.[119] She made clear distinctions on these three terms, and states that the use of אַלְמָנָה in the Hebrew Bible indicates the plight of the lowest end of the financial spectrum of widows. Interestingly, this is the term generally used by the scholars to define the economic status of widows in the Old Testament. She rightly states that their economic circumstances should not be generalized as the lowest stratum in the society as there were also inherited widows presented in the Old Testament.[120] It is to be understood that, widows become vulnerable if they did not have adult sons to support them. In this case, they are either forced to return to their father's house where they become a financial burden to them or to make living on their own, even to the extent of becoming prostitutes.[121]

Basing on the archaeological evidence of Israel during the Iron Age I Period, Jennie Ebeling supports the view that, generally widows were in a vulnerable situation as they did not have the inheritance rights. This was due to the fact that the inheritance law did not provide for them, thus resulting in their vulnerability.[122] As a result they are often mentioned together with other poor people in the Israelite society.

Donald E. Gowan also claims that there is enough evidence in the Old Testament to show that a widow did own property. He cites the example of Proverbs 15:25 which talks about Lord maintaining the boundaries of widows.[123] He refers to Old Testament passages about widows who lived in their own houses and owned livestock.[124] He argues that, the death of husband, father or male members in the family did not necessarily leave the family without resources but according to him, the problem for them was how to maintain those resources.[125]

---

[119] This word is found in Ruth 4:5 and Deut. 25:5.

[120] Galpaz-Feller also states that, not all the widows in the Bible are socially inferior. She is of the opinion that the inferiority status of widow must have been derived from being an outsider in the paternal household that she joined when she married. Cf. Pnina Galpaz-Feller, "The Widow in the Bible and in Ancient Egypt," in *ZAW* 120/2 (2008): 233–4.

[121] Kathleen M. O'Connor, "The Feminist Movement Meets the Old Testament: One Woman's Perspective," in *Engaging the Bible in a Gendered World: An Introduction to Feminist Biblical Interpretation in honor of Katharine Doob Sakenfeld* eds. Linda Day and Carolyn Pressler (London: Westminster John Knox, 2006), 4.

[122] Jennie R. Ebeling, *Women's Lives in Biblical Times* (Auckland, New Zealand: T&T Clark International, 2010), 134.

[123] Donald E. Gowan, "Wealth and Poverty in the Old Testament: The Case of the Widow, the Orphan, and the Sojourner," in *Int* 41/4 (October 1987): 344.

[124] 1 Kgs. 17:9–24; 2 Kgs. 4:1–7; Job 24:3.

[125] Gowan, "Wealth and Poverty," 345.

There are also frequent warnings against coveting the land of widows or defrauding them which imply that widows in fact owned land.[126]

Before examining the Israelite situation in more detail, it is worth comparing it with other ancient societies which did give women much greater freedom when they became widows. Like many other ancient societies, Ugarit was also a patriarchal society but by comparison with other similar societies women were given so much freedom with no evidence of oppression. Their opinions were respected, and they participated in all kind of activities.[127] A "WILL" which was excavated from Ugarit Text says:

> As of this day, before witnesses, Yarimanu spoke as follows: "Now therefore, whatever I possess (and) that which Bidawe acquired together with me: my large cattle, my small cattle, my asses, my male slaves, my female slaves, my bronze bowls, bronze kettles, bronze jugs, baskets, the field of Bin-Harasina (bordering) upon the Ra'abani stream—I have bequeathed to Bidawe, my wife. And now therefore, my two sons Yatlinu, the elder, and Yanhamu, the younger—whichever of them shall bring a lawsuit against Bidawe, or shall abuse Bidawe, their mother, shall pay 500 shekels of silver to the king; he shall set his cloak upon the doorbolt, and shall depart into the street. But, whichever of them shall have paid respect to Bidawe, his mother—to that one will she bequeath (the possessions)."[128]

Here in this "WILL," husband leaves the property to his wife upon his death. She was given the right and responsibility to manage the estate, and also the right to distribute them.

Returning to the Israelite situation, no doubt there may have been widows who were poor and without any inheritance as there are passages in the Old Testament that refer to poor widows, but this does not mean that all widows were poor or without an inheritance (Job 22:9; Zech. 7:10 Isa. 1:23;).[129] To

---

[126] Deut. 10:18; 27:19; Isa. 1:17, 23; Jer. 7:6; 22:3; See, Robert L. Hubbard, *The Book of Ruth: The New International Commentary on the Old Testament*, eds. R. K. Harrison et al., (Michigan: William B. Eerdmans Publishing Company, 1988), 55.

[127] Quoted by Marsman, *Women in Ugarit*, 35.

[128] (17) Will and Testament, Ugarit Text: R S 8. 145, F. Thureau-Dangin, Syria, xviii (1937), 246; transliteration and trans. G. Boyer, *Archives royales de Mari (ARMT),* (Paris, 1950–), 249 f., in *Ancient Near Eastern Texts Relating to the Old Testament,* 3rd ed. with Supplement, ed. James B. Pritchard (Princeton, New Jersey: Princeton University Press, 1969), 546.

[129] Frank Frick ,clearly explains about the status of widow in the Israelites society, and also the inheritance rights of widows. See, Frank S. Frick, "Widows in the Hebrew Bible: A Transactional Approach," in *Feminist Companion to Exodus to Deuteronomy* (Sheffield: Sheffield Academic Press, 1994), 148–9; Cf. Philip E. Satterthwaite and J. Gordon McConville, *Exploring the Old Testament: A Guide to the Historical Books* vol. 2 (Illinois: InterVarsity Press, 2007), 221.

demonstrate this, let us consider Naomi, a widow with an inheritance in the Old Testament.

Naomi (Ruth 4:3)

> And he said to the kinsman, "Naomi, who has come back from the country of Moab, sold the portion of the field that belonged to our kinsman Elimelech."[130]

Background of the Book of Ruth

The Book of Ruth is about women and their struggle in a patriarchal society with an authentic expression of a female voice. The narrative opens in Bethlehem which is from the Hebrew words בֵּית לֶחֶם "house of bread." Ironically there is no bread in the "house of bread," as the land is in famine. Elimelech, along with his wife Naomi and two sons, travelled to Moab in search of food. Another irony is that, Moabites failed to give food to the Israelites during the Exodus, and Moabites were cursed as a result.[131]

According to Robert L. Hubbard, "The Book of Ruth is profoundly human, a story with down-to-earth features, one can easily identify with."[132] The reader empathizes readily with poor Naomi, who is battered by life's tragic blows—famine, exile, grief, loneliness—and may recall own bitter experiences.

According to the narrative, Naomi, after the death of her husband and two sons, had the right to inherit the land of her deceased husband and sell it. There are scholars who cite the Book of Ruth (especially Ruth 4:3) as evidence for assuming the practice of inheritance by widows.[133] Derek Beattie further claims that the author of Ruth would not knowingly represent a legal situation which was not practiced at that time.[134] The author presents Naomi as being in possession of property, indicating that it was possible in Israelite law for a widow to inherit husband's property.

Evidence of Widows with inheritance from Non-biblical Text

Interestingly, some scholars have compared Naomi to Judith, an outstanding Jewish heroine, who is pictured as young, apparently childless, wealthy and well respected widow, the very antithesis of the traditional picture of a biblical

---

[130] Translated from *BHS*.

[131] Diane Jacobson, "Redefining Family in the Book of Ruth," *W&W* 33/1 (2013): 5–6.

[132] Hubbard, *The Book of Ruth*, 1.

[133] Zevit rightly states that, the Book of Ruth details three distinct socio-legal institutions: levirate marriage, land redemption, and a widow's right in matters of inheritance. Cf. Zevit, "Dating Ruth," 576; See also, Derek Robert George Beattie, "Book of Ruth as Evidence for Israelite Legal Practice," in *VT* (July 1974): 255–6.

[134] Beattie, "Book of Ruth," 252.

widow.[135] Naomi was also compared with a widow named Babatha, whose legal records have been discovered among the documents dating to the second century CE. She is said to be the only child of her parents. After the death of her parents she inherited all the property.[136] Babatha's archive of documents is said to be found in *Nahal Hever* that reveals about her personal history, her family and business.[137] For example, in one of the occasions, she filed law suit against her son's guardian for failing to support her son; for this reason she wanted the land to be given back to her.[138]

It is therefore, evident that the histories of AWA brought clarity regarding the position of widows with inheritance to a greater extent than are mentioned in the Hebrew Bible. This would be understandable as Israelites shared in large measure in custom, institutions and practices with the neighbouring nations. In the case of widow whose husband died leaving inheritable property, she remained as a continuing part of the property.

A Hebrew ostracon from the Iron Age, dating to the 7th century BCE, which is named "A Widow's Plea to an Official," gives evidence to a story where a widow made claim to the property that was given to the brother of deceased husband.[139] The ostracon contained the plea of a widow to an official asking for transference of her late husband's land. The English translation of the ostracon reads as follows:

> 1 May *YHWH* bless you in peace: And now: May[140]
>
> 2 my lord the official listen to your maidservant. My husband
>
> 3 died without sons. (I request politely that the following) happen: (let) your hand (be)
>
> 4 with me and entrust to your maidservant the

---

135 Frick, "Widows in the Hebrew Bible," in *Feminist Companion to Exodus* ed. Brenner (Sheffield: Sheffield Academic Press, 1994), 148.

136 Tal Ilan, *Jewish Women in Greco-Roman Palestine: An Inquiry into Image and Status* (Massachusetts: Hendrickson Publishers, 1996), 51.

137 Nahal Hever is in Judean desert near the western shore of the Dead Sea. Several biblical scrolls were said to have been discovered from this cave in early 1950's by the Bedouins; Cf. Peter W. Flint and Andrea E. Alvarez, "The Preliminary edition of the First Numbers Scroll from Nahal Hever," in *BBR* 9 (1999): 137–43.

138 Frick, "Widows in the Hebrew Bible," 149–50.

139 An ostracon is archaeological remains, a piece of pottery usually broken off from a vase or other earthenware vessel. It contains scratched-in words or other forms of writing which may give clues as to the time when the piece was in use. The languages are Hebrew, Canaanite, Phoenician or Moabite. For detail study on Ostragon see, Alan Millard, "The Ostracon from the Days of David Found at Khirbet Qeiyafa," in *TB* 62/1 (2011): 1– 2.

140 The blessing formula in this document has the same blessing formula found in the Hebrew Bible, a form of the Priestly Blessing known from the Book of Numbers (Num. 6:26). Cf. Pierre Bordreuil, Felice Israel, and Dennis Pardee, "King's Command and Widow's Plea: Two New Hebrew Ostracon of the Biblical Period," in *NEA* 61/1 (March 1998): 9.

[5] inheritance about which you spoke to Amas
[6] yahu. As for the wheat field that
[7] is in Naamah, you have (already) given (it) to
[8] his brother.[141]

This is said to be an occurrence in Northwest Semitic epistolary tradition basing on the formula used as, "May such-and-such a divinity bless you."[142] The geographic name Naamah is possibly the town that is mentioned in Joshua 15:41, which was located in the Shephelah and assigned to the tribe of Judah.[143] It is a plea for a hearing addressed to a superior by someone of inferior status asking him to let her have the legal right over the portion of her deceased husband's property.

Going back to the Book of Ruth, some scholars like Hubbard and others have argued that the Book of Ruth seems more concerned with inheritance matters than with Naomi's poverty.[144]

Chapter four opens by recording the speech of Boaz to the kinsman and the assembled witnesses at the city gate of Bethlehem. Boaz speaks about Naomi's return from Moab, and her plan to sell the plot of land that she inherited from her husband. He presented the custom and procedure in the matter of redemption of land.

4:3: As Boaz prepares to address his kinsman, he begins with this word הַשָּׂדֶה חֶלְקַת which literally means "a portion of the field." It is an expression of technical term used in property law.[145] Boaz specified that "the property belonged to our brother Elemelech." The word אָחִינוּ literally means "our brother." The noun אָח often refers to people related by blood, family members, kinsmen and it also refers to the members of the same tribe.[146]

The word מָכְרָה literally means "Naomi sold," it is from the root מכר "to sell." This verb is in perfect tense, thus, a straight-forward statement that the sale has taken place in the past. Normally, the perfect indicates an action already completed, but that sense does not suit this context. Yair Zakovitch states that the past tense of the verb indicates Naomi's determination.[147]

The root word מכר, according to Bush has two meanings: to sell movable goods outright and also specific kind of land transfer. He claims that, this verb is used in the context of selling meat (Deut. 14:21), oil (2 Kgs. 4:7), garments (Prov.

[141] Bordreuil, Israel, and Pardee, "King's Command," 7.

[142] Bordreuil, Israel, and Pardee, "King's Command," 7.

[143] Bordreuil, Israel, and Pardee, "King's Command," 8.

[144] Hubbard, *The Book of Ruth*, 55; Ilan, *Jewish Women in Greco-Roman*, 51.

[145] Hubbard, *The Book of Ruth*, 142.

[146] Cornelius I., "אח," in *NIDOTTE*, vol. 1, 345.

[147] Yair Zakovitch, "מכרא ליראל," *A Biblical Commentary for Israel*, (רות) (Magnes: The Hebrew University Magnes Press, 1990), 155; Quoted by Andre LaCoque, *Ruth: A Continental Commentary*, Trans. K. C. Hanson (Minneapolis: Fortress Press, 2004), 128.

31:24), or even the sale of a human being into slavery (Gen. 37:27, 28; Deut. 21:14). The other meaning with regard to land is that, it refers to a transaction in which only the legal right of the land is transferred for a specific value and stipulated time.[148] This passage clearly implies that Naomi had the legal right over the land.

The biblical text is clear enough in pointing to Naomi in possession of the land. Naomi's land is the issue of a legal discussion at the city gate. Comparative studies with other figures like Judith and Babatha have given a clearer picture that not all widows were poor, but they were also inherited widows. The fact that the author represents Naomi as being in possession of property which belongs to Elimelech serves to indicate that it was possible in Israelite law for a widow to inherit her deceased husband's property.

7. Inheritance Rights of Wife

The status of wife carries with it certain customary rights, usually stipulated in a marriage settlement. Whatever she acquired as marriage gift, acquired independently and before marriage remains at her disposition, but her property acquired after marriage automatically falls under her husband's control. It is true that women appearing in the context of inheritance in the Old Testament are related to men in one way or another either as wives or as daughters.

Divorce is regulated by laws in Sumerian society. The law permits the man to divorce his wife on the ground of adultery. However, wife was punished by death for repudiating her husband.[149] She is permitted to retain the marriage portion which she had brought to the home. She also had a share with her children in the divorced husband's property at his death.[150]

In Babylon, it is said that wife could acquire property, take legal action, be a part of the contract and have certain shares in her husband's inheritance.[151] The LH 150 has a provision for wife and it reads as follows:

> If a man awards to his wife a field, orchard, house, or movable property, and makes out a sealed document for her, after her husband's death her children will not bring a claim against her; the mother shall give her estate to whichever of her children she loves, but she will not give it to an outsider.

Based on the evidence of the existence of the sealed document, wife has the right to her entitled property. This property cannot be claimed by anybody

---

[148] Frederic W. Bush, "Ruth," in *WBC Ruth, Esther*, vol. 9 eds. David A. Hubbard at al., (Texas: Word Books, Publisher, 1996), 200–1.

[149] C. H. W. Johns, *Babylonian and Assyrian Laws, Contracts and Letter* (Edinburgh: T&T Clark, 1904), 141.

[150] Johns, *Babylonian and Assyrian Laws,* 141.

[151] Vaux, *Ancient Israel*, 40.

including her own children. There is also a stipulation that she must leave her estate to one of her children in order to prevent piece of property to be given to a person outside the family.

The biblical account in 2 Kings 4:8 and 8:1–6 records the story of a wife exercising authority over the land, therefore, the following is an attempt to study the story of a Shunemmite woman who is depicted as being in possession of land.

7.1. Shunemmite Woman (2 Kings 4:8; 8:3)

> 4:8 And it happened, one day Elisha was passing through Shunem, and there lived a great woman, and urged him to have bread. So, it was as often as he passed that way, he would turn there to eat bread.
>
> 8:3 And it happened at the end of the seven years, the woman returned from the land of the Philistines, and she went and cried out to the king for her house and her field.[152]

Background of the Book of 2 Kings

The Book of Kings as it indicates covers the era of Israel's monarchic rulers. It begins with the transition of power from David to his son Solomon and continues until both the Northern and Southern kingdoms were exiled. It narrates the story of Israel's life from the conquest of the Promised Land to the Babylonian exile. It is clear that 1 Kings 12 to 2 Kings 17, the narrative alternated between the Northern and Southern kingdoms.[153] The present story is a disconnected piece of account of a faithful Israelite woman and the prophet Elisha.

The stories concerning prophets Elijah and Elisha dominate this book. Philip E. Satterthwaite states that, the story of Shunemmite woman was incorporated here to magnify Elisha's reputation.[154] 2 Kings chapters 2–8 contains most of the prophet Elisha's narrative, of which most narratives are not related to the context.[155] This could account for the story of the Shunemmite woman being included here.

Elisha's involvement ranges from politics to performing miracles. His involvement in political affairs is seen in supporting the rebellions of Jehu (1 Kgs. 9:1–13), Hazael (1 Kgs. 8:7–15). He also intervened directly in the wars (1 Kgs. 6:8–23), foretold the victory (1 Kgs. 13:14–19). Several strands are woven together in the narratives. The book should be read in the context of the larger narrative of Kings of which they form a part.

---

[152] Translated from *BHS*.

[153] Lissa Wray Beal, *1 & 2 Kings*, Apollos Old Testament Commentary series, eds. David W. Baker and Gordon J. Wenham vol. 9 (Illinois: IVP Academic, 2014), 22.

[154] Philip E. Satterthwaite, "The Elisha Narratives and the Coherence of 2 Kings 2–8," in *TB* 49/1 (May 1998): 6–7.

[155] Satterthwaite, "Elisha Narratives," 1–2.

Great Woman

4:8: Returning to the story of the Shunemmite woman, she was introduced as a "great woman" (2 Kgs. 4:8–37), and one without son, who was promised a son by Elisha. The boy child was delivered in the following year as promised by the prophet. As the story unfolds, the boy at one point became ill and was at the point of death, but the prophet revived him. The story ends abruptly here, but is later resumed from 2 Kings 8:1–6.

As the narration goes, Elisha foresaw famine and warned the woman to relocate to another place. In this way she indeed survived the famine that lasted for seven years by staying in the land of Philistines. As she returned home after the famine was over, she found that her entire property was taken by someone else. It could be assumed that the property must have fallen to king's hand.[156] The story is interpreted in many ways from different perspectives but, here the researcher's interest is in the woman's social status and possession of land.

The woman supported Elisha by providing housing and food.[157] She is also an unnamed woman like most of the female biblical characters. But, she is depicted as woman with voice that speaks for her. She makes decisions, and acts independently as a citizen with full rights. For this, she was even called, the real miracle worker and the most powerful woman.[158]

The Old Testament narratives about wife consist of three major thematic components: that is, the initial barrenness of wife, divine promise of future conception and the birth of a son.[159] The character of the great Shunemmite woman was different in that, it was the first time in the Old Testament where a woman taking a leading role was not described as childless or barren.[160] Fuchs suggests that, it was in fact the prophet who discovers she does not have a son and so does something about it. Lee follows this argument:

> In the miracle stories of Elijah and Elisha, the wonder workers are males, and most of the recipients are women. Each of these women is very poor and in desperate situations. Either she has nothing to eat

---

[156] Walter Dietrich, "1 and 2 Kings," in *The Oxford Bible Commentary,* eds. John Barton and John Muddiman (Great Clarendon: Oxford University Press, 2007), 252; See also, Beal, *1 & 2 Kings*, vol. 9, 360.

[157] For further reading, Alice Ogden Bellis, *Helpmates, Harlots, and Heroes: Women's Stories in the Hebrew Bible* (Louisville: Westminster John Knox Press, 2007).

[158] Quoted by Kyung Sook Lee, "1 and 2 Kings," in *Global Bible Commentary,* eds. Daniel Patte et al., (Nashville: Abingdon Press, 2004), 114.

[159] Gen. 17:15–16; 25:21; Judg. 13:2–3.

[160] As she appears in the biblical narrative, she was presented as great woman, taking very active role in providing food and shelter to the prophet Elisha, and making decisions by herself. It was the prophet himself who found out that she did not have son and so he himself promised that she would give birth to a son. Cf. Esther Fuchs, "The Literary Characterization of Mothers and Sexual Politics in the Hebrew Bible," in *Semeia* No. 46 (1989): 151–66.

> e.g., 1 Kings 17:8–18, no son, her only son is dead, or she is a poor widow in debt as in 2 Kings 4:1–7. It is a pity that these stories gave us the general impression that women are always in need, and that man, like priests or prophets should protect them. Happily, the story of Shunemmite woman breaks this pattern.[161]

"Great woman" (אִשָּׁה גְדוֹלָה) is also sometimes translated as "wealthy woman" which is a descriptive adjective for persons of esteem and status.[162] Brent Plate and Rodríguez Mangual describe the wealth as not limited to financial status, and claim that the woman gave without expecting anything in return where her sole desire was to give.[163]

8:1: When the prophet Elisha said "you and your household" (אַתְּ וּבֵיתֵךְ), he implies that the woman is responsible for the welfare of her household. In 4:14, her husband is described as old and the state of her husband whether dead or alive is not indicated by the author. According to the narrative, she has power to control the property. In both the episodes, she was depicted as an active woman playing important role.

John Gary comments that, the word וְגוּרִי (8:1) indicates a גֵּר (sojourner) temporary dweller, or a protected stranger in an alien community. It means to live abroad for a season in the intention of returning to enjoy one's rights and property in one's native land.[164]

V.3: The word "and she went and cried out" (וַתֵּצֵא לִצְעֹק), is a phrase used in legal procedure. Since the king was the chief magistrate of the country, responsible for the welfare of his subjects, she went to him with a complaint regarding her house and field. The King took the woman's plight seriously after hearing her case, and he appointed an official to be in charge for the restoration of the property. The procedure whereby someone else could possess her property was not told. The only mention is that, it had passed from her hand. In order to claim what was rightfully hers, she appealed, literally "she cried out," to the king. The outcome was that, all that belonged to her was restored.

Generally, in the Old Testament women are depicted as powerless, dependent on the male members of the family, but this unnamed woman played a contrary role. She was depicted as woman of means, because she built for the Elisha a chamber. Her further actions and words describe her as an independent woman in her own right with a legal power over the property both house and land.

When Elijah asked her what she needs, she responded saying, she dwells among her people, she is fine and wants nothing. This response shows her

---

161 Lee, "1 and 2 Kings," in *Global Bible Commentary*, 114.

162 M. G. Abegg, "גדל," in *NIDOTTE,* vol. 1, 823.

163 S. Brent Plate and Edna M. Rodríguez Mangual, "The Gift that stops Giving: Heline Cixous's "Gift" and the Shunammite Woman," in *BibInt* 7/2 (April 1999): 119–20.

164 John Gray, *I and II Kings: A Commentary* (Philadelphia: Westminster Press, 1971), 527.

sufficiency. Her response to the offer is one that affirms her own status in the community and her independence.[165]

In the second episode when she returned from the land of the Philistines after seven years, her property has been possessed by someone, so she went and got the things done without anyone's help. It is something that she had earlier tried to tell the prophet that she could do. It is clear evidence of wife holding land.[166] Her status is revealed through the description as great women and her appearance in the court regarding land.

7.2. Strong Wife (Proverb 31:16)

> She considers a field and takes it; from the fruit of her palm she plants a vineyard.[167]

Background of the Book of Proverbs

Hebrew Bible is divided into three parts: the Law, the Prophets and the Writings. The Book of Proverbs along with Job and Ecclesiastic are known as the writings or the Wisdom Literature, as it is dominated by wise counsel and least dominated by priestly and prophetic interests. Wisdom literature is a distinctive literature of professional group of sages that have produced these writings whose truths are based on human experience rather than divine revelation.[168]

The Hebrew word for "Proverb" is מָשָׁל which is related to the verbal stem משל "to rule, master." The overall shape of the work communicates the sages' purpose, that is, to bring order out of the chaos of daily life.[169] The major theme of the book is the surpassing value of wisdom which is the gift of God that is founded on the fear of the LORD. The book comprises of principally two types of materials. Firstly, it is a series of didactic discourses comprising parental instructions and speeches by personified wisdom (chaps. 1–9). These discourses also serve as an extended introduction to the collections that follow. Secondly, it is a collection of chiefly short proverbial sayings (chaps. 10–31).

---

[165] Mary E. Shields, "Subverting a Man of God, Elevating a Woman: Role and Power Reversals in 2 Kings 4," in *JSOT* 58 (June 1993): 60.

[166] Edward F. Campbell, *Ruth: A New Translation with Introduction, Notes, and Commentary*, 4th ed. AB vol. 7 (Garden City, New York: Doubleday & Company, 1978), 157; Cf. Mordechai Cogan and Hayim Tadmor, *2 Kings: A New Translation with Introduction and Commentary*, vol. 2 AB (USA: Doubleday & Company, INC., 1988), 88.

[167] Translated from *BHS*.

[168] James L. Crenshaw, *Old Testament Wisdom: An Introduction* (Atlanta: John Knox Press, 1998), 28–9.

[169] Anthony R. Ceresko, *Introduction to Old Testament Wisdom: A Spirituality for Liberation* (Mumbai: St Paul Press, 2005), 66.

The sages' recognition of wives as having great potentials has been articulated by Carole Fontaine as follows:

> Despite regular delineation of women as potential troublemakers, the sages see an able, active, fruitful wife as an undisputed prerequisite for male advancement in the public world . . .[170]

In the final chapter of Proverb (chap. 31) there are two female figures of relatively different kinds. In the first part, the poem in 31:1–9 is about the queen who instructs her son in his kingly duties and royal behaviour. The second part of this chapter 31:10–31, is in praise of the virtuous wife. This passage presents a woman exercising a many-sided responsibility. It is an evidence of the degree of managerial domestic responsibility assumed by well-to-do wives in ancient Israel.

Christine Roy Yoder, reads Proverbs 31:10–31 in the context of the post exilic period, specifically the Persian period in the light of the epigraphic and biblical evidence.[171] She claims that during the Persian period royal women and other women of affluent position were property holders and estate owners. Therefore, she is of the view that this strong wife too acquired real estate and developed it for income.[172] To her she is a composite figure of real Persian period women that reflect the socio-economic realities of the writer's period. In the words of Beth Szlos also, it is the description of an ideal woman, a carefully crafted literary piece.[173] Almost all of the relevant characteristics described here fit in with other periods too.

This strong woman embodies no one particular woman as the entire poem is arranged alphabetically, a pattern known as an acrostic. Here each verse of 22 lines begins with successive letters of the Hebrew alphabet. Such a structure points to a complete and ordered description of strong and noble woman. What is important in this research is the depiction of this strong wife with an independent right to plan and buy a field. She invests her own assets in land purchase and development. She bought a field which she made more productive by turning it into a vineyard.

V. 10: The Hebrew word for this strong woman is אֵשֶׁת־חַיִל). The word חַיִל emphasizes the quality of person and the basic meaning is "strength and power." The word is also applied to variety of people including a warrior (1 Sam. 2:4), an army (Deut. 11:4), landowners (Ruth 2:1), a person who is capable of doing

[170] Fontaine, *Smooth Words: Women Proverbs,* 19.

[171] Christine Roy Yoder, "The Woman of Substance (lyx-tva): A Socio-economic Reading of Proverbs 31:10–31," in *JBL* 122/3 (September 2003): 427–31.

[172] Yoder, "Woman of Substance," 444–5.

[173] M. Beth Szlos, "A Portrait of Power: A Literary-Critical Study of the Depiction of the Woman in Proverbs 31:10–31," in *USQR* 54/1–2 (2000): 98.

things (Exod. 18:21).[174] Samuel Goh states that, the word אֵשֶׁת־חַיִל here hints to the importance of her status.[175]

V. 16: the Hebrew word זָמַם is used here, and it is translated as "think, plan, purpose, devise." Here in this verse, the verb stands for putting together a plan to act on, such as considering purchasing a field and executing the plan.[176] This verse pictures the wife as engaged in real estate and agricultural ventures. Here, she is depicted as going out by herself to find a field to buy and with her own resources she plants a vineyard.

She is a wealthy woman who runs a household estate with servants and conducts business. The poem briefly refers to the husband mentioning merely the respected position he enjoys sitting at the city gate (31:23) that is the public sphere assigned for men. The poem describes how wife excels in the discharge of her domestic duties related essentially to the production of clothing and the preparation of food, the space traditionally assigned to women. It is clear that, she acts with much independence in her own sphere. Even though the woman presented here is a symbolic figure, a type of literary form, yet it is tied to a socio-historical setting. Undoubted the poet's portrayal is based on particular conceptions that the Israelite society had about women.

8. Inheritance Rights of Daughter

בַּת is the Hebrew word for daughter which is found 585 times in Old Testament. It is less than one eighth as often as בֵּן (son).[177] The word בַּת generally refers to a young girl. The social position of the daughter in Hebrew society was rather complex.[178] According to the Israelite inheritance law, they received support from the father's estate. It is stated that if male heirs to the property exists, daughters receive only maintenance, and if there are no sons, the daughters received the property. They also receive a sum from the property for their dowry, and some generous and rich father provides even land.[179] Roth claims that, in many countries it is customary to give equal inheritance to sons and daughters.[180]

Before looking at examples of Israelite daughters who claimed property rights, let us review briefly the situation in neighbouring countries.

One of the earliest clear indications of the rights of a daughter to inherit from the father comes from a royal inscription (in Sumerian) of Gudea, king of Lagash,

---

[174] Robin Wakely, "חיל," in *NIDOTTE,* vol. 2, 116.

[175] Samuel T. S. Goh, "Ruth as a Superior Woman of חיל?: A Comparison between Ruth and the "Capable" Woman in Proverbs 31:10–31," in *JSOT* 38/4 (June 2014): 488.

[176] John E. Hartley, "זמם," in *NIDOTTE,* vol. 1, 1112.

[177] Chrys C. Caragounis, "בת," in *NIDOTTE,* vol. 1, 779.

[178] The status of daughter in Israelite society has been discussed in the first chapter.

[179] Kaufman, *Woman in Jewish Law,* 202.

[180] Cecil Roth, *House of Nasi: Dona Gracia* (Philadelphia: Jewish Publication Society of America, 1947), 105–6, 202.

dating to the late 22nd century BCE. The text reads as follows: "In a household that has no male child, the daughter becomes its heir (of the household)."[181]

The laws of Lipit-Ishtar (LL), king of Isin (Sumerian c.1930 BCE) states:

> If a man dies without leaving a male heir, (his) unmarried daughter shall be his heir.[182] The Legal adoption document recovered from Old Babylon records the adoption of a daughter by the name Belizuna by her aunt Tabni-Istar. The adopted daughter was made the sole heir of Tabni-Istar's estate on the condition that the adoptee honours her adopted mother.[183] This is clear evidence where a real estate that belonged to a mother has been handed down to adopted daughter.

Under the title "Litigation over Inheritance," James B. Pritchart mentions a court case from Old Babylonian Period over inheritance. The priestess Amat-Shamash left her adopted daughter a house plot before her death. After her death, her brothers contested the bequest, arguing that Amat-Shamash did not leave any house for the adopted daughter. After thorough investigation the judges delivered the verdict in favour of the adopted daughter. The witnesses in the case testified that a 'WILL' indeed was drawn up by Amat-Shamash.[184] Later another brother reinstituted the suit against the judges' verdict. It is mentioned that as a punishment for filing a non-contestable document, the authorities shaved half his head of hair, pierced his nose, extended his arm and marched him around the city as an act of humiliation.[185]

There is a separate law that regulates the inheritance of priestesses. The LH has provision for priestesses upon their father's death.[186] Legally brothers are required to support their priestess-sisters through regular allowances. If the brothers failed to give her needed support, then priestesses had the right to reclaim the land that is given to her by her father prior to his death. She has the right to give her land to any agricultural tenant she pleases, and they will support her. She will not sell it, as it belongs only to her brothers, therefore, upon her death, she must leave it

---

181 Gudea Statue B, vii, 44–46. For the inscription, cf. Dietz Otto Edzard, *Gudea and His Dynasty* vol. 3/1 (Toronto: University of Toronto Press, 1997), 36.

182 Laws of Lipit-Ishtar paragraph B. Cf. Roth, *Law Collections from Mesopotamia,* 26.

183 M. Schorr, Urkunden des altbabylonischen Zivil-und Prozessrechts, 1913/13A, quoted by Nathanael Warren, "Adoption-Alienation in Ezra 47:22–23 and in the Ancient Near East," in *ZAW* 126/3 (2014): 422.

184 (4) "Marriage Contract," Old Assyrian, 19th century BCE Text: B. Hrozny, *Inscriptions Cuneiformes du Kultipi* 1 (Praha, 1952). Transliteration and trans., Hrozny, in *Symbolae Koschakjer (Studia ei Documenta* 11, 1939), 108 ff., in *Ancient Near Eastern Texts,* 543–4.

185 4) "Marriage Contract," in *Ancient Near Eastern Texts,* 544.

186 LH 178.

to her brothers.[187] Unlike LH 178, law 179 permits woman to permanently own her share of property, with a right to invest or sell as she chooses. However, this does not dismiss the disputes over inheritance.

In Egypt, the daughters were legally entitled to a share of their father's estate equal to that of sons.[188] They had the right to own land, represent themselves in legal proceedings, and conduct a business.[189] Tablets from Arraphe and Nuzi mention about daughters as potential heir. The document reads as follows:

> This is the tablet of the testament of Unaptae to his daughter, Shilwaturi. He drew up a will for her. This is what Unaptae said: "I have established my daughter Shilwaturi as a son. All of my fields, my buildings . . . all of my property . . . its entirety . . . I have given to Shilwaturi, my daughter, whom I have established as a son." Unaptae also said: "I have established my wife, Shakutu, as a father for my daughter, Shilwaturi. As long as Shakutu is living, Shilwaturi shall care for her. When Shakutu dies, Shilwaturi shall mourn her, and she shall bury [her]."[190]

According to this document if a man had only daughter for potential heir, she would be adopted as son and inherit the father's real estate without any condition.

The above cited laws and cases are some of the indications that daughters inherited or owned land in southern Mesopotamia and Egypt. It also gives evidence to the mother handing over real estate to the adopted daughter and daughter adopted as son. However, there is virtually less evidence in the Old Testament comparable with these quoted examples from other neighbouring countries.

Besides the daughters of Zelophehad, there are few passages in the Old Testament concerning daughters with property inheritance. The following is a study on it.

8.1. Achsah (Judges 1:12–15)

> 12 And Caleb said: "whoever attacks Kiriath-sepher, and captures it, I will give him my daughter Achsah as wife."
>
> 13 And Othniel son of Kenaz, Caleb's younger brother took it; and he gave him his daughter Achsah as wife.

---

[187] LH 178; Cf. David P. Wright, *Inventing God's Law: How the Covenant Code of the Bible used and Revised the Laws of Hammurabi* (New York: Oxford University Press, 2009), 142.

[188] Bruce Wells, "Law and Practice," in *A Companion to the ANE*, ed. Daniel C. Snell (Oxford: Blackwell Publishing, 2005), 192.

[189] Graves-Brown, *Dancing for Hathor*, 32.

[190] E. Lacheman, *Tablets from Arraphe and Nuzi in the Iraq Museum*. Sumer, 32, 113–48, (1976), 133–4, text 2.

> 14 When she came, she urged him to ask for field from her father. As she dismounted from her ass, Caleb said to her, "What do you wish?"
>
> 15 She said to him, "Give me a blessing; since you have given me the land of Negeb, give me also springs of water." So, Caleb gave her upper and lower springs.[191]

Achsah (עַכְסָה), Caleb's daughter's name appears five times in the Old Testament, and her tale is found also in Joshua 15:15–19 in the biblical conquest account.[192] She was understood not only as woman but as a local or tribal dependent of the powerful Caleb clan of Hebron during the settlement history, but many scholars do not support this view.[193] The following is a background of the Book of Judges in brief.

Background of the Book of Judges

The Book of Judges presents an astonishingly rich collection of thrilling war stories of individual heroism in the Israelites' battles against their neighbours. There is a connection between the Books of Joshua and Judges which is found in Judges chapter 1. It presents the Israelites' entry into the land which had been allotted to the tribes and settled by dispossessing the Canaanites. The book begins with a prologue (1:1–3:6) setting the stage for the judge.

The theology of the book is made very clear at the beginning of the book. The people of Israel will be rewarded if they maintain their uniqueness as a special people of God and keep all the commandments. On the other hand, failure to obey would lead to divine judgment, if they assimilate with the neighbouring nations.

The Israelites were separated by their tribal allotment into regions and there was no federal government to administer the nation. Joshua was a devoted and a successful leader. After the death of Joshua, the succeeding generation broke *YHWH's* covenant and experience the covenant's curses including long period without rest in the land. Joshua claims the land for *YHWH* by erecting altars to Him, the next generation builds altars to Baal.[194] The worship of Baal is well attested in Judges (2:11–13; 3:7; 6:25–32; 8:33; 9:4). They failed to obey *YHWH*, therefore, as the name of the book implies the divinely inspired righteous leaders called "judges" were raised to deliver the people. Their disobedient behaviour

---

[191] Translated from *BHS*.

[192] Josh. 15:16–17; Judg. 1:12–13; 1 Chr. 2:49.

[193] John Gray, "Joshua, Judges, Ruth," in *New Century Bible Commentary* (Grand Rapids: Eerdmans Publishing Company, 1986), 137; Cf. Danna Nolan Fewell, "Deconstructive Criticism: Achsah and the (e)razed City of Writing," in *Judges and Method: New Approaches in Biblical Studies,* ed. Gale A. Yee (Minneapolis: Fortress Press, 2007), 126.

[194] Bruce K. Waltke and Charles Yu, *An Old Testament Theology: An Exegetical, Canonical, and Thematic Approach* (Grand Rapids, Michigan: Zondervan, 2007), 589.

provoked *YHWH* to anger and *YHWH* disciplined them by handing them over to oppressive enemies. As they cried out for deliverance *YHWH* raised judges to deliver them.

The book as a part of Deuteronomistic History was compiled in Judah in the 7th century during the time of King Josiah. The book expresses Israelites hopes and political aspirations.[195] The history of Israel presented in this book reflects an era of great disorder without unified leaders. The period was marked by everyone doing what was right in their own eyes (Judg. 21:25).

One can easily understand that the writer of the book inherited a large number of individual stories related to the acts of deliverance from oppression and deeds of heroic valour.[196] The Deuteronomic historian shaped the material by brilliantly gathering the stories into a unified historical account.

Narrowing down to the first chapter, it is regarded as possessing a possible reliable nucleus of memories of ancient victories. This chapter tells us about the tribes that made up the core of the Southern Kingdom Judah and Simeon. It further narrates about the execution of the sacred mission in conquering the Canaanite cities within their territories. The narrative also elaborates on the inability of the Israelites to drive away all the Canaanites. It is reported that, many Canaanite cities survived the Israelites conquest.

The setting of the Book of Judges, the field of battle, is an arena traditionally reserved for the affairs of men. In this arena, Achsah appears like a pawn and fighting men's fodder in a war time game of chess.[197] She was given up by her father to achieve his purpose that is, to capture Debir, the town of Kiriath-sepher.[198] Othniel claims her as his trophy of war.

V. 14: Achsah spoke out, urging Othniel her bridegroom to ask her father for a marriage gift of land. This act informs the readers that she was at first still identified as being in her pawn-like status. But, the contradiction appears in the following verse where she quickly takes over the charges of asking her father Caleb for land. This action highlights her ability to act as an agent independent of him. Ackerman further claims that, she begins as pawn character and at the end shift and presents herself as assertive, practical and laying claims to land ownership.[199]

---

[195] Finkelstein and Silberman, *Bible Unearthed*, 121.

[196] Brevard Springs Childs, *Biblical Theology of the Old and New Testaments: Theological Reflection on the Christian Bible* (Minneapolis: Augsburg Fortress; SCM Press, 1992), 149.

[197] Susan Ackerman, *Warrior, Dancer, Seductress, Queen: Women in Judges and Biblical Israel* (New York: Yale University Press, 1998), 1.

[198] The Book of Joshua describes the capture and destruction of key sites such as Jericho, Ai, Debir, Lachish, Hazor by the Israelites. Archaeological work has been done in nearly all of these sites and concludes that there was considerable destruction in these towns about 1250 BCE. Cf. Joel F. Drinkard, "The History and Archaeology of the Book of Joshua and the Conquest/Settlement Period," in *R&E* 95/2 (1998): 177.

[199] Ackerman, *Warrior, Dancer*, 219.

She demonstrated herself as the dominant partner in her marriage by assuming the responsibility of petitioning her father for land and water resources which were normally not available to women in ancient Israel.[200] She received what she asked for.

The word וַתְּסִיתֵהוּ is a Hiphil form from the root word סוּת, which literally means "to allure, incite, instigate." וַתְּסִיתֵהוּ לִשְׁאוֹל means "she incited him to ask for." Paul Mosca asserts that it is a perfect grammatical construction which consequently renders the sentence, "When she arrived, she incited him to ask from her father arable land."[201]

V. 15: גֻּלֹּת מָיִם means "bowls/springs of water." She already possessed land in the dry Negeb, now she demands land with water supply and she wants it now. Caleb grants her more than she demands, as she was given two water supplies, the upper and the lower. She makes a claim in her own interest and for the benefit of the family she is about to establish. What she received might well be her dowry that is, her share of the inheritance.[202] This is because she receives not only her own land but also sets of springs. Having access to fresh water was considered a great luxury in ancient times.

To a modern reader Caleb's vow may sound unfair. But in the biblical world, especially during the settlement period clan loyalties take precedence over personal and individual interest. In Israelite society father often exercised his power and authority in giving away his daughter in marriage.[203]

In the beginning, Achsah was treated like a spoil of war, as she was bestowed upon the conqueror as battle trophy to Othniel. On the other hand, she did not continue in her pawn or victim status. She soon took the opportunity into her hands, went to her father and asked for land with water sources. Owing to her assertiveness, there are some scholars who claim that the story has happy ending as she winds up possessing her own watered land.[204]

Achsah's role can be taken as good example for empowering women. In the genealogy of 1 Chronicles (2:49), there is a specific reference to her. The story allows Achsah to make an entrance. Not only that, but she is also given character,

---

[200] Jo Ann Hackett, "Violence and Women's Lives in the Book of Judges," in *Int* 58/4 (October 2004): 364. Cf. Julia Myers O'Briens, "Achsah," in *Women in Scripture: A Dictionary of Named and Unnamed Women in the Hebrew Bible, the Apocryphal/Deuterocanonical Books, and the New Testament,* eds. Carol Meyers, Toni Craven, and Ross Shepard Kraemer (Michigan: William. B. Eerdmans Publishing Company, 2001), 46.

[201] Paul G. Mosca, "Who Seduced Whom: A Note on Joshua 15:18; Judges 1:14," in *CBQ* 46/1 (January 1984): 120–1.

[202] Marsman, *Women in Ugarit*, 105.

[203] Daniel I. Block, "Judges," in *Zondervan Illustrated Bible Backgrounds Commentary: Joshua, Judges, Ruth, 1 & 2 Samuel*, vol. 2 ed. John H. Walton (Grand Rapids, Michigan: Zondervan, 2009), 109.

[204] Tikva Frymer-Kensky, *Reading the Women of the Bible: A New Interpretation of Their Stories* (New York: Schocken, 2004), 101.

speech and name and allowed to take initiatives. She was given away as prize yet she grabbed the opportunity to present her own demand. She was able to realize the rights to inherit property as a daughter whereby she stood up and took the initiative to speak to her father for a gift of fertile land and received it. This is one of the rare cases in the Old Testament that a daughter asks for a fertile land.

8.2. Daughters of Job (Job 42:15)

> 15 No women were found more beautiful like the daughters of Job in all the earth; and their father gave them an inheritance along with their brothers.[205]

Background of the Book of Job

The Book of Job is classified under the heading of Wisdom in the Old Testament along with Proverbs and Ecclesiastes. It is a story of a man who loses all his possessions and his children as a result of a wager between God and Satan. The prologue (chaps. 1–2) and epilogue (42:7–17), is written in prose with poetic dialogue in between. There is difference between the narrative section and the rest of the book on several counts. John Hartley states that, the prologue and epilogue represent an old epic account reworked by the author to serve as a framework for the central dialogue.[206]

There are various contradicting opinions regarding the date. It varies from the time of patriarchs to the post-exilic era. Post exilic date is generally considered to be more likely by many scholars.[207] Clines, Hartley and others, have given later date to sometime between the 7th and 2nd centuries BCE. Their argument is based on the language of the book which is Aramaic.[208] One of the views has been that, the book is very old and that points to the patriarchal period with Moses as its author.[209] The language of the dialogue is said to have relations with Ugarit,

[205] Translated from *BHS*.

[206] John E. Hartley, *The Book of Job,* New International Commentary on the Old Testament series (Grand Rapids: Eerdmans, 1988), 21.

[207] Scholars in general agree that the book was written during exilic or early part of post exilic period. There are no references to particular historical people or events, because of which it is difficult to supply a definite date. cf. Leo G. Perdue, *The Sword and the Stylus: An Introduction to Wisdom in the Age of Empires* (Grand Rapids, Michigan: Eerdmans, 2008), 117–8; Sean P. Kealy, *The Wisdom Books of the Bible–Proverbs, Job, Ecclesiastes, Ben Sira, Wisdom of Solomon: A Survey of the History of their Interpretation* (UK: The Edwin Mellen Press, 2012), 80–1; Murphy and Carm, *Wisdom Literature: Job*, 8; Ceresko, *Introduction to Old Testament*, 92.

[208] David J. A. Clines, "Job 1–20," in *WBC,* vol. 17 (Waco, Texas: Word Books Publishers, 1989), lvii, lix; Cf. Hartley, *Book of Job,* 20.

[209] R. Laird Harris, "The Book of Job and its Doctrine of God," in *Presbyterion* 7/1–2 (March 1, 1981), 5.

Aramaic and Arabic languages.[210] The author shows no interest in historical details. The book clearly represents the early Persian period marked by severe socio-economic crisis. Therefore, it is understood that while exilic and post exilic period represent the historical context for the Book of Job, the motivation in writing was the struggle to survive and preserve the identity of the race.

Wisdom compositions in the AWA are as old as the 2nd millennium BCE. Thought of "after life" was popular among the Mesopotamians and Egyptians.

There are evidences of parallel stories found in the extra-biblical literature of the AWA. In Babylonia there is a work known as "I Will Praise the Lord of Wisdom." Here the sufferer, a God-fearing man, was accused by his friends and family members as a wrongdoer. Despite all the accusations, he trusted in divine mercy and acted in the proper cultic manner. At the end, he experienced restoration.[211] The book can be seen as an independent creation giving answer to the question of suffering which was common among the AWA, although the theme is unique to the Israelite.

The present study about the daughters' inheritance in 42:15 falls under epilogue (42:7–17). It describes the restoration of Job's health and his former possessions. In the story, Job regained twice what he lost before together with ten new children. According to the biblical account son was more desirable than daughter. However, in a quite unusual way in this text only the names of the daughters, who are praised for their beauty, are mentioned. The first daughter was named *Jemimah* "turtle dove," the second *Keziah* "the name of the aromatic plant, a prized variety of cinnamon." The third *Keren-Happuch* "a horn of eye paint," that is, black rouge used to highlight the eyes.[212] The writer here keeps the Old Testament standpoint in naming, because "name" in the Old Testament is more than the person's identity. The name reveals the person's character, personality and destiny. Therefore, the person's name is related to what he/she is. The daughters of Job reveal certain aspects of Jewish women's lives in antiquity.

Jewish feminist scholars like Judith Plaskow, Rebecca Lesses, and others, give particular attention to the women in the Old Testament who are being silenced in the texts.[213] Lesses gives a commentary on the daughters of Job from *Pseudepigrapha* comprising chapters 46–53 which has a clear ascription of mystical

---

[210] C. Hassell Bullock, *An Introduction to the Old Testament Poetic Books* (Chicago: Moody Press, 1988), 71.

[211] There are also other parallel stories from Egypt, Canaan, Sumer. cf. Martin H. Manser, *Critical Companion to the Bible: A Literary Reference* (New York: Facts on File, 2009), 170; James L. Crenshaw, "Job," in *OBC*, 332.

[212] Hartley, *Book of Job*, New International Commentary, 543; See also, Carol A. Newsom, *The Book of Job a Contest of Moral Imaginations* (Oxford: Oxford University Press, 2009), 258.

[213] Judith Plaskow, *Standing Again at Sinai: Judaism from a Feminist Perspective* (New York: HarperCollins, 1991), 35; Cf. Rebecca Lesses, "The Daughters of Job," in *Searching the Scriptures: A Feminist Commentary*, vol. 2 eds. Elisabeth Schussler Fiorenza (New York: The Crossroad Publishing Company, 1994), 139.

powers and insight to women.[214] According to her, Job's daughters are not just ordinary young women, but they possess mystical powers.

V. 15: The manner of Job being blessed is recorded in 42:12. His three daughters were given inheritance along with the sons which is in fact unique in biblical custom.[215] F. Delzsch states: "It sounds more Arabian than Israelite."[216] It is because the Israelites have their unique way of maintaining their boundaries within the nation. This is also evidence that the custom of giving inheritance to daughter was in general common practice in the AWA, prior to the Mosaic history.

Job gave his daughters a share of inheritance in his estate, and it is an extraordinary case with no legal ramification. The purpose of this detail is to suggest Job's incomparable wealth.[217] Norman Habel stresses that the speakers in the book draw widely on nature imagery, ancient mythology, verbal irony and literary technique.[218] In his comment on the daughters' inheritance, he states that Job displayed the policy of justice and equity in his life by giving his daughters an inheritance with their brothers.[219]

Compared to rest of the books in the Old Testament, the epilogue of Job is very brief. Nevertheless despite its brevity several points are highlighted of which the most important issue was the daughter's inheritance rights.

9. Inheritance Rights of Mother

There are many indications in the Old Testament where mothers play vital roles both in spiritual and social realm which is often overlooked.[220] Only occasionally in the writers' androcentric agenda did the mothers emerge in the biblical text shaping the plot but they never did this in their own right.[221] In fact, they are not absent from the narrative. The mother's teaching role is also found in Proverb

---

[214] Pseudepigrapha refers to 52 texts written between 200 BCE and CE 200, but ascribed to various prophets and kings in the Hebrew Scriptures, many are apocalyptic in nature. For commentary on daughters of Job see, Lesses, "Daughters of Job," in *Searching the Scriptures,* vol. 2, 139–40.

[215] Ellen F. Davis, "Job and Jacob: The Integrity of Faith," in *Reading Between Texts: Intertextuality and the Hebrew Bible* eds. Danna Nolan Fewell et al., (Kentucky: Westminster/John Knox Press, 1992), 220.

[216] F. F. Delitzsch, *Biblical Commentary on the Book of Job,* vol. 2 trans. Francis Bolton (Grand Rapids, Michigan: Wm. B. Eerdmans Publishing Company, 1961), 391.

[217] Yael Shemesh, "A Gender Perspective on the Daughters of Zelophehad: Bible, Talmudic Midrash, and Modern Feminist Midrash," in *BibInt* 15/1 (2007): 89.

[218] Norman C. Habel, *The Book of Job: A Commentary* Old Testament Library (Philadelphia: The Westminster Press, 1985), 60.

[219] Habel, *Book of Job*, 585.

[220] Christopher J.H.Wright, "אב," in *NIDOTTE,* vol. 1, 219.

[221] J. Cheryl Exum, *Fragmented Women: Feminist (sub)versions of Biblical Narratives* (Sheffield: JSOT Press; TPI, 1993), 97, 104.

1:8, 6:20 and even for the benefit of kings in Proverbs 31:1–9. There are also plenty of evidences of mothers taking public initiative and exercising considerable influence, domestically and particularly as queen mothers.[222]

Before looking at the role of one of the Israelite mothers, it is worth noting that a civilization so close to Israel's as Egypt had the exact opposite situation—a matrilineal society in which common roles were reversed. It is popularly believed that ancient Egyptian societies were matrilineal society that passed their succession or inheritance through female lineage.[223] Consequently Egyptian mothers are said to have enjoyed a far higher status. They certainly enjoyed good deal of independence by the standards of the ancient world.

Greek historian Herodotus of the 5th century BCE, wrote about Egyptian mother as, "The Egyptians in most of their manners and customs exactly reverse the common practice of mankind. The women attend the market and trade, while men sit at home at the loom."[224]

Herodotus claims that the Egyptians had completely reversed normal roles as he saw women in the market place. This does not mean that women did not involve themselves in the domestic affairs. In fact, they were involved in every aspect. Egyptian mothers were shown in most portrayals as dutiful women.

The scope of this study does not extend to going into detail regarding the mother's role in the Israelite society. However, we will examine a heroic figure in the Old Testament, the unnamed mother of Micah, who own property.[225]

Micah's Mother (Judges 17:2–3)

> 2 He said to his mother, "The eleven hundred pieces of silver which were taken from you, about which you uttered a curse and spoke it in my ear, behold, the silver is with me; I took it." And his mother said, "Blessed be my son by the YHWH."
>
> 3 He returned the eleven hundred pieces of silver to his mother, and his mother said, "I wholly dedicate the silver to YHWH from my hand for my son to make an idol and a molten image; and now I will return it to you.[226]

The Book of Judges, asserts right from the opening the failures and the wickedness of the people of Israel. The final chapters 17–21 climax the process

[222] Gen. 27; Judg. 17; 1 Kgs. 1:11; Cf. Wright, "אב," in *NIDOTTE,* vol. 1, 220.

[223] Graves-Brown, *Dancing for Hathor*, 47; See also, Troy D. Allen "Problems in Egyptology: Ancient Egyptian kinship," in *JBS*, 31(2) (2000): 139–48.

[224] Quoted by Joyce Salisbury, *Encyclopedia of Women in the Ancient World* (California: ABC–CLIO, 2001), 92.

[225] Brief survey of the Book of Judges has been done under the title "Achsah," in 8.1.

[226] Translated from *BHS*.

of deterioration. These final five chapters present two episodes which the biblical tradition connects with the time of the Judges.

The story states that, there was a man named Micah who stole eleven hundred pieces of silver from his mother. The mother, ignorant of the fact that the thief was her son, utters a curse condemning the criminal.[227] At this point, Micah, in danger of incurring God's wrath, confesses his guilt to his mother. In order to save her son from the consequences of her curse, she consecrates two hundred pieces of silver to *YHWH*, to be made into a graven image.

The story of Micah's mother reflects the extent of the syncretism and the complete corruption of the nation. According to the textual narrative she was involved in the irreligious behaviour of their time. She has a graven image made to cancel a curse she had spoken.[228] She is clearly depicted as wealthy woman who owned property and could provide money to have a graven image cast.

Gale A. Yee, in reading Judges 17–21, uses ideological criticism and proposes that the unnamed mother to be Delilah, who according to the preceding chapter, betrays Samson to the Philistines for precisely the same amount (Judg. 16:5).[229] Such conclusion cannot be drawn so easily just because of the equal amount of silver mentioned.

The reference to Micah's household and absence of public temple buildings in Israelites villages points to the period of non-centralized political and social life.[230] The narrative reveals a multiple family household compound of the period of Judges. Moreover, several functional collective roles of family are revealed in this narrative that points to pre-monarchic period. Israel during the pre-state period was characterized by strong patrilineal, kinship and village-based social grouping where family was the basic unit.[231]

V. 3: The Hebrew word אָלִית means "to make a solemn oath." According to C. F. Burney, it was a solemn promise to devote the silver for *YHWH's* service. Such an oath brought a curse upon the person who violated it, anyone who misappropriated the consecrated thing.[232] The fear of this curse caused Micah to confess to the theft and to make restitution.

---

[227] In ancient times it was believed that, words spoken as curse or blesing had power to achieve the desired rresult; Cf. Bernhard W. Anderson, *Understanding the Old Testament* (Eaglewood Cliffs, New Jersey: Prencetice–Hall, INC., 1961), 69.

[228] This study's focus is not on the curse or the graven image, but in the fact of her clearly being in possession of wealth.

[229] Gale A. Yee, "Ideological Criticism: Judges 17–21 and the Dismembered Body," in *Judges and Method*, 144.

[230] The period when ceremonial observances were largely family centered.

[231] Biblical passages such as this, relates well to the archaeological and anthropological evidence for the existence of households larger than the simple conjugal unit.

[232] Burney C. F., *The Book of Judges, with Introduction and notes, and notes on the Hebrew Text of the Books of Kings, with an Introduction and Appendix* ed. Harry M. Orlinsky (New York: KTAV Publishing House, 1970), 418.

The word פֶּסֶל, etymologically denotes an idol carved or hewn out of wood or stone. On the other hand וּמַסֵּכָה, denotes one which is cast of metal in a mould. However, it has been suggested that פֶּסֶל may also denote a cast-metal idol.[233] Micah restored the silver to his mother and from there she took two hundred shekels of silver, and gave them to the silversmith to make graven image.

There is constant emphasis on the disintegration of Israel's cult worship during the tribal period with references to such things as homemade idols of stolen silver, private shrines, and personal priests. This biblical passage points to the tribal period which highlights a wicked age when there was no king in Israel.

Women during the pre-state period wielded considerable power and authority in family household management. This narrative depicts a senior mother's authority at home including her right to perform efficacious religious acts to the extent of commissioning cultic objects.[234]

In ancient society, only a wealthy person is said to be prone to have some of the gold and silver cast into an idol. This text is one of the proofs. It clearly shows that, Micah's unnamed mother was a rich mother who owned the property, so she consecrated the returned silver to make graven image.

10. Critique on Women's Property Inheritance Rights

Having studied the description of ancient Israelite women in the light of the AWA and Egyptian context, one commonality we find in the ancient societies was that it was centred in a milieu of patriarchal cultures. In a male dominated family, wives and children did not have much property rights. In most cases, they can be independent only after father's death.

AWA laws reveal that men and women operated under a marital system composed of marriage contracts. Compared to other societies in AWA, women in ancient Egypt and Babylon enjoyed higher rights and freedom. Egypt was a matriarchal society and women were managing the family holdings, contesting claims and acting as witnesses. Babylonian wife had many rights which Israelite legislation appears to know nothing about.[235] They could acquire property, take legal action, be a part of the contract and have certain shares in her husband's property. LH has provision for the divorced wife or the widow.[236] No such provision is made for the Israelite women. Even Nuzi women and men were able to participate equally in the social and economic life of the community. On the contrary, in Assyrian society, women are said to have exercised very few rights. The above studies show that, throughout the AWA history, women have had nearly as much legal capacity as men.

---

[233] Burney, *Book of Judges*, 418.

[234] Carol L. Meyers, "Was Ancient Israel a Patriarchal Society?" in *JBL* 133/1 (2014): 22.

[235] Eichrodt, *Theology of the Old Testament*, 81.

[236] LH 137–140.

Under the Sumerian law, wife had various legal rights, for example she could be witness to a contract, own property and administer it. She could also engage independently in business, and was entitled to the income from any assets she received from her husband.[237]

Reading about women in AWA time shows that in pre-biblical time women enjoyed good deal of independence. She received her inheritance mainly through dowry. This dowry was not entitled to merge to the families that she has established in marriage, and cannot be sold without her consent. Marriage contracts records were important to women who were in a legally vulnerable position and also to those who possess property. Although, inheritance was generally passed through male members of the family with father as the head, nevertheless, there are a number of instances in the Old Testament where the property and inheritance of property rights passing to women are specifically mentioned or alluded to.

The study of the six biblical passages that dealt with women with property inheritance rights bear witness to ancient Israelite women exercising power over the land and wealth. The extant evidence in the Old Testament and other AWA sources bear witness that women did have property and inheritance rights.

CONCLUSION

The three ancient civilizations, that is, Israel, Mesopotamia and Egypt differed sharply in numerous respects, including religion, language, and writing system. There is uniqueness in each separate culture, yet the individual cultures of each society were not isolated from each other but were subject to mutual influences.

The picture that emerged from the above studies is that women appearing in the context of inheritance are related to men in one way or another, either as wives, widows or daughters. The inheritance laws regarding women aim basically at keeping the immovable property within her family.

AWA sources have contributed immensely to the understanding of biblical narratives. Archaeological findings in the AWA within the last century have added to our knowledge of the historical, cultural and religious background of the Old Testament world. Prior to that, the Scripture was often misunderstood because its readers were unfamiliar with their times. The discovery of the ancient law codes bear witness to the antiquity of Mosaic legislations that are found in the biblical account.

Marriage was an important aspect in ancient society. It was viewed as a means for the continuation of families. Procreation rather than companionship was the main purpose of marriage in ancient times. The marriage settlement was basically organized along patriarchal rules. Mesopotamia has yielded wealth of documents on marriage laws. Comparatively in Egypt, there is no evidence of betrothal or of a bride price. It could have been an unwritten practice. Marriage

---

[237] Harris et al., eds., *Ancient Egypt*, 70.

customs and practices that we see are mainly based on those practiced by people of power and influence in society.

In all these three societies, the custom of giving pride price and dowry was practiced. In most cases, women have control over the dowry that she brought in marriage. In the case of a divorce, the wife could take her dowry with her if she were blameless.

The above studies show that there are similarities in their practice of inheritance laws. In most cases wives could inherit property, but could be mostly managers of the holdings. The property they managed was either given by their husbands or fathers. There are also cases of some women who inherited or owned land in southern Mesopotamia and Egypt. It also gives evidence to the mother handing over real estate to the adopted daughter and daughter adopted as son.

Evidences from the AWA brought clarity regarding the position of widows with inheritance to a greater extent than are mentioned in the Hebrew Bible. Widows are shown in a better position.

Within the patriarchal construction, women enjoyed substantial amount of autonomy and freedom.[238] This foregone survey unfolds two pictures about women: Firstly, women can own goods and immovable property; and secondly, women can act as a person in the juridical sense of the word.

In fact, the Bible portrayed women in a defenceless situation, robbed of their worth. Nevertheless, not all the Israelite women were in a vulnerable state and completely dependent on the male members of their family. The six passages from the Old Testament studied above clearly depict women in possession of wealth and property. They were afforded a degree of material security.

The Bible has been instrumental in shaping and influencing ideas about the place of women. Therefore, the Bible, especially the Old Testament, needs to be approached from a critical feminist perspective. It is not possible to explicitly say that women had equal legal rights with men. This opens the avenue to explore further on the issue of women's legal rights. In a contemporary society where women may be treated unfairly, feminist biblical scholarship has the task of unwrapping the women's legal status that is concealed in the Old Testament in order to explicitly affirm that women do have inheritance rights sanctioned by God.

[238] Wells, in his studies on the AWA Law and Practice, claims that women in AWA have much legal capacity to the extent of owning land. See, Wells, "Law and Practice," in *A Companion to the Ancient*, 192.

Chapter 4

Exegetical Study on Numbers 27:1–11; 36:1–13

INTRODUCTION

Extensive studies have been done in the previous chapter on property inheritance rights of women in the Old Testament in the light of ancient West Asia and Egypt. This was done for the better understanding of the daughters' inheritance rights in ancient Israel.

The present chapter intends to take a closer look at the acts of the daughters of Zelophehad in the Book of Numbers 27:1–11. They challenge the judicial system with reference to the query of female inheritance rights. The grievances brought by their tribal elders in 36:1–13 will also be dealt.

Critical investigation will be made using multiple methods so as to unlock the textures imbedded in the text.[1] The essential questions to be raised in this chapter include "Did the event actually occur?" Women standing at the tent of meeting were unusual, so this chapter will inquire the significance of their act of standing at the sacred place before the leaders, and the consequences of their act for the legal system in Israel. Another curious question is, "Why did the tribal leaders insist on the revision of the law?" The insights gained from the exegetical studies of the select texts will be summarized. The method employed to access the texts will include historical, sociological, literary, to name some.

[1] The word "critical" is derived from the Greek word *krino* which means to distinguish, differentiate, judge after careful consideration of all aspects of a matter. Cf. Werner Kahl, "Growing Together: Challenges and Chances in the Encounter of Critical and Intuitive Interpreters of the Bible," in *Reading Other–Wise: Socially Engaged Biblical Scholars Reading with their Local Communities*, ed. Gerald O. West No. 62 (Atlanta: SBL, 2007), 149.

1. Background of the Book of Numbers

The Book of Numbers records the Israelite experience during the wilderness period, a schematic time-frame that begins with the exodus from Egypt and concludes as they stood in the plains of Moab, east of Jordan. The book contains law and history of the wilderness period. It concentrates on the preparations for entering the land which was promised to the patriarchs by *YHWH*. The promise began to come to fruition but it was beset by questions and negations.

As far as the history of the Old Testament scholarship is concerned, the Book of Numbers is the most neglected book, the reason being the most disorganized, formless collection of miscellaneous materials.[2] It is held to be the most diverse of *Torah* books as it incorporates historiographical narratives, collection of early Hebrew poetry and wide-ranging legal and ritual texts.[3] The book presents the reader with a vision of new beginning and hope as it narrates the transition from the old generation that left Egypt and died in the desert to the new generation that stand on the brink of the Promised Land.

The Book of Numbers preserves a wide variety of priestly texts that consists of four main types of writings: narrative, law, administration records, and description of ritual celebrations that are associated with important events in the religious history of Israel.[4]

Concerning the organization of the book, the researcher here finds the contribution of Dennis Olson most beneficial as his theory of organizing the book is based on the shift of focus from the old generation who failed the test and perished in the desert to the new generation who replaced them.[5] According to him Numbers has two parts, that is, chapters. 1–25 and 26–36.[6] The first part of Numbers focuses on the tabernacle and the various responsibilities of priests and Levites along with taking census. It also covers placement of the entire people within the wilderness camp to conquer the Promised Land which is the land of

---

[2] Robert Kugler and Patrick Hartin, An Introduction to the Bible (Grand Rapids: William B. Eerdmans Publishing Company, 2009), 90; See also, Terence E. Fretheim, *The Pentateuch: Interpreting Biblical Texts Series* (Nashville, TN: Abingdon Press, 1996), 138; Horst Seebass, "'Holy' Land in the Old Testament: Numbers and Joshua," in *VT* 56/1 (2006): 92.

[3] Baruch A. Levine, *Numbers 21–36: A New Translation with Introduction and Commentary*, AB vol. 4A (New York: Doubleday, 2000), 48.

[4] It is generally agreed that the bulk of the Book of Numbers was composed of Priestly material, especially chaps. 1–10 and 26–36 are said to have originated after the exile of Judah in Babylon. Cf. Olson, "Book of Numbers," in *Dictionary of the Old Testament: Pentateuch*, eds. Alexander and Baker, 613; Elmer E. Flack, "Flashes of New Knowledge: Recent Study and the Book of Numbers," in *Int* 13/1 (January 1959): 6–7.

[5] Dennis T. Olson, *The Death of the Old and the Birth of the New: The Framework of the Book of Numbers and the Pentateuch* Brown Judaic Studies No. 71 (Chicago: Scholars Press, 1985).

[6] Olson, *Death of the Old*, 1; See also, John D. Litke, "The Daughters of Zelophehad," in *CTM* 29/3 (June 2002): 208.

Canaan. It is based on the theological distinction between the disobedience of the old generation and the obedience of the new generation.

The second part begins with census of the new generation. After many years of journeying in the wilderness, they reached the plains of Moab. Encamped at the very edge of the Promised Land, the new generation was numbered. Further instructions were given by *YHWH* regarding the manner in which the allotment of land and offering were to be made in the Promised Land. It also deals with different issues and sacrifices of the daily, weekly and annual feast, then validity of vows, the stations of the wandering, the borders of the land, the installation of Levitical and asylum towns, and ends with inheritance rules for women.[7]

It is noteworthy that several issues in the concluding chapters are about legal matters pertaining to women. Israel will enter the land with a legal system already subject to change and revision even while they are still encamped in the wilderness.

1.1. Title and Authorship

The Hebrew title of the book בְּמִדְבַּר "In the Wilderness," is taken from the first line of the first verse as it is done with other books of the Pentateuch.[8] The book was entitled Numbers because of the number of the children of Israel which is often mentioned in the book. It also relates to the two census lists, one at Mount Sinai (chap. 1), and the other in the plains of Moab (chap. 26).

Traditionally Jewish and Christian scholars have assigned the writing of Numbers to Moses.[9] This claim is based on one reference to Mosaic writing in Numbers 33:2, but this is limited to the itinerary of the Israelites during their journey from Egypt to Moab.[10] The book appears to be more fragmentary which is particularly evident in chapters 20 and 21. The original form was probably in the nature of short topographical notes.[11] This difference has led many scholars to challenge Moses' authorship from the beginning of the advent of rationalistic biblical criticism during the enlightenment period. Scholars now agree that the Book of Numbers likely was written by a group from priestly school somewhere between the seventh and the fifth century BCE.[12] Evidence suggests that later

[7] Rainer Albertz, "A Pentateuchal Redaction in the Book of Numbers? The Late Priestly Layers of Numbers 25–36," in *ZAW* 125/2 (2013): 222.

[8] Levine, *Numbers 1–20: A New Translation*, vol. 4A, 47.

[9] Herbert Livingston states the traditional meaning of Mosaic Authorship in his book, G. Herbert Livingston, *The Pentateuch in its Cultural Environment* (Grand Rapids: Baker Book House, 1977), 218–9.

[10] Andrew E. Hill and John H. Walton, *A Survey of the Old Testament*, 2nd ed., (Grand Rapids, Michigan: Zondervan, 2000), 114.

[11] R. K. Harrison, *Introduction to the Old Testament* (Grand Rapids: William B. Eerdmans Publishing Company, 1969), 616.

[12] Juliana Claassens, "Give us a Portion Among our Father's Brothers": The Daughters of Zelophehad, Land, and the Quest for Human Dignity," in *JSOT* 37/3 (March 2013): 323; See also,

editors drew the writings together and incorporated additional information to produce the five Books of Moses known as Pentateuch.

The Book of Numbers Chapters 27 and 36 are considered to be written by two different authors because of the variation in style and expression. For example, in 27:1 it is written as "sons of Manasseh from the clan of Manasseh son of Joseph," and in 36:1 it is written "from the clans of the sons of Joseph." Another variation is found in 27:2 in their difference of approach. Zelophehad's daughters approached "Moses, Eleazar, chieftains and the congregation," whereas in 36:1 the tribal elders spoke before "Moses, chieftains, heads of the fathers belonging to the sons of Israel." These variations are a clear indication that these two passages were written by different authors.

1.2. Place in the Pentateuch

The Book of Numbers is an integral part of the Pentateuch. It has no meaningful structure as a whole when read separately. However, one begins to understand the overall structure of the book by noting the larger context of the Pentateuch in which it is set. Pentateuch records the beginning of God's redemptive work. In the Book of Genesis, God promised to Abraham that God would make him fruitful and make his descendants numerous. God also promised Abraham that He would be their God and to give them land.[13] The book ends with Jacob and his family moving to Egypt to ensure their survival. The Book of Exodus continues by describing how God fulfilled the covenant made with Abraham. The book narrates God's leading of the people through the wilderness towards the land of Canaan. The Book of Leviticus continues the narration by giving them the law at Mount Sinai. In Leviticus, laws were important for Israelites to identify themselves as the people of God. It also made them distinct from other nations' rituals with other meanings.[14] The important generational transition in Pentateuch is made in the Book of Numbers. This transition between generations provides a context for the Book of Deuteronomy that follows. Deuteronomy is the story of Moses' review of history and law for a generation that did not experience all these events themselves.

There are so many similar themes that Numbers shares with the other Pentateuchal books and the Book of Joshua, such as the conquest and distribution of the land.[15] All these clearly affirm that theologically and thematically there is unity in the five books of the Pentateuch.

Albertz, "A Pentateuchal Redaction," 221.

[13] Daniel S. Diffey, "The Royal Promise in Genesis: The Often Underestimated Importance of Genesis 17:6, 17:16 and 35:11," in *TB* 62/2 (2011): 315.

[14] Alexi E. George, "Leviticus," in *South Asia Bible Commentary: A One-Volume Commentary on the Whole Bible*, eds. Brian Wintle et al., (Rajasthan, India: Open Door Publications, 2015), 135.

[15] J. Gordon McConville, *Law and Theology in Deuteronomy*, JSOTSup Series 33 (Sheffield: *JSOT* Press, 1984), 11.

1.3. The Book of Numbers in the Canonical Context

The theological significance of the Book of Numbers cannot be properly appraised in isolation from other books of the Pentateuch, particularly Exodus and Leviticus. There is an inner unity of theology that underlies them all. *YHWH's* redemptive plan for humanity was made through his covenant with Abraham. Abraham received a divine promise of land, progeny and blessings that would extend to all nations. The three Books namely Exodus, Leviticus and Numbers provide details of that divine promise. Exodus concentrates on the deliverance from Egypt, covenant at Sinai, and the construction of the tabernacle. Leviticus highlights the nature of true worship and holiness, and Numbers focuses on the Promised Land and the journey towards it.

The Pentateuch highlights the relationship between God and the descendants of Abraham which was both happy and stormy by turn. The Book of Numbers restates the value of faith and obedience. The count of people in the first census of Numbers was 603,550, excluding the Levites, who were not subject to military service (Num. 1:46), the second census taken forty years later was 601,730 (Num. 26:51).[16] Even though God preserved the nation in the wilderness, in fact God did not prosper them as in Genesis and Exodus, as the two census lists show. The count in the first census list was greater. Therein lies the theological significance, that is, it is a story of God's faithfulness in the face of Israel's faithless rebellion.

1.4. Purpose of Census

The two census lists of the twelve tribes in the Book of Numbers serve as primary pillars. It divides the book into two major halves, that is, chapters 1–25 and 26–36.[17] The first census in chapter 1 narrates the eventual death of nearly all the members of the old generation who came out of Egypt. The second census list in chapter 26 introduces the second half of the book and narrates the emergence of a new generation of Israelites as they prepare to enter the Promised Land with life and hope as its theme.

There are basically three reasons for taking census; firstly, to form a military group;[18] secondly, to demonstrate to the people the extent of God's faithfulness in the provision of the Abrahamic covenant as recorded in Gen. 12:2 and; thirdly, to provide a clear sense of family and clan identity for the individual and to provide the means for an orderly march of the people to the new home in Canaan.[19]

---

[16] Jerry Waite, "The Census of Israelite Men after their Exodus from Egypt," in *VT* 60/3 (2010): 487–9.

[17] Dennis T. Olson, "Book of Numbers," in *DOTP*, eds. T. Desmond Alexander and David W. Baker (Illinois: IVP Academic, 2003), 612.

[18] Carol L. Meyers, *Discovering Eve: Ancient Israelite Women in Context*, (New York: Oxford University Press, 1988), 166.

[19] Ronald B. Allen, "Numbers," in *The Expositor's Bible Commentary Abridged Edition: Old Testament*, vol. 1 eds. Kenneth L. Barker and John R. Kohlenberger III (Grand Rapids, Michigan:

The first census was taken according to the numbers of individuals in each tribe but the second census was taken according to the families.[20] The second census was to include all males from twenty years and above by divine direction (Num. 26). The main object was in view of the approaching apportionment of the land which Israel was to possess. According to the names of the families listed in the second census the inheritance will be allotted to each tribe by lot. Zelophehad, of the tribe of Manasseh, had died in the wilderness. His family was not listed in the census because he did not have son. The proposed division of land brought up special question raised by his daughters, a legal dispute involving claims to inheritance of land in Canaan.

1.5. Literary Structure

The Book of Numbers is a patchwork of four or more literary sources as it is a mixture of narration, laws, legal cases and ritual instructions. It is undoubtedly exilic with significant post-exilic additions. The priestly editors crafted the text competently weaving the diverse collection of materials into a story about the distant past. The basic pattern in the priestly sections of Numbers is the introduction of a novel law through the medium of a story.[21]

Adriane Leveen argues that the Book of Numbers is a complex literary composition with its own internal logic.[22] She seeks to show how the Book of Numbers' tradition was shaped and ordered by the concept of memory. She examines how the editors of Numbers created a narrative of the forty years journey through the wilderness. She had thoroughly considered the dynamics of the transmission of tradition, memory and values in an environment of crisis as the new generation witnessed their parents die in the wilderness. Despite the absence of critical text and linguistic work in her book, her far reaching treatment of the literary structure of Numbers, of memory and of the uses of memory in the *Torah* is to be valued. She firmly states that Numbers promote a priestly vision for Israel and that vision transpired out of an arrangement of multiple texts derived from a collection of sources.[23]

Zondervan, 1994), 175–6.

[20] Alfred Edersheim, *Bible History: Old Testament*, new updated ed., (Peabody, Massachusetts: Hendrickson Publishers, 1995), 289.

[21] Levine, *Numbers 1-20*, 4A, 102.

[22] Adriane Leveen, *Memory and Tradition in the Book of Numbers*, (Cambridge: Cambridge University Press, 2008), 25.

[23] Leveen, *Memory and Tradition*, 22; Rooted in the findings of literary and historical criticism, Budd too claims that, Numbers is a complex accumulation of traditions. He further claims that it is not a factual account of Israelites journey in the wilderness. cf. Philip J. Budd, "Numbers," in *WBC* vol. 5 eds. Hubbard et al., (Texas: WB, Publisher, 1984), xxvi.

The author had used complex tradition and this assertion is based on the story that is tied in with the Korah incident and census list.[24] It is therefore suggested that the author brought out the traditional material to resolve certain burning issues of the author's time, that is, during the Babylonian exile and return. The question of access to land and the rights associated with it was raised and there is a clear and definitive answer concerning the rights of daughters.

1.6. Theme and Structure

The theme of land occupies an important place in the Book of Numbers. It deals with the liberated community and with the possession of land as the goal of the journey.[25] The whole Book of Numbers looks forward to the occupation of the land of Canaan. Canaan is the ever present goal of the people of Israel. As rightly pointed out by Gordon Wenham, three aspects of land are emphasized in the Book of Numbers, firstly, YHWH has given it to Israel (32:7,9); secondly, the land of Canaan was to be holy land, sanctified by God dwelling among the people (35:34; cf. Lev. 26:11–12); and thirdly, the land was to be Israel's permanent possession.[26] The book emphasizes that YHWH had given it to Israel as He had sworn to give it to Abraham, Isaac and to Jacob (32:11 cf. Gen. 17:8; 26:3; 28:13). These promises guaranteed that Israel would be able to conquer the land at the right time. The land was to be Israel's possession and each tribe must cleave to its own inheritance.

Regarding the structure of the Book of Numbers, Philip Budd claims that in spite of its diverse materials and long compositional period, there is a basic threefold structure with three different important geographical references: firstly, the wilderness of Sinai (Num. 1:1); secondly, the wilderness of Paran (Num. 10:12); and thirdly, the plains of Moab (Num. 22:1; 36:13). The present event took place in the plains of Moab.[27] It describes the journey of the Israelites from Mount Sinai to the borders of Canaan.

The structure of the book should be understood keeping in mind the larger contexts of the Pentateuch. Reading the entire setting of the Pentateuch, one can comprehend that old generation of Israelites who occupied the centre-stage in the Books of Exodus and Leviticus disappeared and was now replaced by new

---

[24] Budd, "Numbers," in *WBC*, 302.

[25] Numbers is a mixture of some old traditions and many later elements, mostly in Priestly tradition with the land as the book's unifying theme that looks forward to Joshua as bringing the fulfilment of this theme. See, Seebass, "'Holy' Land," 92–3; Ada Taggar-Cohen, "Law and Family in the Book of Numbers: The Levites and the Tidennutu Documents from Nuzi," in VT 48/1 (January 1998): 74–5; John Marsh, "Numbers: Introduction," in *The Interpreter's Bible Leviticus–1&2 Samuel*, ed. George Arthur Buttrick et al., vol. 11 (New York: Abingdon Press, 1953), 137–8.

[26] Gordon J. Wenham, *Numbers: An Introduction and Commentary, Tyndale Old Testament Commentaries*, eds. D. J. Wiseman et al., (Leicester: InterVarsity Press, 1981), 43–4.

[27] Budd, "Numbers," in *WBC*, xvii.

generation. The transition from old generation to new generation is made in the Book of Numbers and it forms the primary structure for the entire book.

1.7. Date

The Book of Numbers is believed to be completed after the Israelites' experience in the Babylonian exile in 587 BCE. As they returned to the homeland of Judah in 539 BCE, the transition from an old generation who had died in the wilderness to a new generation of hope who were born in the wilderness would have spoken powerfully to a people coming out of exile. The author of the Book of Numbers is using this old fragment of remembered tradition about Zelophehad's daughters to illustrate the author's concern for proper apportionment of the new land.[28]

According to source analysis, the Book of Numbers underwent expansion, revision, and rewriting until it took its final form at the hands of Priestly editors in the 5th century BCE.[29] Clearly the editors felt the story of Zelophehad's daughters was important enough to retain in the final form of the book.

2. Law

The study of law is important because it reflects the values of the societies and it is also beneficial in assessing how women functioned and were esteemed within these cultures. The Hebrew word for law is תּוֹרָה which is usually connected with the root word ירה in Hiphil conjugation meaning "to point, direct and teach." It includes legal codes along with the teaching and instructions.[30]

Pentateuch contains five major collections of legal materials: firstly, the Book of the Covenant (Exod. 20:22–23:1); secondly, the Decalogue (Exod. 20:2–17; Deut. 5:6–21); thirdly, the Deuteronomic Code (Deut. 12–26); fourthly, the Holiness Code (Lev. 17–26); and fifthly, the Priestly Code (Exod. 25–31; 34:29; Lev. 16; some parts of Num.). As the Israelite community becomes larger and requires more guidance, the covenant is expanded upon in the Decalogue.

Israelite laws articulate Israel's vision and values, requiring equal treatment for all citizens. It also promotes loyalty to Israel's covenant with YHWH as it represents Israel's practical response to God's gracious acts—election of Israel, rescue from slavery, and covenantal relationship.

Israelites' legal practice is similar to that of its neighbours in many ways but the framework of understanding is different. The law of AWA is dominated by economic and political evaluation whereas biblical law is governed by religious

---

[28] Katharine Doob Sakenfeld, "Zelophehad's Daughters," in *PRS* 15/4 (Winter 1988): 42.

[29] Hill and Walton, *Survey of the Old Testament*, 115.

[30] This is also the reason that first section of the Hebrew canon which comprised of both narrative and laws bears the name *Torah*. Cf. Robert L. Hubbard, "Law in Israel and in Judaism," in *The Eerdmans Companion to the Bible* eds. Gordon D. Fee and Robert L. Hubbard Jr. (Grand Rapids, Michigan: William B. Eerdmans Publishing Company, 2011), 153.

evaluation.[31] For instance in Mesopotamia the king was the author of the law.[32] On the other hand, for Israelites the lawgiver is YHWH.[33] The wrongdoings do not merely affect human relationships but relationship between God and people. There is God's judgment in failing to keep the law. Since law comes from God all life is related to God. It is the responsibility of every Israelite to know and obey as well as teach the law to every other individual.

Biblical laws show evidences of a process of growth and adaptation long past Moses' time. Albrecht Alt, a German scholar, was the first person who made a major contribution to biblical studies by separating two types of laws.[34] He expands the classical distinction between apodictic laws (absolute) and casuistic laws (conditional) in Pentateuch in 1934.[35] The following section is a brief survey of both forms of the laws.

2.1. Apodictic Law

Apodictic or absolute form of law is unconditional and stated in sharp and terse language.[36] It has no "ifs," or "buts." There are two main Hebrew words that are employed to express a prohibition: אַל with jussive and לֹא with imperfect. לֹא prohibitive has a much stronger force than the אַל prohibitive.[37]

Apodictic laws are found throughout the Pentateuch and the best biblical example of this type is the Ten Commandments (Exod. 20:1–17).[38] It demands the exaction of the death penalty by the community. These laws are absolute prohibitions of the "you shall not" variety that are usually concerned with religious or moral issues.[39] It is associated with the Israelites cults and expresses the

---

[31] Anthony Phillips, *Essays on Biblical Law*, (London: T&T Clark International, 2004), 12.

[32] It is said that, in Egypt the word of the Pharaoh became law immediately as the people believed him to be having the quality of the high god–the sun. Cf. *Livingston, Pentateuch in its Cultural Environment*, 121–2; Gordon J. Wenham, "law," in *NBD*, eds. I. Howard Marshall et al., (Secunderabad: OM-Authentic Books, 2007), 674.

[33] For further reading on "*YHWH* as the source of law," see, James W. Watts, *Reading Law: The Rhetorical Shaping of the Pentateuch* (Sheffield: Sheffield Academic Press, 1999), 105.

[34] Albrecht Alt, "The Origins of Israelite Law," in *Essays on Old Testament History and Religion* trans. R. A. Wilson (Garden City, New York: Doubleday, 1967), 89, 104–5.

[35] Alt, "Origins of Israelite Law," 104–5.

[36] Bernhard W. Anderson, Steven Bishop, and Judith Newman, *Understanding the Old Testament*, 5th ed. (Upper Saddle River, New Jersey: Pearson Prentice Hall, 2007), 87.

[37] John Bright has elaborated in detail about the two prohibitive uses of words: la prohibitive and al prohibitive. According to him, la starts with a wish or request and culminates in direct negative command "Do not." On the other hand al prohibitive expresses a prohibition of binding validity both for the present and the future. It characteristically takes the 2nd mas. sing. "You shall not." This subject is too vast to be dealt adequately here. For further information see, John Bright, "The Apodictic Prohibition: Some Observations," in *JBL* 92/2 (June 1973): 185–6.

[38] Cf. Livingston, *Pentateuch in Its Cultural Environment*, 175–6.

[39] J. W. Marshall, "Decalogue," in *DOTP*, 174.

unconditional demand of the covenant with the understood penalty being death even if it is not prescribed directly. Unlike the casuistic law which have parallels in the legislation of other people in the AWA, the apodictic form of the law is the product of the genuine Israelite heritage.[40]

2.2. Casuistic Law

Casuistic law or case law is a conditional concept noted for its "if–then" structure. It deals with a specific problem and provides legal remedies for the situation envisioned. It introduces a conditional clause with an "כי" (if or when) to state the actual case under consideration and follows with a "then" clause. It is associated with administration of justice that deals with human states of affairs. Anthony Phillips states that casuistic laws originated from the new situation in Canaan caused by the entry of the Israelites into the land.[41]

The casuistic laws are defined as remedial, describing the violation of someone's rights or retaliation for the person found guilty.[42] Take as an example Exodus 21:22, a law concerning striking of a pregnant woman and causing a miscarriage. It is an example of remedial law as it prescribed compensation.[43] Exodus 22:24–26 also contains a set of casuistic laws governing a relationship between lender and borrower. This law has a characteristic pattern "כי" (if).

2.3. The Birth of Four Laws in Pentateuch

The Pentateuch contains four sets of stories that are normally considered case laws that served to actually establish the precedent—the case of the daughters of Zelophehad, the case of the blasphemer, special case concerning Passover observance and the case of the man who collected firewood on the Sabbath day.[44] These four laws emerged as new situations developed for the people of Israel in the desert. Jacob Milgrom, who had contributed enormously on the subject of Old Testament laws and rituals, upholds his view that all these four cases have

---

[40] Moshe Weinfeld, "Origin of the Apodictic Law: An Overlooked Source," in *VT* 23/1 (January 1973): 63.

[41] Phillips, *Essays on Biblical Law*, 20; in this connection, Livingston also states that this kind of law in amply illustrated in the pagan legal documents. He further claims that the "eye for an eye" legal policy in Exod. 21:23–25 is paralleled in the code of Hammurabi; Cf. Livingston, *Pentateuch in Its Cultural Environment*, 176–7.

[42] Bernard S. Jackson, *Studies in the Semiotics of Biblical Law* (Sheffield: Sheffield University Press, 2000), 171; Cf. Dale Patrick, "Casuistic Law Governing Primary Rights and Duties," in *JBL* 92/2 (1973): 180–1.

[43] Patrick, "Casuistic Law," 180; See also, Assnat Bartor, "The Representation of Speech in the Casuistic Laws of the Pentateuch: The Phenomenon of Combined Discourse," in *JBL* 126/2 (2007): 235–6.

[44] The additional three laws in Pentateuch are taken into consideration here in this section because they are directly related to the present study.

arisen in the wilderness having their origin in Israel's early history.[45] It is clear that the law of Israel was not presented as code unlike the law codes of the AWA or in contemporary societies. It was integrated with the on-going story of the people of God. This section briefly surveys the three laws other than Zelophehad's daughters' case which will be studied in detail hereafter.

2.3.1. The Case of the Blasphemer (Lev. 24:10–16)

This is a narrative about a man of mixed ancestry who engaged in an act of blasphemy and received punishment after Moses consulted God.[46] This narrative has much in common with the other three narratives in the Book of Numbers which were all set in the wilderness period.[47] The Hebrew word used for "to curse" is וַיְקַלֵּל which is from the root word קלל (24:11 in Piel form). It is a law against blaspheming God.[48] In fact the narrative does not exactly specify what constituted the blasphemer's actual transgression, or how he engaged in this act, because the text only says "he cursed." There is a prohibition against blasphemy in Exodus 22:28. So, the only clear indication is that he had gone against this commandment.

Mark Leuchter argues that this narrative belongs to the legislative Holiness Code, and he states that there is no mention of the tent of meeting, unlike other Holiness passages where the community and sanctuary are highlighted.[49] He states that it was an issue addressed to the exilic community. According to him, the Holiness author developed the language from earlier collections and developed that narrative law in holiness school of thought although the present narrative took its final form during the post exilic period.[50] In this text the new divine law was conveyed through Moses affirming that insult to the divine name was a severe transgression and the penalty to be exacted was execution by public stoning for his offence. The narrative ends with a whole set of provisions about penalties for homicide and injury.

---

[45] Jacob Milgrom, *Leviticus 23–27: A New Translation with Introduction and Commentary*, vol. 3 AB (New Haven: Yale University Press, 2001), 2105.

[46] This law along with the Sabbath gatherer is called "religious" infraction and impose the death penalty for it. Cf. Raymond Westbrook, *A History of Ancient Near Eastern Law*, Handbook of Oriental Studies (Leiden: Brill, 2003), 979.

[47] Mark Leuchter, "The Ambiguous Details in the Blasphemer Narrative: Sources and Redaction in Leviticus 24:10–23," in *JBL* 130/3 (September 2011): 431–2.

[48] John E. Hartley, "Leviticus," in *WBC*, vol. 4 eds. Hubbard et al., (Dallas: Word Books Publishers, 1992), 406.

[49] Leuchter, "Ambiguous Details," 448–9.

[50] Leuchter, "Ambiguous Details," 448–9.

2.3.2. Special Case Concerning Passover Observance (Num. 9:1–14)

This section narrates about the keeping of Passover. Vv. 1–5 recount that in the second year after the exodus, the Israelites were commanded to observe the פֶּסַח (Passover) sacrifice at the appointed time. The following Vv. 6–13 report about some men who had to bury a dead person just before the Passover and consequently became unclean. They were forbidden to offer the Passover sacrifice because of their state of ritual impurity at the appointed time.[51] On this particular issue Moses consulted God and secured the answer. A new law was given (9–14) specifying that such person must observe the Passover a month later. The deferral was specifically intended for those who were impure at Passover as well as for those people on a journey in a foreign country, or those who were too far away from the sanctuary to participate at the appointed time.

2.3.3. The Man who Collected Firewood on the Sabbath Day (Num. 15:32–36)

It is a story about an individual who gathered firewood on the Sabbath defying the law of Sabbath. It is an individual case of sin, which is essentially legal. The issue was also settled by Moses after consulting YHWH.

Jonathan Burnside took narrative approach to examine the case of Sabbath gatherer and he puts forward three questions: Firstly, Did the wood gatherer violate the Sabbath? Secondly, if so, did the particular form of Sabbath violation attract a capital punishment? And thirdly, if so, what form should this capital punishment take?[52] The case must be resolved by two parties concerned and since God is the only offended party only God can determine for any sort of punishment. This is because Sabbath is associated in personal terms with YHWH Himself. Humanity is to imitate God by keeping the Sabbath holy as it is also a sign of covenant between God and Israel. Under this circumstances Moses had to take the matter before God, and God gave the verdict that he should be stoned to death outside the gate. He stated that the verdict was made because the act of the Sabbath gatherer brought to mind the Israel's condition of total servitude. It is said that, this act reflected a desire to return to the economic condition associated with Pharaoh and thus signifies the rejection of YHWH's Lordship.[53]

These three stories involve pleas from parties to remedy their situation and establish social institutions. In all these cases Moses' intervention is sought, but since he cannot resolve the legal problem, accordingly he sought divine intervention. Michael Fishbane explains that all the above mentioned passages shadow one another structurally manifesting four stages in the development of

---

[51] Levine, *Numbers 1-20*, 4A, 79.

[52] Jonathan Burnside, "'What Shall We Do with the Sabbath-Gatherer?' A Narrative Approach to a 'Hard Case' in Biblical Law (Num. 15:32–36)," in *VT* (January 1, 2010): 54.

[53] Burnside, "What Shall We Do?" 59.

the adjudicatory process. In all these passages firstly, a case is brought to Moses, secondly, the law is unknown and God is consulted thirdly, a divine decision is given to Moses for the case at hand and finally, a compliance formula is used which states that the law was enacted.[54]

These cases demonstrate the development of Israelite legal traditions and they also cast YHWH as the principle instigator of change within law. In all these cases YHWH reacts to new circumstances and developed alternative means for compliance. These case laws characterize YHWH as judge, legal interpreter, reformer and law-giver. These cases have further implication for the case of Zelophehad's daughters which is to be studied hereafter.

2.4. The Laws in the Book of Numbers

There are laws and statistical summaries interwoven upon the thread of narratives and geography in the Book of Numbers. There are regulations concerning the Levites (chaps. 1–4), the treatment of lepers and related defilement, contributions to be made to the priesthood in case of breaking faith with YHWH, the law of the Nazirite (chaps. 5–6). Directions with regard to the lampstand of the tabernacle and purification and dedication of the Levites are given (chap. 8). There are laws concerning ceremonial uncleanliness due to contact with dead body (as studied earlier in chap. 9:1–14), direction for blowing of the two silver trumpets, sacrifice of cereals and animals and elaboration on witting and unwitting offenses (chaps. 9–15). There are laws concerning proper functions of the Levites (chap. 18). All these religious and civil laws are placed without regard for suitability of context. [55]

These laws are without any doubt assigned to P source of high antiquity set by the priestly community during and following the exile. The motif behind it is that, Israel was to be a holy people consecrated to YHWH, for which reason YHWH has set her apart for His service. During the exile, the priestly community had devoted themselves to the study and elaboration of the divine law. It was done with an aim to preserve the holy community within an alien environment.[56]

It is generally accepted that Numbers 25–36 are among the latest texts of the Pentateuch and most of them have assigned the date to 4th century.[57] There are inconsistencies found in these chapters and to explain this, Rainer Albertz, states

---

[54] Michael A. Fishbane, *Biblical Interpretation in Ancient Israel* (New York: Clarendon Press 1985), 98, 102.

[55] Dentan finds this subject completely irrelevant to the context. Cf. R. C. Dentan, "Book of Numbers," in *The Interpreter's Dictionary of the Bible: Illustrated Encyclopedia Identifying and Explaining All Proper Names and Significant Terms* (K–P), vol. 3 eds. George Arthur Buttrick et al., (Nashville: Abingdon Press, 1962), 570.

[56] W. J. Harrelson, "Law in the Old Testament," in *The Interpreter's Dictionary of the Bible*, vol. 4 eds. Buttrick et al., (Nashville: Abingdon Press, 1962), 86–7.

[57] Albertz, "Pentateuchal Redaction," 221–2.

that the author used several sources for the composite text.[58] There is a possibility because there are differences in details, and structure in various places.

It is clear that the law of Israel rests upon the initiative of God, who has redeemed particular people and entered into covenant with them and provided the basic stipulations of this covenant relationship in the form of the covenant law. The following is a detailed study about the daughters of Zelophehad who initiated change in the Israelite legal system.

3. Daughters of Zelophehad

We will now consider in detail the fourth story—the inheritance issue of the daughters of Zelophehad which is the primary focus here. Zelophehad, son of Hepher and grandson of Gilead died in the wilderness leaving behind five daughters namely, Mahlah, Noah, Hoglah, Milcah and Tirzah. His death raised an inheritance issue because he did not have any son to claim his share of inheritance—the land that would normally be allotted to him or to his son. Because he had left no son, his name, and thus his family, would be wiped off the census—they would no longer exist for the purposes of gaining an allocation of land. This was because the land would be distributed only among the names that were listed in the census (Num. 26:2).[59]

The important thing to remember here is that ancient Israelite society was predominantly a non-urban, agriculture-based society. The people of Israel upon entering the Promised Land have their plans to execute. They have a calendar of events for the entire year and all the events are based on the agricultural activities. They possess a calendar of yearly sacrifices and festival celebrations. Therefore it was needed for each individual to be connected to the land through father, brother or any of the male relatives. On reaching the land of Canaan the land will be distributed according to the names listed in the census through lot. Zelophehad's daughters found themselves disconnected from the land as their father had died in the wilderness. This is why they felt the need to present their case which is recorded in 27:1–11.

The last chapter of Numbers (36:1–12) presents a further amendment on this law. The elders from the tribes of Manasseh complained to Moses saying that allowing the daughters to inherit the estate would result in reducing the portion of land allotted to their tribe if the heiresses marry to other tribes. Moses consulted YHWH and further amendment was made declaring that an heiress should marry within her tribe.

There are two histories of scholarships in the study of the narrative of Zelophehad's daughters, that is, real story or work of fiction. Scholars like Zafrira Ben Barak, Pikka, Philip Budd, and others argue that it was a historical affair

---

[58] Albertz, "Pentateuchal Redaction," 227.

[59] A. Noordtzij, "Numbers," in *Bible Students Commentary* (Grand Rapids, Michigan: Zondervan Publishing House, 1983), 252.

that happened during the settlement period which had led to Numbers 27 and 36 and created a precedent and shattered a taboo.[60] To Barak especially, the story is derived from the real life situation where she sees women taking radical initiatives bringing change upon the existing legal system that denied women inheritance rights. To support her claim she provides a series of documents of the AWA spanning the period from 3rd millennium BCE Nippur (605–562) which are arranged geographically, covering the entire area from the Mediterranean in the West to Elam in the East and as far north as Anatolia and Greece.[61] Pekka Pitkanen too argues that names of the daughters are the same as districts in the area of Manasseh.[62] He further claims that it was historical event, and the names reflect the allotment and early settlement of these areas.[63]

On the other hand David H. Aaron firmly states that it is a fiction without any reality. He argues that the story was all fabrication with fictitious characters.[64] He states that the issue of women inheritance rights need not have a verse in the *Torah*. To him it was a dominant legal practice that existed. In order to justify his claim, he brought the example of marriage arrangement and wedding tradition. According to him, there was no text that describes the structure of marriage arrangement as well as no record of wedding traditions of which it is absolutely certain that the legal traditions and rituals existed.[65] Therefore, to him it is the literary strategy of the author to describe the dominant social behaviour.

To consider such an important historical event as something fictional and simply a literary work of the author is unacceptable. The five daughters' names are recorded not just once but thrice.[66] The scriptures also mentioned about the land allotted to the half tribe of Manasseh to which they belong. Numbers 26:28–34 and Joshua 17:3–6 clearly mentioned that Zelophehad's daughters received territory on the Western side of the Jordan. Moreover, as mentioned earlier, the daughters name and their ancestors' names mentioned in this section also occurs as place names in the area allotted to the tribe of Manasseh.[67] They indeed help us to form a picture of the territorial situation of this region. The whole story of the Book of Numbers has been one of movement towards the land of promise and the

---

[60] Zafrira Ben-Barak, *Inheritance by Daughters in Israel and the Ancient Near East: A Social, Legal and Ideological Revolution* (Michigan: Archaeological Centre Publications, 2006), 105; Cf. Pekka Pitkanen, "Ethnicity, Assimilation and the Israelite Settlement," in *TB* 55/2 (2004): 176.

[61] Ben-Barak, *Inheritance by Daughters*, 181–6.

[62] The following are the references in the Bible where the daughters' names appear as name of places Josh. 12:24, 17; Num. 26:31–32.

[63] Pitkanen, "Ethnicity, Assimilation," 176; Cf. Levine, Numbers 21–36, vol. 4A, 300.

[64] David H. Aaron, "The Ruse of Zelophehad's Daughters," in *HUCA* (January 1, 2009): 8.

[65] Aaron, "Ruse of Zelophehad's," 8.

[66] Num. 26:33; 27:1; and 36:11.

[67] Joseph Blenkinsopp, "Deuteronomy," in *The New Jerome Biblical Commentary*, eds. Raymond E. Brown et at., (Bangalore: Theological Publications of India, 1990), 97.

story of Zelophehad's daughters does provide a fitting conclusion to the Book of Numbers itself. The following section attempts to see the connection of the story to the entire Pentateuch.

3.1. Narrative of Daughters in the Context of Pentateuch

Pentateuch is a single work in five volumes that describes the manner in which Israel came into existence as a people. It defines their history and religious institutions beginning from the creation account to the occupation of the Promised Land.[68] It describes in detail about God's revelation to the people of Israel and choosing them for His service. The role of Moses is pre-eminent in all these formulations. He is a great mediator of the ancient law.

The indication in the Pentateuch is that the land of Canaan that the Israelites are about to possess will be Israel's forever (Gen. 13:15; 17:8). It is the conviction of Numbers 27 and 36 that the entry to Canaan is both certain and imminent. The story of the daughters of Zelophehad begins in Numbers 26:29–33, where their names appear in the second census list as members of the new generation who will inherit the land. As the new generation prepares to enter the land of Canaan, the book narrates the importance of land and laws to be followed in the land that they are about to possess. It is the theme that runs through the Pentateuch.

Budd comments that the author of this book intended to point out that daughters indeed have a right of inheritance. He further argues that, this text is about the rights of daughters to inherit the property.[69] Indeed, the focus of the story is not on the placement but the ancestral rights of the daughter to inherit the land.

3.2. Five Daughters' Names Listed Three Times in the Book of Numbers

The names of Zelophehad's daughters were listed three times in the Book of Numbers alone (26:33; 27:1; and 36:11). It is very unusual to see the female names listed in the census because as mentioned above the main purpose of taking census was to form a military group to fight against the Canaanites, the original inhabitants of the land. In fact they were the only female names mentioned in chapter 26 when the second census was taken.

The names of the daughters corresponded to the name of the towns in the west of the Jordan that is, Noah in Zebulun (Josh. 19:13), Hoglah in Judah (Josh. 15:6), and Tirzah in Manasseh (Josh. 12:24; I Kgs. 15:21) and the same applies to Mahlah (I Chr. 7:18) and Milcah.[70]

[68] Harrison states that the Pentateuch can be regarded as the first stage of a nine-volume work, that is, from Genesis to Kings that narrates from the creation to the subsequent fall of Jerusalem in 587 BCE. Cf. Harrison, *Introduction to the Old Testament*, 496.

[69] Budd, "Numbers," in *WBC*, vol. 5, 300–1.

[70] Budd, "Numbers," in *WBC*, vol. 5, 300.

Yonathan Grossman states that the purpose of mentioning their names was the story's desire to emphasize the initiatives the daughters have taken.[71] The probable reason for mentioning their names in 26:33 was to set the stage for the narrative of chapter 27:1–11 on the issue of inheritance of women on entering the land. The third time their names were mentioned in 36:11, it was to make the point that they must marry within their own tribe so as to retain the land within their tribe. At the year of Jubilee, all the problems of line of inheritance were to be resolved but land transferred to another tribe through marriage cannot be resolved because of the twin lines of right to the land: through wives and husbands from different tribes.[72]

Leveen rightly asserts that the entire generation of Zelophehad was going to be wiped out in an abrupt manner. Countless names were to be erased just because they had no male members in the family. This very issue had motivated the daughters to present the matter before Moses and the male elders.[73] Thus, for this very reason, the names of the five daughters were listed not just once but thrice.

3.3. Significance of "Name" in the Bible

שֵׁם is the Hebrew word for name, reputation and fame. Names represented more than mere labels to distinguish one person from another. For example, the word Abram which literally means "great father" was given to him because of his eminent place in the patriarchal line. However, in the course of time he was renamed Abraham meaning "father of a multitude" according to his new role that a multitude would spring from his descendants.[74] Fame and esteem are implicit in name associated with Abraham's imputed genealogical status, for with him Israel comes into being.

Allen P. Ross in his article asserts that the name frequently means "reputation" where God promised Abraham and David that their names will be made great (Gen. 12:2; 2 Sam. 7:9).[75] Names represent a person's personality and therefore, the bearers are concerned with good reputations.[76] A person acquires a name through mighty deeds and through property.

[71] Yonatan Grossman, "Divine Command and Human Initiative: A Literary View on Numbers 25–31," in *BibInt* 15/1 (2007), 62.

[72] Allen, "Numbers," in *Expositor's Bible Commentary*, vol.1, 235.

[73] Leveen, *Memory and Tradition*, 175–6.

[74] Eugene H. Merrill, *Everlasting Dominion: A Theology of the Old Testament* (Tennessee: B&H Publishing Group, 2006), 40; Cf. Fabry. V. Reiterer, "שֵׁם," in *TDOT*, XV Trans. David E. Green, eds. G. Johannes Botterweck et al., (Grand Rapids, Michigan: William B. Eerdmans Publishing Company, 2006), 153.

[75] Allen P. Ross, "שֵׁם," in *NIDOTTE*, vol. 4 eds. VanGemeren et al., (Michigan: Zondervan, 1997), 148.

[76] A. S. Vann Der Woude, "שֵׁם," in *Theological Lexicon of the Old Testament*, vol. 3 eds. Ernst Jenni and Claus Westermann trans. Mark E. Biddle (Peabody, Massachusetts: Hendrickson

According to the biblical account, we see that YHWH intends to blot out rebellious Israel's name, because the blotting out would result in cutting off their memory (Deut. 9:14). The text says that the name would be destroyed, cut off, blotted out, and covered over forever.[77] Naming brought things into describable existence. Similarly in the Bible, to have the name cut off was to cease to exist.

The perpetuation of a name is a matter of great importance as the name is linked to land ownership and therefore, it is important to prevent any land from being removed from the family, clan or tribe. In describing the distribution of the land, the Book of Numbers (26:55) states that the land is to be apportioned by lot according to the individual names of the ancestors, and distributed in hereditary portions. The name is associated with entitlement of land. Hence, the daughters of Zelophehad noted in Numbers 27:4 that their father's name would still be associated with the land as Israel's patrilineal system sough to ensure the continuation of the family name.[78]

3.4. Significance of Genealogy

Zelophehad belongs to the tribe of Manasseh. The daughters' genealogy was traced back to the lineage of Manasseh, son of Joseph. The tracing back of their genealogy to Joseph was not an accidental. Therefore, the following is a survey on origin of the tribe of Manasseh.

Jacob, the father of Joseph took to himself Joseph's two sons (Manasseh and Ephraim) and made their descendants tribes of Israel. Joseph's two sons were made legitimate to receive an inheritance which was done through the device of adoption formula a common practice in the AWA, thus making them legal heirs to inherit ancestral lands.[79] It is understood that Jacob's adoption has given them legal right to become family group and made them legitimate to receive the inheritance. This act gave Joseph a double portion of the patrimony.[80] Joshua 16:1–17:18 is a narrative about the inheritance of the tribes of Joseph and according to this narrative much space was allotted to the clans of Ephraim and Manasseh.[81]

Publishers, 1997), 1357.

[77] Reiterer, "שֵׁם," in *TDOT*, XV, 168; Cf. Ross, "שֵׁם," in *NIDOTTE*, vol. 4, 148–9.

[78] Terence Fretheim, "Numbers," in *OBC*, eds. John Barton and John Muddiman (Great Clarendon: Oxford University Press, 2001), 130.

[79] Nathanael Warren, "Adoption-Alienation in Ezekiel 47:22–23 and in the Ancient Near East," in *ZAW* 126/3 (2014): 422.

[80] Gen. 41:45 mentioned about Joseph marriage to an Egyptian. In place of one tribe of Joseph there were two tribes, namely, Ephraim and Manasseh. Cf. Robert L. Hubbard, "Joshua," in *Eerdmans Companion to the Bible,* 179.

[81] Elizabeth Bloch-Smith and Beth Alpert Nakhai, "A Landscape Comes to Life: The Iron I Period," in *NEA* 62/2 (June 1999): 70–1.

There is an intricate relationship between Numbers 26 and 27 regarding the status of the tribe of Manasseh. Numbers 26 presents the second census of the wilderness period and the demographic of the census were also to serve as a basis for the apportionment of the land to the various tribes according to their respective populations. This chapter has a link with Numbers 27:1–11, and both the chapters are linked to the tradition of Joshua chaps. 16–17 that narrates about the land allotted to Ephraim and Manasseh. Therefore, Numbers 27 provides an etiological legitimation of the claim of the tribe of Manasseh to settle territory west of the Jordan.[82] To establish these as Manassite, Zelophehad's daughters were given title after the death of their father.

4. Daughters Rights to Inherit: An Exegetical Study of Numbers 27:1–11

The law of inheritance is clearly mentioned in Deuteronomy 21:15–17. It is said that the property will pass on to the male heirs. The law of primogeniture provides a double portion of the inheritance as the birth-right of the eldest son and the rest of the sons get equal share.[83] Neither widows nor daughters, receive any portion of the estate. The male relatives were obliged to care for them. But, what would happen in the event when there is no male heir? It is this reality that obligates the daughters to take their case to the divine authority.

Numbers 27 fittingly opens with a story that concerns the new generation and very unusually the story about a new generation of daughters.[84] As the Israelites prepare to enter the Promised Land, laws were laid before them but the issue of women's inheritance rights was not covered in their given laws. Prior to this incident, the system of land ownership was something they have not experienced. In Egypt they lived as slaves without any right to ownership. And for forty years they were wandering in the desert. This text deals with the case put forward by the daughters who were to be deprived of their patrimony.

[82] Levine, *Numbers 21–36*, vol. 4A, 320.

[83] MAL B.1 also says, "If brothers divide the estate of their father, the eldest brother will select and take two shares of the orchards and wells on the land, and thereafter his brothers will divide and take. As regards the arable (?) land and the appurtenances thereto, the youngest brother will sketch out shares, the eldest brother will select and take one share and cast lots with his brothers for his second share."

[84] Recent postcolonial treatments of this narrative point out that the daughters of Zelophehad form part of the group of conquerors who are on the verge of entering the land. With their request for land, they wittingly or unwittingly participated in the imperial agenda of the Israelites which divides up the land without regard to the people who are already living there. By means of their request, they participated in the dispossession of Canaanites. No doubt the researcher here agrees that they participated in the imperial agenda but in their society they were also greatly impacted by patriarchy, having limited access to the resources. In deed they were the oppressed section of people so they raised this inheritance issue because their rights have been denied, Dora Rudo Mbuwayesango, "Can Daughters be Sons? The Daughters of Zelophehad in Patriarchal and Imperial Context," in *Relating to the Text: Interdisciplinary and Form-Critical Insights on the Bible* eds. Timothy J. Sandoval and Carleen Mandolfo (London: T&T Clark International, 2003), 251–62.

4.1. Form, Structure and Setting

This passage falls under the provenance of the priestly writers which is revealed by paying close attention to the content, language and inner coherence. Numbers Chapters 26–36 narrates the story of the new, obedient generation, who were allotted portion in the Promised Land. This provides the larger context for the daughters of Zelophehad narrative. Numbers 27 attends to two essentially unrelated subjects in the priestly agenda: inheritance law and the transfer of leadership from Moses to Joshua by divine degree.

In terms of its form, the story is a legal confrontation between YHWH and the daughters of Zelophehad. The story has obvious affinities with other case laws embedded within the priestly literature (cf. Lev. 24:10–23; Num. 9:6–14; 15:32–36). It is a traditional legal material, which according to Martin Noth is relatively late.[85]

The story intends to resolve a particular issue which had become pressing in the author's time and resolved in the light of previously given legal principle. The circumstances of exile and return made the question of access to land and the associated rights a real and very live issue. The author makes a point that women too have right of inheritance through divine pronouncement. The divine ruling given here also ensures that the land is kept within the family.

The composition of Numbers involves changes from narrative to law and from law to narrative, the special unifying factor behind the Book of Numbers.[86] This abrupt change from narrative to law is also best illustrated by 27:1–11. The preceding chapter 26 clearly records the survey of Israel's clans after which in 27:12–23 Moses got the order to climb the mountains of Abarim (עֲבָרִים) to install Joshua as his follower. This flow of narrative was interrupted by 27:1–11 that emphasizes the law of succession to landed property.

This text is clearly concerned with retaining the territorial integrity of certain family units, legislation designed to keep clan property within the paternal line of descent. Although, written much later, the story is set in a period of Israel settlement, located at the plains of Moab and the narrative spans 11 verses.

4.2. The Case (27:1–5)

The present narrative is a legal case that Moses and the leaders encountered during their wandering in the wilderness. A problem arose without previous precedent because there was no male member of the family, only the five daughters. Zelophehad's daughters protested their exclusion from their father's estate. They presented their specific case at the entrance to the tent of meeting, seeking the land be given to them. Moses then sought YHWH's direction.

---

[85] Martin Noth, *Numbers, Old Testament Library Series*, trans. by James D. Martin (London: SCM Press, 1968), 211–2.

[86] Seebass, "'Holy' Land," 94; Levine, *Numbers 1–20*, 78–9.

Numbers 27:1–5 *BHS*

1 וַתִּקְרַבְנָה בְּנוֹת צְלָפְחָד בֶּן־חֵפֶר בֶּן־גִּלְעָד בֶּן־מָכִיר בֶּן־מְנַשֶּׁה לְמִשְׁפְּחֹת מְנַשֶּׁה בֶן־יוֹסֵף
וְאֵלֶּה שְׁמוֹת בְּנֹתָיו מַחְלָה נֹעָה וְחָגְלָה וּמִלְכָּה וְתִרְצָה׃

2 וַתַּעֲמֹדְנָה בַּעֲדַת־קֹרַח לִפְנֵי מֹשֶׁה וְלִפְנֵי אֶלְעָזָר הַכֹּהֵן וְלִפְנֵי הַנְּשִׂאִם וְכָל־הָעֵדָה
פֶּתַח אֹהֶל־מוֹעֵד לֵאמֹר׃

3 אָבִינוּ מֵת בַּמִּדְבָּר וְהוּא לֹא־הָיָה בְּתוֹךְ הָעֵדָה הַנּוֹעָדִים עַל־יְהוָה
כִּי־בְחֶטְאוֹ מֵת וּבָנִים לֹא־הָיוּ לוֹ׃

4 לָמָּה יִגָּרַע שֵׁם־אָבִינוּ מִתּוֹךְ מִשְׁפַּחְתּוֹ כִּי אֵין לוֹ בֵּן תְּנָה־לָּנוּ אֲחֻזָּה בְּתוֹךְ אֲחֵי אָבִינוּ׃

5 וַיַּקְרֵב מֹשֶׁה אֶת־מִשְׁפָּטָן לִפְנֵי יְהוָה׃

Translation

1 Then approached the daughters of Zelophehad, the son of Hepher, son of Gilead, son of Machir, son of Manasseh[87] belonging to the clans of Manasseh,[88] son[89] of Joseph. These are the names of his daughters: Mahlah, Noah,[90] Hoglah,[91] Milcah,[92] and Tirzah.

2 And they stood before Moses, Eleazar the priest, the leaders, and all the congregation, at the entrance of the tent of meeting[93] (saying),

3 Our father died in the wilderness; he was not among the congregation of those who gathered themselves together against YHWH in the company of Korah, but he died[94] for his own sin; and he had[95] no sons.

---

[87] "Son of Manasseh" is lacking in the G. There is no particular reason for it.

[88] Here the word מִשְׁפָּחָה is translated as clan. Sometimes the word is synonymous with tribe (שֵׁבֶט). Sometimes even the entire Israelites are called one large מִשְׁפָּחָה. The P writers had a preference for combining discrete terms of reference to produce composite terminology, and for this Levine claims that it was undoubtedly the priestly writers' effort to embrace the common bonds uniting all Israelites. Levine, *Numbers 1-20*, vol. 4A, 131.

[89] In G. it is written as των υιων "of sons," and the BHS has suggested לִבְנֵי which can be translated as "belonging to the son of." This translation follows the proposal made by *BHS*.

[90] Few manuscripts such as the Sam., Syr., Tg., and Vg. have conjunction word added, וְנ "and Noah." In Num. 26:33; 36:11; and Josh. 17:3 the name Noah is with conjuction "וְ."

[91] Some manuscripts like the Sam., and others do not include conjunction.

[92] Here as well some manuscripts like the Sam. and others, the name ומלכ is written without conjunction.

[93] פֶּתַח אֹהֶל־מוֹעֵד (entrance of the tent of meeting) this location is understood literally, "at the very entrance and not inside."

[94] The Sam. has added the word אָבִינוּ translated as "our father died," instead of "he died."

[95] The Sam. has used the word הָיָה trans. as "he had" instead of הָיוּ (qal pf. 3c.p) trans. as "they had," which is not relevant. According to the context it is talking about Zelophehad not having son,

4 Why should the name of our father be withdrawn[96] from his clan, because he had no son? Give[97] to us a possession,[98] in the midst of our father's brothers.

5 Moses brought[99] their case[100] before the YHWH.[101]

Immediately upon Israel's arrival at the threshold of the fulfilment of the promise, they renewed the census of the people in the plain of Moab by the Jordan of Jericho (Num. 26:3). After accomplishing the census, the division of the land is commanded 26:53–56. It is at this point, Zelophehad's daughters raised their plea. Moses brought the daughters' case before YHWH for divine direction.

The Significance of קרב (Approach)

Vv. 1, 5. The five daughters' act of coming together is described by the word וַתִּקְרַבְנָה (qal form) from the root קרב meaning "to approach, come near, draw near."[102] It is found throughout the entire Semitic domain.[103] The motivation for "approaching" includes hostile, cultic, legal, and sexual reasons.[104] In this narrative the word וַתִּקְרַבְנָה "came near" is used in legal context where a group of

---

it cannot be read as they had no son. So Sam. renders the right translation, same textual problem is also found in Num. 26:33.

[96] The root word גרע is withdraw, diminish. Here it is used in Niphal form, so it means "be withdrawn or diminished." The daughters' case reveals a concern that the name of an Israelite should not be withdrawn just because he had no son.

[97] The word תְּנָה is singular. Other Mss. like Sam., G., Vg. has plural ending תְּנוּ which is more appropriate because it is not an individual claiming the land but group of people.

[98] In Sam. it is written as אֲחֻזָּה נַחֲלָה "possessions of inheritance" instead of just אֲחֻזָּה. The word אֲחֻזָּה is generally translated as "possession" denoting inalienable property. Milgrom states that the two terms אֲחֻזָּה and נַחֲלָה are not interchangeable. He claims that אֲחֻזָּה is a technical term denoting inalienable property received from a sovereign and that נַחֲלָה denotes inalienable property transmitted by inheritance. Cf. Jacob Milgrom, Leviticus 1–16: A New Translation with Introduction and Commentary, vol. 3 AB (New York: Doubleday, 1992), 6.

[99] Hiphil "to bring near."

[100] The letter ן (pronominal suffix) in the word מִשְׁפָּטָן "their case," is written in bold. For this, Allen states that the writer used this unusual letter to bring special attention to the fact that, this was an appeal from women. Cf. Allen, "Numbers," in *The Expositor's Bible Commentary with NIV: Genesis, Exodus, Levitcus, Numbers*, vol. 2 eds. Frank E. Gaebelein et al., (Grand Rapids, Michigan: Zondervan Corporation, 1990), 942–3.

[101] Translated from *BHS*.

[102] Lubitch interprets this word as indicating a sense of great closeness and intimacy between the sisters when they appeared in person to appeal before the leaders. Cf. Rivkah Lubitch, *Creative Feminist Midrash*, Women in Judaism No. 11 (Ramat Gan: Bar-Ilan University, 2000), 25.

[103] R. E. Gane, J. Milgrom, "קָרַב," in *TDOT*, vol. XIII eds. Botterweck et at., trans. David E. Green (Grand Rapids: William B. Eerdmans Publishing Company, 2004), 136–7.

[104] Gane, Milgrom, "קָרַב," in *TDOT*, vol. XIII, 137.

people came near to other persons demanding an authoritative decision.[105] The five daughters brought a claim which is a just case (מִשְׁפָּט, v.5). This word plays an important role in this story. The basic meaning usually denotes physical and spatial proximity.

As the story unfolds, it starts as the daughters "came near" (qal). The same root is also used in v. 5 in Hiphil form (to bring near).[106] It is used in the sense of presentation which is expressed as וַיַּקְרֵב מֹשֶׁה "and Moses brought their case."[107] קָרַב is integral to the juridical process, thus, the Hiphil וַיַּקְרֵב "and he brought" (27:5) is talking about bringing one near, so in this instance it is the "case" that Moses brought before YHWH.

The daughters' act of coming near to the central shrine was an act of incredible courage, conviction and faith.[108] The people were not in the land yet, but these women knew that they would enter it soon, and because of that they made this just claim. According to the biblical account, with the exception of Mariam, sister of Moses and Aaron, there is no record about woman coming to such sacred place.

Zelophehad's daughters' genealogy was traced back to Joseph. This has an important historiographic significance. Their names are listed within the tribe of Joseph, more specifically within the tribe of Manasseh.[109] In dealing with Old Testament genealogies, M. Noth argues that one must distinguish between primary and secondary genealogies.[110] Thus, the present genealogies antedate their narrative settings and are, therefore, potential historiographic sources.

---

[105] Levine, *Numbers 21–36*, 346; Cf. Gane, Milgrom, "קָרַב," in *TDOT*, vol. XIII, 138; J. Kuhlewein, "קרב," in *Theological Lexicon*, vol. 3, 1165.

[106] The word is also used in Josh. 17:4, in the context of daughters approaching Eleazar the high Priest, Joshua and before the tribal leaders to remind them about their father's inheritance to be given to them as commanded by God through Moses.

[107] Grossman, "Divine Command," 64–5.

[108] McKinlay reads this text from the New Zealand context with the painful history of colonialism. In her reading she struggles while trying to balance gendered interpretation and postcolonial reading. In spite of the tension she faced in reading the daughters act yet she acknowledges the daughters' courage that challenged the highest authorities; Cf. Judith E. McKinlay, "Playing an Aotearoa Counterpoint: The Daughters of Zelophehad and Edward Gibbon Wakefield," in *Postcolonialism and the Hebrew Bible: The next Step*, ed. Roland Boer (Atlanta: SBL, 2013), 12.

[109] Their genealogy has been explained in detail above under the title, "Significance of Genealogy."

[110] According to Martin Noth, primary genealogy is one which once existed apart from the narrative in which it is now found. Contradictory to that, secondary genealogy is one which had no existence as a genealogy outside the narrative in which it appear which is simply a literary construct. Cf. Martin Noth, *A History of Pentateuchal Traditions*, trans. Bernhard W. Anderson (Eaglewood Cliffs, New Jersey: Prentice Hall, 1972), 214–9.

The Role of Eleazar

Eleazar was the third son of Aaron and Elisheba (Exod. 6:23; Num. 3:2). He was also consecrated as priest along with his father and three brothers. According to the biblical narrative, he succeeded his father Aaron the high priest. As commanded by *YHWH*, he along with Moses and Aaron climbed the Mount Hor and there Moses removed Aaron's garments and put them on Eleazar. After this Aaron died and Eleazar started to assist Moses with the second census.[111] This is how he succeeded his father Aaron as the high priest. He then served as the leading priest alongside Moses (Num. 27:3, 21–22; 31) and Joshua (Josh. 14:1; 19:15; 21:1). He assumed an important role in the administration of the nation of Israel especially in the enumeration of the clans of Israel in preparation for the apportioning of Canaan. He along with Moses and other elders of Israel heard the inheritance plea of the daughters of Zelophehad.

Significance of וַתַּעֲמֹדְנָה לִפְנֵי (Standing Before)

> **V. 2:** There are five references to an individual standing לפני (before) other human being in a judicial context in the Old Testament. Here is Zelophehad's daughters' standing לפני Moses and leaders with their case described as משפט in v. 5. The other four references are Numbers 35:12 and Joshua 20:6, 9 that narrates about an Israelite who has killed someone unwittingly is expected to stand לפני the congregation for judgment. Also in 1 Kings 3:28 it is mention about the dispute between the two prostitutes standing לפני Solomon.[112] In all these five cases the people concerned are standing in close proximity to those לפני whom they stand.

וַתַּעֲמֹדְנָה "and they stood" is from the root word עמד "stand, take one's stand, take position, be present" in qal form.[113] In the Old Testament, the word is used to denote the physical act of standing. It is used in a context where one enters into the presence of human dignitary like Moses standing before Pharaoh (Exod. 9:10), Joseph standing before Pharaoh (Gen. 41:46), David standing before Saul (1 Sam. 16:21), to name some.[114] In this passage the daughters of Zelophehad took their place by standing before Moses, Eleazar the high priest, chieftains and all the congregation.

---

[111] Robin Gallaher Branch, "Eleazar," in *DOTP*, 214–5.

[112] Ian Wilson, *Out of the Midst of the Fire: Divine Presence in Deuteronomy*, ed. Michael Fox (OT), SBL Dissertation Series 151 (Atlanta, Georgia: Scholars Press, 1995), 172.

[113] David J. A. Clines et al., eds., "עמד," in *DCH*, vol. 6 (p-s) (Sheffield: Sheffield Phoenix Press, 2007), 463.

[114] Elmer A. Martens, "עמד," in *NIDOTTE*, vol. 3, 432.

The Role of עֵדָה (Congregation)

The phrase וְכָל־הָעֵדָה "and all the congregation" is a significant word in this context. The meaning of the noun עֵדָה is concentrated in two areas: Firstly, a general assembly or gathering of a people for legal and cultic purpose; Secondly, a swarm of animals. This word which is found more than 149 times in the Old Testament is said to be associated with the priestly writers.[115] It is used commonly as a corporate designation for the people of Israel for social, political and cultic purposes.[116] This "congregation" also had a legal function to perform. In Leviticus (24:10–16), the עֵדָה is responsible for stoning to death the blasphemer after *YHWH* has announced the sentence. In Numbers (15:32–36), the Sabbath gatherer was brought before Moses, Aaron, and the עֵדָה to be judged. In this case as well *YHWH* pronounced the sentence and the עֵדָה executed the punishment.[117] In a similar manner, the case of the daughters of Zelophehad was presented before Moses, Eleazar, chieftains and the עֵדָה. Since it was an extremely difficult case, God rather than the עֵדָה passed the judgment.

The Significance of אֹהֶל־מוֹעֵד (Tent of Meeting)

V. 2: Justice comes from YHWH as an oracle, a divine decision so the leaders led by Moses and the high priest sit at the entrance to the tent of meeting. אֹהֶל־מוֹעֵד is a Hebrew word for "tent of meeting." This is the site where Zelophehad's daughters stood and presented their case. The tent of meeting is first mentioned in connection with the sojourn at Sinai (Exod. 33:7–11) and later in connection with Kadesh and the wilderness (Num. 11, 16–17; 27:2; Deut. 31:14–15).[118]

Exodus 16:16; 33:10 mentioned that the Israelites lived in tents during the exodus and also when they went out to war (1 Sam. 17:54). The phrase אֹהֶל־מוֹעֵד is frequently used in the Old Testament to designate the pre-Solomomic sanctuary. Exodus 33:7–11 also notes that it was a place where Moses met with *YHWH* and was said to be located outside the camp, a temporary structure used until the more permanent shelter was constructed. Moses visited this tent whenever the need arises to meet YHWH.[119] The phrase probably derived from the belief that this structure served as the meeting place between God and Moses (Lev. 1:1), and between God and the people of Israel (Exod. 29:42–43). The tent of meeting was

---

[115] Eugene Carpenter, "עדה," in *NIDOTTE,* vol. 3, 326; Cf. D. Levy, J. Milgrom, "עֵדָה," in *TDOT,* vol. X, 470.

[116] Philip A. Harland, "Congregation," in *New Interpreter's Dictionary of the Bible*, vol. 1 (A–C), eds. Katharine Doob Sakenfeld et at., (Nashville: Abingdon Press, 2006), 718.

[117] Levy and Milgrom, "עֵדָה," in *TDOT,* vol. X, 472.

[118] Anderson, Bishop, and Newman, *Understanding the Old Testament*, 106.

[119] Exod. 33:7–11. Cf. Walter C. Kaiser, "Exodus," in *Expositor's Bible Commentary*, OT, vol. 2 eds. Kenneth L. Barker and John R. Kohlenberger III (Grand Rapids, Michigan: Zondervan), 121; Anderson, Bishop, and Newman, *Understanding the Old Testament*, 106.

said to be a series of enclosures, as the place itself being the outer covering of the tabernacle in which they kept the Ark of the Covenant (Exod. 26:7–14).[120]

YHWH chose to appear in special locales whose boundaries were clearly circumscribed and where He could be approached by individuals and communities to manifest himself in special ways. It was in such places, he said that "I cause My name to be remembered" (Exod. 20:24). Numbers presents an understanding of Israel, the people of God, as a community organized around the tent of meeting, the centrality that bears witness to the presence of God among them. The Book of Deuteronomy further expands upon the need for the community to meet YHWH at the designated places.[121] The text clearly indicates that it was in this kind of sacred site where they pitched the tent with the Ark of the Covenant inside and at the outer layer was a dwelling place for the high priest, Moses and the leaders. The community is divided among the people, their leaders, priest, with the tabernacle in its midst which reinforces a clear hierarchy of authority.

The Daughters Disassociate their Father from Korah's Rebellion

V. 3: Zelophehad's daughters' rhetorical move is to give assurance that their father was not guilty of a capital offense of rebellion. Korah's rebellion was mentioned in the previous chapter (26:9–11) and again the daughters mentioned it in v. 3. They made it clear about their father's death as a natural death. According to the biblical text, the punishment that God imposes on all mortals is natural death. It indicates that those found guilty of serious religious offences were not only put to death but that their property was confiscated as well.[122] This reality is alluded to in the statement of Zelophehad's daughters that their father had not perished as one of Korah's faction, but he died because of his own sin, that he committed only the ordinary sins of human frailty.

According to Korah's narrative in Numbers 16 and 17, in the course of the journey from Sinai to Edom, Korah joins with Dathan and Abiram to lead a revolt of two hundred and fifty dignified leaders of Israelites against the authority of Moses, objecting Moses' appointment of his brother Aaron to the post of high priest.[123] As Levites, Korah and his followers believed that they too have the right to share equally in the priestly status. This angered Moses and upon his specific urging, the ground under them split apart and swallowed up Korah, Dathan, Abiram and their families.[124] The Priestly writers of the Book of Numbers view Korah's sin in a very serious light.

[120] Gary Alan Long, "אהל," in *NIDOTTE*, vol.1 eds. VanGemeren et al., (Grand Rapids: Zondervan, 1996), 300–1.

[121] Merrill, *Everlasting Dominion*, 346.

[122] Wenham, *Numbers: An Introuction*, 193.

[123] Allen, "Numbers," in *Expositor's Bible Commentary*, vol. 2, 834.

[124] Ronald M. Green, "The Korah Episode: A Rationalistic Reappraisal of Rabbinic Anti-Rationalism," in *ASCE*, (1981): 103.

Zelophehad's daughters strongly asserted that their father has never belonged to the wrong assembly. Their rhetorical move here is to declare that their father's estate should not be confiscated because his death was unrelated to the Korah rebellion. They are anxious to show that their father was in no way implicated.

Significance of שם (Name)

V. 4: This is one of the important verses where the daughters appealed for a change in the legal system.[125] One of the issues they mentioned was about the preservation of their father's name. The potential disappearance of the family's name is a matter of grave concern leading to the extent of societal abandonment. Katharine Sakenfeld affirms that the main motivating factor for the daughters' courageous action was not so much their own situation of injustice, but to preserve their father's name.[126] Jione Havea also claims that the daughter's primary beneficiary was the dead father whose name should not be lost to the clan because he had no sons.[127] Both of them fail to see the strategy the daughters used to gain the right that was denied to them. We see that in doing so, their father Zelophehad's name which would have been forgotten got mentioned and their names as well in the biblical text. No doubt, they were naturally anxious about their father's name being wiped out, but that is not the main motivating factor. They were right to be concerned because the existing rule failed to consider their situation in a census in which only male heads were counted.

Their father Zelophehad's name would be forgotten if his daughters do not receive an inheritance in the land, while they themselves will be absorbed in their husbands' clans.[128] It is very clear that within this framework that is, "preservation of the father's name" they asked for the father's share of land. They desire status and inheritance rights within the clan of Manasseh. Hence, the importance of the phrase the daughters used in 27:4: "Why should our father's name be withdrawn. ..?" It was a rhetorical form of a question because name occupies an important place in the Israelite life. Certainly it was used to persuade and to convince the people in authority.

Baruch Levine and Westbrook argue that the term "name" in this passage should be fully equated with "title to landed inheritance."[129] It is a clear indication that only that which has a name exists.

---

[125] Harrison asserts that it was possible for the ancient Hebrews to interpolate additional laws to replace the existing law whenever necessary. Cf. Harrison, *Introduction to the Old Testament*, 264.

[126] Sakenfeld, "Zelophehad's Daughters," 41.

[127] Jione Havea, *Elusions of Control: Biblical Law on the Words of Women, Semeia Studies* (Atlanta: SBL, 2003), 56.

[128] Noordtzij, "Numbers," in *Bible Students Commentary*, 252.

[129] Levine, *Numbers 21–36*, vol. 4A, 77.

The expression יִגָּרַע is from the root word גרע that conveys many meanings such as, "to diminish, take away, erase, reduce, lessen, shave."[130] Here the word is in Niphal form, a term used in the legal context meaning "to be withdrawn."[131] This is a passage that deals with taking away of the name. The same root word is also used in 36:3 to describe the tribal elder's fear of land being "lost." Eugene Carpenter claims that the verb יִגָּרַע in 27:4 is used to indicate the total disappearance of a man's name from Israel.[132]

Zelophehad's daughters based their claims by citing the reason of the consequences of wiping out one's name. Thus, the basis upon which the daughters construct their case was very important. They petitioned the court that they should be given the legal status to inherit his property. By doing so their family would not be passed over in the apportionment and thereby their name would remain in posterity.

Another important phrase to be considered here is, "give to us" (27:4, qal imperative). This phrase appears with the two objects namely, possession (27:4,7) and inheritance (27:9–11) to signify the granting of an inheritance to family members. The Hebrew word for "give to us," is תְּנָה־לָּנוּ. The root word נתן means "to give, offer, present, permit, surrender, deliver, set, put, place." This verbal root is the fifth most common word found more than 2010 time in the Old Testament.[133] This word encompasses a broad concept whose fundamental meaning is not "give, or make a gift," but "to extend the hand" in order to place an object at a specific place or to give over to another person as a possession.[134]

The Hebrew word נָתַן frequently denotes the tribal land inheritance of the Israelites.[135] The same root word is also found in the following verse 7 with participle conjunction וְנָתַתָּ֫ם "and you shall give" to mean that an inheritance is apportioned according to the inventory lists.

The term אֲחֻזָּה designates land acquired through grant or purchase, a term widely used in priestly writings. In the Old Testament it usually refers to three things, that is, a piece of agricultural real estate (Lev. 25:10; Gen. 23:4), refers to whole countries, especially Canaan as Promised Land (Lev. 14:34; Josh. 22:4),

[130] In Jewish Aramaic, Syriac, Old South Arabic, the root word [rg is used to refers to "to shave." In the Middle Hebrew and Jewish Aramaic it means "to diminish, take away." Ringgren assumes that the original meaning was "to cut (off);" Cf. Ringgren, "גָּרַע," in *TDOT*, vol. III, 66.

[131] Carpenter, "גָּרַע," in *NIDOTTE*, vol. 1, 895; Cf. Gilad J. Gevaryahu, "The Root G-R-A in the Bible: The Case of the Daughters of Zelophehad and beyond," in *JBQ* 41/2 (April 1, 2013), 112.

[132] Carpenter, "גָּרַע," in *NIDOTTE*, vol. 1, 895.

[133] Michael A. Grisanti, "נתן," in *NIDOTTE*, vol. 3, 205.

[134] E. Lipinski, "נָתַן," in *TDOT*, vol. X, 90–1.

[135] The word also occurs with the object אֲחֻזָּה in Gen. 17:8; Lev. 14:34; Num. 32:5, 29, and with the object נַחֲלָה in Num. 16:14; 26:54. Cf. Grisanti, "נָתַן" in *NIDOTTE*, vol. 3, 207.

and to non-Israelite purchase of slave (Lev. 25:45).[136] Here in the present context the daughters approached the leaders demanding the right to inherit the real estate. They asked for the possession among their father's brethren.

Moses Brought Their Case Before *YHWH*

V. 5: Moses heard the daughters' case and then he brings it before YHWH. In the wilderness period, an inability to decide on any important issue often resulted in a formal consultation of YHWH using Moses as the intermediary to pose the question and receive the answer.[137] Deuteronomy 1:17 clearly says, ". . . Any case that is too hard for you, bring to me, and I will hear it." According to this text, Moses appointed the officials and gave them authority over the people of Israel to administer justice, civil order and military discipline. He impressed upon them the duty to be fair and impartial.[138] But, the case of the Zelophehad's daughters is something serious which even Moses could not address, and he sought for divine judgment. This is a verse referring to human (Moses) presenting a case before YHWH.

The arena where the daughters presented the case points to the localized presence of the Deity at the chosen place. In v. 2 there is a mention of the tent of meeting. In the light of this observation, conclusion can be drawn that they presented the case before YHWH. Thus, this episode ends with the daughters and all Israelites awaiting the decision from YHWH.

4.3. The Verdict (27:6–11)

Numbers 27:6–11 *BHS*

6 וַיֹּאמֶר יְהוָה אֶל־מֹשֶׁה לֵּאמֹר׃

7 כֵּן בְּנוֹת צְלָפְחָד דֹּבְרֹת נָתֹן תִּתֵּן לָהֶם אֲחֻזַּת נַחֲלָה בְּתוֹךְ אֲחֵי אֲבִיהֶם וְהַעֲבַרְתָּ
אֶת־נַחֲלַת אֲבִיהֶן לָהֶן׃

8 וְאֶל־בְּנֵי יִשְׂרָאֵל תְּדַבֵּר לֵאמֹר אִישׁ כִּי־יָמוּת וּבֵן אֵין לוֹ וְהַעֲבַרְתֶּם אֶת־נַחֲלָתוֹ לְבִתּוֹ׃

9 וְאִם־אֵין לוֹ בַּת וּנְתַתֶּם אֶת־נַחֲלָתוֹ לְאֶחָיו׃

10 וְאִם־אֵין לוֹ אַחִים וּנְתַתֶּם אֶת־נַחֲלָתוֹ לַאֲחֵי אָבִיו׃

11 וְאִם־אֵין אַחִים לְאָבִיו וּנְתַתֶּם אֶת־נַחֲלָתוֹ לִשְׁאֵרוֹ הַקָּרֹב אֵלָיו מִמִּשְׁפַּחְתּוֹ וְיָרַשׁ אֹתָהּ
וְהָיְתָה לִבְנֵי יִשְׂרָאֵל לְחֻקַּת מִשְׁפָּט כַּאֲשֶׁר צִוָּה יְהוָה אֶת־מֹשֶׁה׃

---

136 Clines et al., eds., "אֲחֻזָּה," in DCH, vol. 1 (a) (Sheffield: Sheffield Phoenix Press, 2007), 187–8.

137 Litke, "Daughters of Zelophehad," 209.

138 Luciano C. Chianeque, Samuel Ngewa, "Deuteronomy," in *Africa Bible Commentary*, eds. Tokunboh Adeyamo et al., (Nairobi, Kenya: Word Alive Publishers Zondervan, 2006), 212.

Translation 27:6–11

6 And YHWH spoke[139] to Moses (saying),

7 "Thus the daughters of Zelophehad are right, give to them[140] possession of inheritance among their[141] father's brothers and cause the inheritance of their father to pass to them."

8 And you shall speak to the sons of Israel,[142] (saying) "If a man dies, and has no son,[143] and his inheritance should cause to pass[144] to his daughter.

9 If he has no daughter, then you shall give his inheritance to his brothers.

10 If he has no brothers, then you shall give his inheritance to his father's brothers.

11 And if his father has no brothers, then you shall give his inheritance to the nearest kinsman[145] of his clan, and he shall possess[146] it.[147] It shall be[148] for the sons of Israel a statute of judgment as YHWH commanded Moses"[149]

God's verdict was indeed to give the daughters their father's share of inheritance accompanied by a general law regarding such a case.

---

[139] Two other Mss. that is, Sam. and G. write וַיְדַבֵּר from the root word rbd "to speak."

[140] In the *BHS* the pronoun לָהֶם "to them" is masculine plural. It is referring to daughters, so feminine is required here. Multiple Mss. like Sam. and others write in feminine gender as לָהֶן. There is a proposal regarding the inconsistency in gender that claims that since it was passed from the colloquial language into literature, and masculine suffixes especially in the plural are frequently used to refer to feminine substantives. Cf. GKC, *Hebrew Grammar*, (135 o), 440.

[141] In the *BHS*, it is masculine gender אֲבִיהֶם 3mas.pl. "their father," which should be in feminine gender. Here as well multiple Mss. like Sam. have feminine gender written as "אֲבִיהֶן," the proposal of GKC, Hebrew Grammar, applies here as well (135 o), 440.

[142] NRSV, NIV, and others translate as "Israelites," but here it is translated literally "sons of Israel."

[143] It is a conditional legal formulation that expresses condition or circumstance.

[144] Sam. and Syriac write וּנְתַתֶּם "shall give" instead of וְהַעֲבַרְתֶּם "cause to pass over."

[145] לִשְׁאֵרוֹ refers to a person having blood relation, from the word raev. "flesh" the nearest blood relative; Syr. and Vg. write לַאֲשֶׁר "to which."

[146] Sam. writes in imperfect form וְיִירַשׁ "he shall possess."

[147] In *BHS* it is direct object maker with feminine ending, but the Sam. and Syr. has אֹתָהּ with mas. suffix. It is referring to the land so feminine suffix is appropriate.

[148] There is a proposal made to change this feminine suffix with mas. suffix וַתְּהִי.

[149] This phrase "כַּאֲשֶׁר צִוָּה יְהוָה אֶת־מֹשֶׁה" "As *YHWH* commanded Moses," is characteristically P postscript, its intention is to emphasize that all the specifics of the law had been commanded by God, and transmitted directly to Moses. The text is translated from *BHS*.

The ruling then follows that a man who had no sons may pass on his inheritance to daughters.

The Hebrew word מִשְׁפָּטָן (Noun construct with suffix) is derived from מִשְׁפָּט meaning "judgment, legal case, legal claim."[150] This particular word has several meanings especially when it is used in the context of resolving of disputes. Here, Moses is settling the case of Zelophehad's daughters before YHWH and in the presence of Eleazar the priest, the chieftains and the whole congregation.

YHWH Acknowledges the Daughters' Claim

A particular question which was left unanswered in deuteronomic law, concerning the rights of daughters, is here given a clear and definitive answer.[151] The issue was settled for all future occasions, for all the daughters in the family of Israel.

V. 6: The daughters requested for an אֲחֻזַּת "a landed property." YHWH's response went beyond their request. Not only their case was heard, but the daughters of Zelophehad are declared to be right. God affirms that the five sisters have a just case.[152]

V. 7: The term אֲחֻזָּה is an inalienable property derive from the sovereign, which should be rendered as "holding or tenure." On the other hand נַחֲלָה is an inalienable property which is obtained by virtue of belonging to a family. It conveys the notion of permanence, granted by YHWH.[153] In this verse these two words appear in a construct chain as אֲחֻזַּת נַחֲלָה (also in 32:32), which means "possession of inheritance." As the explanation above shows, although these two words are similar in meaning yet they cannot be synonymous.

The daughters' claim was not just inheritance but אֲחֻזַּת נַחֲלָה a hereditary possession of landed property. Albertz asserts that this is a unique phrase and motif used only by the author of the Numbers and can only be explained as a deliberate mixture of Deuteronomistic and Priestly language.[154] The point here is that they received the property along with the right to transfer it to their heir.[155]

---

[150] Peter Enns, "משפט," in *NIDOTTE*, vol. 2, 1142.

[151] Budd, "Numbers," in *WBC*, vol. 5, 302.

[152] Claassens explores the text Num. 27:1–11 focussing on the complex hermeneutical issues such as gender, power and right to land involved in the narrative. She struggles with her attempt to hold gendered interpretation of the five daughters in tension with the postcolonial reading. She states that the daughters emerge as a symbol of the powerless standing up for their rights. Cf. Claassens, "Give us a Portion Among our Father's Brothers," 320.

[153] Milgrom, *Leviticus 23–27*, 2172.

[154] Albertz, "Pentateuchal Redaction," 228–330.

[155] Allen, "Numbers," in *Expositor's Bible Commentary*, vol. 2, 943.

Statement of Law Applicable to all Israelites

Vv. 8–11: The law is stated casuistically with "if' clause, that is, אִישׁ כִּי "if a man." וְהַעֲבַרְתֶּם (hiphil perfect 2. mas. pl.) "And you shall cause to pass on," is the verb used here to express the giving of territory by a father to his daughter in the absence of a son.

The new legislation is spelled out in detail, and it stands thus: On the demise of the father, the estate goes to the son; If there be no son the daughters succeed; If there be no daughter, the brother of the deceased inherits; If there be no brothers of paternal uncles, the estate goes to the brothers of the father; If there be no grand uncles or brothers of the father of the deceased, then the nearest kin succeed. Beyond the fifth degree the law does not proceed. It is because as families of the Israelites were kept distinct in their respective tribes. There must always be some who could be called kinsmen, descended from the patriarch of the tribe.

The line of inheritance outlined here resembles the order of clan obligations pertaining to the redemption of land and from slavery as prescribed in Leviticus 25. If the impoverished land owner (Israelite) was forced to sell part of his possession due to dire poverty, it is the responsibility of the clan members to redeem (Lev. 25:25). Equally, it was the responsibility of the clan members to redeem from slavery if he has sold himself to his non-Israelite creditors (v.47).

The word שְׁאֵר (27:11) meaning "flesh," is used here in the context of persons having very close relation, referring to brothers, uncles, or other kin.[156] Occasionally this word also appears in combination with the terms בָּשָׂר (Lev. 18:6; 25:49), may refer to close family relatives. The intention here was to keep the inheritance as close as possible to the deceased man's family line, as his name and his possession in the land are inseparable.

The two words לְחֻקַּת מִשְׁפָּט "Statute of judgment" is used together in this verse and it implies a legal enactment from YHWH. The word חֻקָּה "something prescribed, enactment, or statute," symbolizes the divine authority prescribing civil law or judgment which is an act of deciding a case for which in Hebrew word is מִשְׁפָּט "judgment." Therefore, the combination of these words characterizes a new law prescribed by YHWH. This is one of the unique phrases employed by the author.[157] This special case is then to be used as a legal precedent for other similar cases.

According to this law the first in line for inheriting father's inheritance was the son and daughter will inherit if there is no son. If there is no daughter, the inheritance would pass to the nearest relatives. The decision becomes a מִשְׁפָּט חֻקַּת, a statutory legal decision and the verse ends by saying that the decision was originated from YHWH mediated through Moses.

---

[156] Levine, *Numbers 21–36*, vol. 4A, 348; Cf. Francis Brown, S. R. Driver, and Charles A. Briggs, "שְׁאֵר," in *NBDB–Gesenius Hebrew and English Lexicon: With an Appendix Containing Biblical Aramaic* (Peabody, Massachusetts: Hendrickson Publishers, 1979), 984–5.

[157] Albertz, "Pentateuchal Redaction," 228.

YHWH sides with Zelophehad's daughters, and together they transgress old custom that limits the rights of women. Jione Havea called it a "procedural law" or "law of procedure" for the Israelites.[158] It means that a complaint which began informally was grown into a law of procedure. The command was executed in Joshua 17:3–6. The daughters commendably challenged the current practice and took an important step toward greater gender equality, for the honour of all Israelite daughters. Through their active initiation they were counted as members of Israel and not only that but they also obtained the right to inherit their father's share of inheritance.

5. A Review Petition 36:1–13

Numbers 36:1–12 introduced an innovation which would ensure tribal inheritance must be preserved.[159] Here is a record of a grievance brought by leaders from the tribe of Manasseh who feared that allowing daughters to inherit their father's estates might result in alienation of land from original family if their marriage is not guided. This matter was brought in order to prevent land transfer to another tribe. The matter is referred to YHWH, and Moses mediated the reply. The rules of inheritance enunciated earlier need no alteration.

5.1. Form, Structure and Setting

Numbers 36 is an addendum for the purpose of qualifying the legalities of Numbers 27:1–11 on the matter of women inheritance rights. In other words, this chapter adjusts the provisions of previous verdict in the light of the land allocation system stipulated in Numbers 32 and 34. The purpose here is that the territory could be retained only if female heirs practice tribal endogamy.

The concluding formula (v.13) does not seem to belong to the present section, but it belongs to the final section of the entire Book of Numbers, the priestly author's own conclusion.

5.2. The Case (36:1–4)

Numbers 36:1–4 *BHS*

1 וַיִּקְרְבוּ רָאשֵׁי הָאָבוֹת לְמִשְׁפַּחַת בְּנֵי־גִלְעָד בֶּן־מָכִיר בֶּן־מְנַשֶּׁה מִמִּשְׁפְּחֹת בְּנֵי יוֹסֵף
וַיְדַבְּרוּ לִפְנֵי מֹשֶׁה וְלִפְנֵי הַנְּשִׂאִים רָאשֵׁי אָבוֹת לִבְנֵי יִשְׂרָאֵל׃

2 :וַיֹּאמְרוּ אֶת־אֲדֹנִי צִוָּה יְהוָה לָתֵת אֶת־הָאָרֶץ בְּנַחֲלָה בְּגוֹרָל לִבְנֵי יִשְׂרָאֵל וַאדֹנִי
צֻוָּה בַיהוָה לָתֵת אֶת־נַחֲלַת צְלָפְחָד אָחִינוּ לִבְנֹתָיו׃

3 וְהָיוּ לְאֶחָד מִבְּנֵי שִׁבְטֵי בְנֵי־יִשְׂרָאֵל לְנָשִׁים וְנִגְרְעָה נַחֲלָתָן מִנַּחֲלַת אֲבֹתֵינוּ וְנוֹסַף
עַל נַחֲלַת הַמַּטֶּה אֲשֶׁר תִּהְיֶינָה לָהֶם וּמִגֹּרַל נַחֲלָתֵנוּ יִגָּרֵעַ׃

---

[158] Havea, *Elusions of Control*, 55–6.

[159] Martin Noth calls it an appendix to the daughters' rights of inheritance found in Num. 27:1–11; Cf. Noth, *Numbers*, 211, 256–7.

4 וְאִם־יִהְיֶה הַיֹּבֵל לִבְנֵי יִשְׂרָאֵל וְנוֹסְפָה נַחֲלָתָן עַל נַחֲלַת הַמַּטֶּה אֲשֶׁר תִּהְיֶינָה לָהֶם וּמִנַּחֲלַת מַטֵּה אֲבֹתֵינוּ יִגָּרַע נַחֲלָתָן׃

Translation 36:1–4

1 And the heads of the fathers[160] of the clans of the sons of Gilead, son of Machir son of Manasseh, from the clans[161] of the sons of Joseph, approached and spoke in the presence of Moses[162] and the leaders of the fathers[163] of the sons of Israel;

2 And they said, "YHWH commanded my lord to give the land among the inheritance by lot to the sons of Israel; and my lord was commanded by YHWH[164] to give the inheritance of our brother[165] Zelophehad to his daughters.

3 But, if they become wives of other tribes of the sons of Israel, and their inheritance will be diminished from the inheritance of our fathers[166] and it will.

be joined[167] to the inheritance of the tribe into which they marry; and the lot of our inheritance will be diminished.

4 And when the jubilee of the sons of Israel comes, then their inheritance will be joined to the inheritance of the tribe[168] into which

---

[160] רָאשֵׁי הָאָבוֹת לְמִשְׁפַּחַת which is translated as "heads/chief of the father's house of the clans," refers to tribal leaders because each tribe comprised more than one clan.

[161] G., Vg. and the Syr. have the singular "clan."

[162] In G. there is a proposal to insert the phrase, καί ἐναντι Ελεαζαρ τού ἱερέως) אֶלְעָזָר הַכֹּהֵן וְלִפְנֵי "and before Eleazar the priest." "Eleazar the priest" is also mentioned in the Peshitta and 4Q Numb, and this appears to be the original version. Cf. Itamar Kislev, "Numbers 36:1–12: Innovation and Interpretation," in ZAW 122/2 (January 1, 2010): 249.

[163] In Sam. it has the definite article הא, "the fathers."

[164] *BHS* proposes two possible ways of reading. The first proposal is to read as וְאֹתָנוּ צִוָּה instead of וַאדֹנִי צֻוָּה בַיהוָה instead of accepting the passive (Pual) "to be commanded." Another proposal is to read as צִוָּה בְּשֵׁם (Piel instead of Pual) with the addition of "the name," further explanation continues in the exegesis that follows.

[165] As in other Sematic languages, here אָח means not "brother," but more generally "kinsmen, close relative." Cf. Cornelius I., "אח," in *NIDOTTE*, vol. 1, 345.

[166] In NRSV it is "ancestors." אֲבֹתֵינוּ the suffix is 1 c. pl., translated as "of our fathers," but Syr. reads אֲבִיהֶן "of their father" suffix in 3.f.pl.

[167] The Sam. reads וְנוֹסְפָה and the BHS is וְנוֹסַף. It is from the root word יסף in Niphal form (*BHS*), so it is translated as "to be joined," qal form is "to add."

[168] The Hebrew מַטֶּה is the consistent term for "tribe," a distinctively priestly term of reference, שֵׁבֶט "staff or tribe" these two terms are interchangeably employed in Numbers. Cf. Levine, *Numbers* 1–20, vol. 4A, 440.

they married; and their inheritance of the tribe of our fathers will be diminished from the inheritance.[169]

V. 1: This verse informs that the heads of the ancestral house from the tribe of Manasseh came before Moses and the leaders and presented a problem arising from the previous new ruling on daughters' inheritance rights. The tribal representatives are designated by the two terms, namely, chieftains and heads. They are also in part identified with רָאשִׁים "heads," from the noun ראשׁ "head." The usage adopted here is unique. There is possibility of influence by more than one source in linking the two epithets together.

The Hebrew word רָאשֵׁי הָאָבוֹת means "the heads of the fathers of . . . " This phrase is used to designate the date to the late priestly redaction because it is considered late title and in the rest of the Pentateuch it is found only in Exodus 6, 25, 29. It is considered to have been inserted by the author of the Numbers.[170] The phrase was used to refer to the family lineage of the daughters of Zelophehad.

The phrase לִפְנֵי מֹשֶׁה וְלִפְנֵי הַנְּשִׂאִים רָאשֵׁי אָבוֹת לִבְנֵי יִשְׂרָאֵל "before Moses, chieftains, and the heads of the fathers belonging to the sons of Israel," refers to the body to which the tribal heads made their appeal. Why Eleazar's name is not mentioned among the leaders to whom the case was delivered? Throughout P whenever Moses or Joshua is mentioned along with the group of tribal leaders, priest is also present.[171] But, the priest who is naturally expected to be mentioned here is not presented in this text. The possible reason could be that the two narratives were written by different authors.[172]

Here the word הַנְּשִׂאִים is derived from the verb נָשָׂא with the fundamental meaning "to lift up, elevate, raise, exalt."[173] So, in this context it is to be understood as "one raised up or exalted." In their juridical function, הַנְּשִׂיאִם (the chieftains) appear with Moses as a panel before which the case was presented. They are similarly involved in the land allotment in Numbers 32:2. Regarding this, Gray asserts that the present passage is a supplement by a later hand. His assertion is based on textual variations both in style and expression. He states that it was

---

169 Syr. reads אֲבִיהֶן, "of their fathers" suffix in 3.f.pl., but *BHS* reads, אֲבֹתֵינוּ suffix in 1c.pl., of our fathers, which is not appropriate. Translated from *BHS*.

170 Albertz, "Pentateuchal Redaction," 228; Cf. Kislev, "Numbers 36:1–12," in *ZAW* 251.

171 Exod. 34:31; Num. 1:44; 13:26; 15:33; 27:2; 31:12; 32:2, 28; 34:17; Josh. 14:1; 19:51; 21:1.

172 These are some of the prominent scholars' names who affirm that the two narratives (Num. 27 and 36) were written by different authors basing on the dissimilarities that exist, see, G. B. Gray, "*Numbers*," in ICC, 1903, 477; P. Budd, "Numbers," in WBC, 389; Jacob Milgrom, "Numbers," 511; Levine, "Numbers 21–36," 575.

173 H. Niehr, "נָשִׂיא," in *TDOT*, vol. X, 45.

probably an insertion from chapter 27 and concludes that the writer was mainly influenced in style by P.[174]

The tribal elders did not raise any dissatisfaction against the former decision from *YHWH* regarding daughters' inheritance. Their worry was, when the daughters were allowed to inherit the estate, then the question arises, "what would happen when they marry to someone who was not part of their tribe?" Marrying from within her own tribe would ensure that estate cannot be transferred to another tribe and she continues to possess the estate.

V. 3: This statement raises a question, that is, "What circumstances underlie if inherited daughters marry to men from other tribes?" They expressed the fear that the tribal land that is inherited by daughters will be added to other tribes that they marry. As the case of Naboth's vineyard shows, Israelites clung to their ancestral property even in the face of royal pressure. The land relates to a social rather than economic position.

The term שֵׁבֶט "tribe" appears only once in this section, and in contrast hJ,m;, which is also translated as "tribe" appears consistently (fourteen times 36:3–9,12). The opinion among the scholars is that the word מַטֶּה is a P designation and שֵׁבֶט is not.[175] In the Book of Numbers the two terms are interchangeably used. The combined usage of both terms is taken as evidence of later dating.[176] It bears witness to the fact that the incident related in chapter 36 does not testify to the continuation of the story in chapter 27:1–11.

V. 4: The clan representatives tried to justify their concern by relating it to the law of Jubilee. The phrase in Leviticus 25:10 clearly says, ". . . it shall be Jubilee for you, and each of you shall return to his possession, and each of you shall return to his clan."[177] Here the individual rather than the tribe is indicated. The P legislators created the Jubilee year, a fixed fiftieth year celebrated as a Sabbath year. During this jubilee year, the properties other than houses were restored to its former owners, and the slaves were freed. The land once lost to the tribe through inheritance would be irretrievable by jubilee provision. Only the property that is sold due to poverty can be retrieved by him or his nearest kinsman. If his relative retrieves, the redeemed land did not return to the impoverished relative but was retained by the purchaser. Therefore, the reference to Jubilee is inappropriate because the Jubilee law has to do with land sold to another party, but it does not

---

[174] Gray George Buchanan, "A Critical and Exegetical Commentary on Numbers," in *The International Critical Commentary*, eds. Samuel Rolles Driver et al., 3rd ed. (Edinburgh: T&T Clark, 1956), 477.

[175] Kislev, "Numbers 36:1–12: Innovation," 251–2; See also, H.-J. Fabry, "מַטֶּה," in *Theological Dictionary of the Old Testament*, vol. 8, eds. Botterweck, Ringgren, Fabry (Grand Rapids, Michigan: William B. Eerdmans Publishing Company, 1997), 245.

[176] Kislev, "Numbers 36:1–12: Innovation," 251–2.

[177] Translated from *BHS*.

apply to inherited land.[178] By making this point it makes clear that the present passage is dependent on the Priestly narrative.

5.3. The Verdict (36:5–13)

Numbers 36:5–13 *BHS*

5 וַיְצַו מֹשֶׁה אֶת־בְּנֵי יִשְׂרָאֵל עַל־פִּי יְהוָה לֵאמֹר כֵּן מַטֵּה בְנֵי־יוֹסֵף דֹּבְרִים׃

6 זֶה הַדָּבָר אֲשֶׁר־צִוָּה יְהוָה לִבְנוֹת צְלָפְחָד לֵאמֹר לַטּוֹב בְּעֵינֵיהֶם תִּהְיֶינָה לְנָשִׁים אַךְ
לְמִשְׁפַּחַת מַטֵּה אֲבִיהֶם תִּהְיֶינָה לְנָשִׁים׃

7 וְלֹא־תִסֹּב נַחֲלָה לִבְנֵי יִשְׂרָאֵל מִמַּטֶּה אֶל־מַטֶּה כִּי אִישׁ בְּנַחֲלַת מַטֵּה אֲבֹתָיו יִדְבְּקוּ
בְּנֵי יִשְׂרָאֵל׃

8 וְכָל־בַּת יֹרֶשֶׁת נַחֲלָה מִמַּטּוֹת בְּנֵי יִשְׂרָאֵל לְאֶחָד מִמִּשְׁפַּחַת מַטֵּה אָבִיהָ תִּהְיֶה לְאִשָּׁה
לְמַעַן יִירְשׁוּ בְּנֵי יִשְׂרָאֵל אִישׁ נַחֲלַת אֲבֹתָיו׃

9 וְלֹא־תִסֹּב נַחֲלָה מִמַּטֶּה לְמַטֶּה אַחֵר כִּי־אִישׁ בְּנַחֲלָתוֹ יִדְבְּקוּ מַטּוֹת בְּנֵי יִשְׂרָאֵל׃

10 כַּאֲשֶׁר צִוָּה יְהוָה אֶת־מֹשֶׁה כֵּן עָשׂוּ בְּנוֹת צְלָפְחָד׃

11 וַתִּהְיֶינָה מַחְלָה תִרְצָה וְחָגְלָה וּמִלְכָּה וְנֹעָה בְּנוֹת צְלָפְחָד לִבְנֵי דֹדֵיהֶן לְנָשִׁים׃

12 מִמִּשְׁפְּחֹת בְּנֵי־מְנַשֶּׁה בֶן־יוֹסֵף הָיוּ לְנָשִׁים וַתְּהִי נַחֲלָתָן עַל־מַטֵּה מִשְׁפַּחַת אֲבִיהֶן׃

13 אֵלֶּה הַמִּצְוֹת וְהַמִּשְׁפָּטִים אֲשֶׁר צִוָּה יְהוָה בְּיַד־מֹשֶׁה אֶל־בְּנֵי יִשְׂרָאֵל בְּעַרְבֹת מוֹאָב
עַל יַרְדֵּן יְרֵחוֹ׃

Translation 36:5–13

> 5 And Moses commanded the sons of Israel according to the word of YHWH (saying), the tribe of the sons of Joseph spoke rightly,
>
> 6 this is the word which YHWH commanded to the daughters of Zelophehad (saying), they must marry to whom they think good in their eyes surely belonging to the clan of their father's tribe.[179]

[178] Lemche and Noth disagree with the reference to the Jubilee year and holds to be meaningless in its present context. According to them, it is an inserted gloss. Cf. Niels Peter Lemche, *Biblical Studies and the Failure of History: Changing Perspectives 3*, Copenhagen International Seminar, eds. Thomas L. Thompson et al., (Sheffield, England: Equinox Publishing Limited, 2013), 40; Noth, Numbers, 257; Snaith, "Daughters of Zelophehad," 127.

[179] As in many Mss., Sam. as well, it is feminine reading אֲבִיהֶן which is more appropriate instead of masculine ending אֲבִיהֶם, the proposal of GKC, *Hebrew Grammar*, applies here as well (135 o), 440.

7 And that no inheritance belonging to the sons of Israel will be sieged[180] from one tribe to another, for the sons of Israel shall cleave to the inheritance of the tribe of his fathers.

8 And every daughter that possessed an inheritance from any tribe of the sons of Israel shall be wife to one of the clans of the tribe of her father, in order that the sons of Israel may possess the inheritance[181] of his fathers.

9 and that no inheritance belonging to the sons of Israel will turn around from one tribe to another[182] for the sons of Israel shall cleave to its inheritance.

10 As YHWH commanded Moses, thus the daughters of Zelophehad did.

11 So Mahlah,[183] Tirzah,[184] and Hoglah,[185] and Milcah[186] and Noah, the daughters of Zelophehad were married to the sons of their uncles.

12 And they were married to men from the clans[187] of the sons of Manasseh the sons of Joseph,[188] and their inheritance remained in the clan of the family of their father.

13 These are the commandments and the judgments which YHWH commanded by the hand of Moses to the sons of Israel in the desert-plains of Moab, by Jordan at Jericho.[189]

Tribal Elders' Claim Recognized as Just

Vv. 5–6: These verses make clear that the tribal elders' complaint was well founded. According to the narrative, YHWH heeds the plea of the leaders from the tribe of Manasseh and commands the daughters to marry within their father's

---

[180] The word תִּסֹּב is from the root word bbs used here in לאק form, which is translated as "to be about in every side, beset, siege, besiege." Here it is translated as "to siege."

[181] There is a slight change in Sam. that reads with the direct object maker as אֶת־נַחֲלַת.

[182] The Sam. reads עַל־מַטֵּה as in verse 7, instead of לְמַטֵּה.

[183] In Sam. the order of the names of the daughters are same with *BHS* Num. 26:33; 27:1, but in G. מַחְלָה is placed at the end. Cf. Budd, "Numbers," in *WBC*, vol. 5, 388.

[184] Some Mss. like Sam., Syr., Vg., read with conjunction וְת.

[185] Sam. reads without conjunction ’ח.

[186] Sam. reads without conjunction ’מ.

[187] G., Syr., and Vg. read singular.

[188] G. υἱῶν.

[189] Translated from *BHS*.

tribe.[190] Anna Vareed Alexander has read this narrative from an Indian woman perspective, and she remarks that they were given the freedom to marry from within their own tribe, a freedom which even today majority of Indian women do not enjoy.[191]

This final legal enactment serves to underline how closely land and possession were connected in the primitive mind. This ruling was made to solve the problem of transferring the land to another tribe and enabled every tribe to cleave to the inheritance of the tribes of their fathers.

Vv. 7-9: The verb יִדְבְּקוּ (qal imperfect) "shall cleave," is from the root דבק "to cleave, adhere." Here the root word דבק is used in a sense "to hold onto" the land, not to allow it to transfer out of the clan and tribe. As recorded in the Genesis account (2:24), as a man is to cleave to his wife so also an Israelite is to cleave to his family inheritance. This root is said to be absent in P except in this chapter which appears two times. There seems to be no explanation why the word is absent in the entire P.

Moses acknowledged their case and additional law was pronounced after consulting YHWH for the marriage of daughters with inheritance rights. Rule and regulation like this was very important to God's people because it is God who owned the land. Every tribe had received a share. Within the tribes, the clans had a share allotted to them, as did, ultimately, the families. Kinship ties and attachment to the land were equally important social values in an agriculture-based society like ancient Israel. To forestall the alienation of family property, the law decreed endogamy for heiresses.

The Compliance of the Daughters

Vv. 10–12: According to these verses the five daughters complied with the ruling without protest in order to ensure that the inheritance would remain within the tribe. In the penultimate verse it is mentioned that the daughters marry wisely as to safeguard the just distribution of land among the tribes of Israel. Marriage within one's own tribe was prescribed in order to uphold their social status determined by property. As informed by anthropological studies marriages in ancient world are formed to keep inheritance of land within the kinship boundaries.[192]

---

[190] In Israelite society, marriage was a fundamental socio-religious principle, a community's primary norm. Men were forbidden to marry foreigners mainly because of the religious reasons as the marriage to foreign women contaminates the pure religion. *YHWH* demands no other gods other than Him. Other nations have their own gods. Here, the inherited daughters of Israel's were given the freedom to marry anyone from within their tribe in order to maintain land boundaries allotted to each tribe. Cf. Blu Greenberg, "Marriage in the Jewish Tradition," in *JES* 22/1 (1985): 3–20.

[191] Anna Vareed Alexander, *Biblical Women: Our Foremothers Women's Perspective* ed. Faria, Stella et al., (Indore: Satprachar Press, 1997), 19–20.

[192] Naomi Steinberg, "Kinship and Gender in Genesis," in *BR* 39 (1994): 47.

This evidence is used to state that the daughters' freedom of choice with regard to whom they could marry was limited.[193] It is clear that their compliance was based on the fundamental issue that is, the interrelationship between *YHWH*, land, people and *Torah*. Moreover, ancient Israelite woman did not arrange their own marriage, rather all through the period their marriage was arranged by father generally.

Summary Statement of the Law

V. 13: This particular verse which follows the grammatical structure of Leviticus 27:34, completes the entire Book of Numbers. Bruce Waltke observes that the geography and time line served as the unifying agent for the Books of Leviticus and Numbers.[194] The events in the Leviticus took place at Mount Sinai and Numbers traces the path of the Israelites from Mount Sinai to the plains of Moab. Leviticus 27:34 reads: "These are the commandments which the LORD commanded Moses for the people of Israel on Mount Sinai."[195]

The two verses expressed the same idea from two different geographical locations, and basing on this evidence some scholars claim that they belong to the same author.[196] The book concludes with the brief notice that gives divine sanction to the law enacted on the eastern side of the Jordan. The concluding formula does not belong specifically to the present chapter, but generally to the final sections of the book.[197] This underscores the fact that behind all the commands and regulations of the law was YHWH himself.

The P narrative in Numbers 36:1–12 repeats the account of the petition of Zelophehad's daughters narrated in Numbers 27:1–11. Moses through divine instructions recognized the daughters' claim as just and instituted a ruling which would affect the nation Israel. In future daughters of Israel were allowed to inherit their father's estate if they had no male siblings.

6. Evaluation on the Acts of the Daughters

The story of the daughters of Zelophehad moves from the lowest level to the highest level. The inferior status of a daughter is clearly depicted in the Old Testament. She could be sold into slavery or into concubinage. Her very life was at the disposition of her father. Biblical women are often portrayed as confined to the home while men are portrayed as out in the broader world functioning as prophets, kings, warriors. Men were obligated to support women and children. Women were given the responsibility to create families by bearing and nurturing

---

[193] Sakenfeld, "Zelophehad's Daughters," 42; Claassens, "'Give us a Portion,'" 325–6.

[194] Bruce K. Waltke and Charles Yu, *An Old Testament Theology: An Exegetical, Canonical, and Thematic Approach* (Grand Rapids, Michigan: Zondervan, 2007), 56–7.

[195] Translated from *BHS*.

[196] Waltke and Yu, *Old Testament Theology*, 57.

[197] Budd, "Numbers," in *WBC*, vol. 5, 388.

children along with so many other household responsibilities. Zelophehad's daughters represent those with the least power in the community in which they lived. Their father was dead, they were unmarried, and they have no brother. By law they could not inherit land or receive an allotment. They knew that if they keep silent then forever they would remain disconnected from land and from sustainable life. So they challenge the existing law.

The narrative makes a remarkable statement about the dignity and value of women particularly daughters as members of the congregation of Israel. They initiated an approach to Moses, chieftains and the entire people of Israel. The arena where they presented their case was in the most sacred public arena possible. It was clearly stated that these women were not hesitant to make a move unprecedented in the history of Israel by publicly taking their stand and boldly asking for their rights. Their act of boldness should be acknowledged.

They initiated significant revisions of customary practice. When a man left no son, his daughters would henceforth inherit his estate. In their effort to acquire the inheritance rights, they cleverly used the one point of appeal that stirred serious attention and that is "the preservation of their father's name."

Moses heard their case and consulted YHWH, and YHWH declared that the daughters of Zelophehad were right. The ruling was then generalized to protect daughters in the future who were in the same situation. It was through them, that the laws governing inheritance and the transfer of landed property to women were promulgated.

There are scholars like Josiah Derby and Zvi Ron, who consider the five daughters as the first feminists because they exercised an influence on the feminist aspects.[198] They were able to raise their voices in the given patriarchal and androcentric context. Indeed, their father Zelophehad's name was mentioned only because of his five daughters. The daughters are the active characters, and a cultural model of a struggle to obtain one's rights under both divine and human morality. They indeed promote the struggle for women's rights. Their courageous acts brought the rights of women to a clearer and recognized legal position within the sphere of property law.

CONCLUSION

The foregone studies revealed the daughters of Zelophehad as one of the charismatic women's stories in the Bible. They emerge as the representatives of the powerless section of people standing up for what is right. The arena where they stood is not an ordinary place, but it is a sacred place. Their act of standing in the chosen sacred place before Moses the man of God, priest, and leaders is a

[198] Josiah Derby, "The Daughters of Zelophehad Revisited," in *JBQ* 25/3 (September 1997): 169; Cf. Zvi Ron, "The Daughters of Zelophehad," in *JBQ* 25/4 (December 1998): 260–2.

courageous act—unheard of in their time particularly in the patriarchal societies of the ancient world.

The manner in which the daughters claimed the estate was remarkable. In the entire Old Testament narrative, they are the only women who stood at the entrance to the tent of meeting and made an astonishing demand using the word, "Give to us." They stand out as people who challenged the existing gender–biased law, and ensured that they change for the benefit of women.

Reading the Zelophehad's daughters' narrative in the light of the AWA and in the wider context of the Pentateuch reveals so many facts that are not mentioned in the Bible. Their case disclosed the fact that the Mosaic Law codes were not a closed law. The important issues accumulated through living experience of the laws were accorded new authority. They challenged the patriarchal system that denied justice to the daughters. They are determined to achieve justice in the name of their father. This is the story of their success. Their claim was admitted and God confirmed to Moses the provision by which Israelite daughters were allowed to inherit land.

They are real historical women who inherited the territory in Northern Manasseh. This claim has been supported by the fact that as confirmed through the above studies, their names appear as district names. Moreover, strangely their names are listed in the census list and their names are stated thrice in the biblical account. This clearly confirms that the event actually took place.

The tribal leaders' insistence that the daughters should marry within the tribe is not an infringement of the rights of the daughters if we take into account the laws prevailing that time. The tribal elders quickly realized that if daughters with inherited land married outside her tribe, the land was lost to the tribe. So, Moses as instructed by YHWH passed another verdict that, in such a case the daughter should marry within her own tribe to ensure that the inheritance would remain within her tribe. The rule for inherited daughters to marry within her tribe did not reduce her rights. If this text (36) is read keeping in mind ancient Israelite understanding of land owning system, and their unique way of maintain their boundaries, one can easily understand why the tribal elders brought the grievance. The tribal elders raised a very important issue about the preservation of the tribal inheritance. The present researcher strongly affirms that the Israelites were in a formational period, and land was allotted to each tribe equally and each tribe was expected to maintain their specific allotted boundaries. If the land is transferred to another tribe through marriage, it is a threat to the concept on which Israel's society rested that is, "the inalienability of land." Therefore, it is a text dealing with the issue of daughters with inheritance as to how the land should remain within their father's tribe. "Retaining the territorial integrity" emerged as the concern of the tribal leaders.

The daughters' narratives depict a community in which potentially disenfranchised household received justice. They are given the status of name bearers of their father and granted lawful receivers of the Sovereign's land grant. It can be said that Zelophehad's daughters were the earliest feminists of Israel. It was through their persistence that the law of inheritance was changed for all the daughters of Israel.

Chapter 5

A Critique on the Inheritance Rights of Women and Its Implication for Chang Women

INTRODUCTION

Land is an integral part of the human community and it is the only permanent and precious property which can belong to a person or a group of people. While humanity and nature are interdependent, nature sustains humanity only if humanity maintains it. For the Chang community, identity is intrinsically attached to the land. The specific aim of this chapter is to investigate and analyse the inheritance rights of Chang women (Chang is a tribe in Nagaland, in the Tuensang District). The significance of land owned by the Chang will be examined, along with an understanding of the landholding system. This chapter will further explore the status of Chang women - how girl children are treated from birth, and the different roles assigned to them. We will also examine women's inheritance rights, as protected under international and national human rights standards. This study will comprise a systematic study of Chang customary laws and discuss how they affect women. Inheritance right are an important issue because menfolk use their decision-making power on women's rights by citing and relying on customary laws. Here we attempt to offer strategies for Chang women, to claim their rights, drawing insight from women in the Old Testament (with particular reference to the act of Zelophehad's daughters – see Numbers 27:1–11).

In order to obtain a clearer picture of the situation for Chang women, the researcher has engaged in inductive field research which included questionnaires, interviews and Focus Group Discussions (hereafter, FGD).

1. Nagaland

Nagaland is a tribal state with 17 tribes, located in the north-eastern region of India.[1] The estimated population is over 1,980,602, of which, according to the 2011 Nagaland Official Census, 10,25,707 are male and 9,54,895 are female.[2] Nagaland covers an area of 16,579 km, with the climate ranging from sub-tropical to sub-temperate and the altitude from 200m to 3800m above sea level.[3] Each tribe has its distinct language, which cannot be understood by others, as well as a distinct culture and customs. It borders the state of Assam to the west, and part of the north, Arunachal Pradesh to the north, Myanmar to the east and Manipur to the south.

The state of Nagaland was a district of Assam for almost 90 years and was known as the "Naga Hills District of Assam." It was renamed the "Naga Hills Tuensang Area" in December 1957, when it became a separate administrative area. Nagaland was granted statehood on 1st December 1963.[4] It is the 16th State of the Indian Union, and comprises 11 districts: Kohima,[5] Mokokchung,[6] Tuensang,[7] Wokha,[8] Mon,[9] Phek,[10] Zunheboto,[11] Dimapur,[12] Longleng,[13] Peren[14] and Kiphire all of which are dominated by three tribes: Sangtam, Yimchunger and Sumi.[15] Kohima is the state capital.

The origin of the word "Naga"' has been a source of much debate among different scholars. The two largely accepted viewpoints are taken from the etymology of the word "Naga" and its varying connotations in the Burmese and

---

[1] Map in the appendix 1.

[2] "Nagaland Ranks 25th in Population in India," *The Shillong Times* 11/12 http://www.theshillongtimes.com (11 July 2012).

[3] Hokishe Sema, *Emergence of Nagaland: Socio-Economic and Political Transformation and the Future* (Delhi: Vikas Publishing House Private Limited, 1986), 9.

[4] Adino Vitso, *Customary Law and Women: The Chakhesang Nagas* (New Delhi: Regency Publications, 2003), 13.

[5] The home of Angami and Rengma tribes.

[6] The home of Ao tribe.

[7] The home of Chang, Sangtam, Khiamnyungan and Yimchunger tribes.

[8] The home of Lotha tribe.

[9] The home of Konyak tribe.

[10] The home of Chakesang and Puchury tribes.

[11] The home of Sumi.

[12] Dimapur, the most populated district is inhabited by Kachari, and all the tribes of Nagaland. It is the commercial centre of the state.

[13] The home of Phom tribe.

[14] The home of Zeliang, Kuki and Rongmai tribes.

[15] This is according to the 2011 census published by Government of India, "Census 2011: Government of India," http://www.census2011.co.in/census/state/districtlist/nagaland.html (9 October 2013).

Assamese languages.[16] In Burma, the Naga tribes are called Na-Ka, meaning "people with pierced ear-lobes" - a common practice among the Naga tribes. Although, it is true that the Naga ancestors, both male and female, had pierced ears to decorate themselves, this term was never acknowledged by the Nagas themselves.[17] Another theory of the origin of the word "Naga" is subscribed to the Assamese people. According to their view, the Assamese were the first people to come in contact with the Nagas. "Noga" in Assamese means "naked." The word is even used today for the Nagas, referring to the primitive people living in natural surroundings in an uncorrupted form.[18]

The place of origin is an unresolved issue, given the fact that many Nagas are nomads, moving from place to place over the centuries. Nagas are also found in three other major states besides Nagaland: Assam, Arunachal Pradesh and North-West Manipur. This dispersion of the Nagas across several boundaries is a result of British colonization. However, this research will focus on the Chang tribe of the Tuensang district, in Nagaland State. The following is an attempt to study the Chang Naga society with, firstly, a brief introduction about Tuensang District itself.

2. Tuensang District

Tuensang, which encompasses an area of 1,728 sq km, is the largest and the eastern-most district of Nagaland with its headquarters in Tuensang, from which the district took its name.[19] When the Nagaland state was created, Tuensang was one of the original districts, which, at the time, included Mokokchung and Kohima. Tuensang shares the whole of its eastern border with Myanmar. It is bordered by the Mon and Longleng districts in the north east, Mokokchung and Zunheboto in the west and Kiphire in the south. Tuensang is inhabited by the Chang, Sangtam, Yimchunger and Khiamnyungan tribes. The "Chang" tribe originates from Tuensang district. Over the past decade, the district has gradually diminished in size, with Mon, Longleng and Kiphire being formed into separate districts.[20]

---

[16] Sema, *Emergence of Nagaland*, 2.

[17] Hewasa and Venusa Tinyi, "Who were we before we Became the "Nagas:?" Exploring the Narrative Discourse," In *Nagas Today: Indigenous Discourse,* eds. Zuchamo Yanthan et al., (Delhi: Naga Students' Union, 2010), 1; Cf. Sema, *Emergence of Nagaland*, 3.

[18] Sema, *Emergence of Nagaland*, 4.

[19] M. M. Thomas, *Nagas Towards A. D. 2000, and Other Selected Addresses and Writings* (Madras: Centre for Research on New International Economic Order, 1992), 153.

[20] Brief Industrial Profile of Tuensang District, Nagaland State, 55 cf. http://dcmsme.gov.in/dips/DIPR–Tuensang–Final.pdf, (9 October 2013).

2.1. Chang Society and its People

The history of the Chang is also marked by obscurity, as with other tribes in Nagaland, due to the lack of a written language. It is said that writing was originally preserved on leather which was eaten by the villagers during a time of famine.[21] It is believed that the term "Chang," is derived from the toponym "Changsang,"[22] Tribal tradition holds it that the tribe emerged from the earth at a place called "Changsang," which at present is situated between Tuensang village and Hakchang village (Hakchang is one of the Chang villages).[23] Their history maintains that trees and tigers were their friends. They claim that the tiger taught them how to make fire by rubbing its paws.[24]

A devastating flood hit the village and compelled the inhabitants to move to the top of *Ngakuson* mountain for shelter.[25] On sensing the danger of the havoc the flood was causing, a beautiful girl, called *Momola* was sacrificed by her mother, who drowned her, after which sacrifice the flood abated. Even today this catastrophe, which passed into folklore, is referred to as "Momola's flood." On account of this tragic incident, the tribe abandoned Changsang and migrated to different areas.[26]

Religion

Animism (a belief in the existence and manifestation of spirits, both benevolent and malevolent), was the religion of the Chang people before the advent of Christianity. Animism, in its broadest sense implies the attribution of a living soul to inanimate objects and to natural phenomena, as well as to the existence of soul or spirit - as distinct and apart from inert matter. It is derived from the word "anima," which originally meant "breath, life force or soul."[27] The onset of troubles was always attributed to the evil spirit. People expressed their awe of the beings, and their fascination for solving the mystery of existence through animism.

2.2. Formation of a Village

The Chang people lived in autonomous village settings – i.e., each village being predominantly run on the principles of democracy, in the form of republic. In the

---

[21] B. B. Kumar, *Society and Culture in a Corner of Nagaland* (Meerut: Pragati Prakashan, 1998), 2.

[22] Chang literally means "East," and Sang means "village."

[23] Nyimangyang, "A Comparative Studies of the Feasts and Festivals of Chang Naga and Israelites," (BD Thesis., Senate of Serampore College/University, 2000), 5; Cf. Impongsoted Chang, *Lilangkhala Khun: The Chang Naga Women Headgear*, (Dimapur, Nagaland: Impongsoted Chang, 2014), 3.

[24] Interview with Mr. Kelap, a senior citizen from Tuensang village (9 May 2014).

[25] Name of the mountain.

[26] An interview with Kelap, Tuensang village (9 May 2014).

[27] Sema, *Emergence of Nagaland*, 35.

past, all tribes existed as independent village societies.[28] In the process of village formation a man from any clan was able to become the head (founder) of a village. One of his responsibilities was to take at least one person from every clan, as no village could be predominated by just one or two clans:[29] intermarriage within the same clan was unacceptable.

2.3. Morung (*Haki*)

The word *Morung,* which in Chang is "*Haki,*" is understood to have derived from the Assamese word meaning "big tree."[30] In olden days it was believed there was a practice of keeping a drum made of big tree near the bachelors' dormitory, so the Assamese people called the dormitory itself *Morung*. It was a bachelor's dormitory, a social institution rather more than the present modern educational institution.[31] Traditionally, on attaining puberty, the male members of the village were required to live away from the family (including female members) and enter the *Morung,* to train in the community spirit. They were taught cultural values, norms, and ethics, and provided systems for the functioning of the village. They were separated into age groups, the highest of which was responsible for teaching the younger groups. Each age group had its own responsibilities. However, *Morung* was considered by missionaries as the house of the heathen, and therefore against Christian values.[32] Consequently, with the advent of Christianity, *Morung* was slowly replaced by a modern education system.

2.4. The Chang Traditional Administrative System

The village is considered the foundation of Chang society - the largest political unit that is found in other Naga tribes.[33] It is the most important part of their lives because the tribe's identity is drawn from the village. Family, clan and village affiliation play an important role in Chang society. The clan system is a customary one among the Chang tribes and consists of a number of families with a common ancestor, under patriarchal control.[34] In many ways, it is the clan that gives security

[28] Charles Chasie, "Administrative and Social Factors: The Change in Naga Society" in *Naga Society: Continuity and Change,* ed., Neivetsi Venuh, (Delhi: Shirpa Publications, 2004), 129–39.

[29] Kumar, *Society and Culture*, 3.

[30] Mar Pongener, *Morung Speaks: Cultural Values and Elements for the Enrichment of Naga Christian Community* (Mokokchung: CTC and the TDCC, 2011), 15.

[31] M. Sashi Jamir, "The Impact of Modernization on the Nagas: Anthropological Analysis and Theological Response, 8." in https://sashi2jamir.files.wordpress.com/2012/07/the-impact-of-modernization-on-the-nagas1.pdf.

[32] Jamir, "Impact of Modernization," 18.

[33] Pongener, *Morung Speaks: Cultural* Values, 54.

[34] Like other tribes in Nagaland, Chang is also a patriarchal society. There are number of definitions for the term "patriarchy." Etymologically it means the "rule of the father," and politically it denotes a hierarchical society in which power resides in the male property-owning father-figure.

and stability to the members by maintaining cohesive and strong ties. Only the male members perform the role of citizens, constituted by chosen representatives of the different clans.[35]

Clan

Every village consists of three or more clans, and each clan is sub-divided. There are five principal Chang clans: first, *Chongpho* which, again, is sub-divided into Shangdi, Houngang, Hagi-ong and Ongpang; second, *Ong*; third, *Lomou*; fourth, *Kangshou* and finally, *Kudamji*.[36] The clan is responsible for protecting the entire community from within and outside. The Chang clans have specific functions allotted to each of them – for example, the clan *Ong* is a priestly clan and *Houngang* appoints the dates on which various village activities and festivals take place. This is because they did not follow the Gregorian calendar but appointed the dates according to the phases of the moon. They are also responsible for communicating any information to the villagers and to delegating works. They act as peacemakers and messengers. The clan *Kangshou* is responsible for sowing the first seed, harvesting and eating the first harvest. The clan *Lomou's* responsibility is to clear the path to the agricultural fields and construct and repair bridges. When there is an infestation of any kind, e.g., locusts, rats, etc., which attack the crops, a ritual is performed by a man from this clan to ward off destruction. The clan *Kudamji* is responsible for rituals inviting rain during times of drought, and good weather in times of flood.[37] This is how every village functioned smoothly, with each clan diligently engaged in their assigned responsibilities.

Head of the Clan

The head of the family becomes the head of the clan and his sons and paternal cousins constitute the clan. As to succession, the surviving eldest son succeeds to become head of the clan. If there is no son then the eldest surviving brother of the chief automatically assumes the role.[38] This system excludes women from any kind of leadership role and therefore women are denied the opportunity to

---

Patrilineal refers to inheritance law that allowed property to be passed from a father to sons, or male members of the family. Cf. Deborah W. Rooke, "Patriarchy/Kyriarchy," in *The Oxford Encyclopedia of the Bible and Gender Studies:* vol. 2 eds. Julia M. O'Brien, et al., (Oxford: Oxford University Press, 2014), 1.

[35] Asangla Paul, states clearly about Naga women's identity and how particularly in Ao Naga culture women are systematically denied the membership in the village, which means that women are not citizens of the village. Cf. Asangla Lemtur Paul, "Naga Women or Women in Nagaland?: Denied Identity," in *Women's Issues and Reflections* ed. Christina Manohar, (Delhi: ISPCK, 2012), 84-5.

[36] An interview with Kelap, a senior citizen form Tuensang village (9 May 2014).

[37] An interview with Limba on 26 October 2015.

[38] An interview with Limba on 26 October 2015.

exercise any form of power or power-sharing or position of importance within the clan.

Formation of the Village Council

According to tradition, each clan in the village selects their representatives to form the village council. Normally the eldest male of the clan is selected. Women are excluded from this role and they have no direct representation on the village council. The chief and the village council constitute the highest court of justice. All kinds of disputes and cases that arise in the village, such as land disputes, thefts and divorce - along with criminal cases, are decided and settled by the village council.

In the traditional governing system, membership is on a clan basis where each clan appoints a male representative to serve on the village council. That means only males experience the role of acting in the public domain while females are restricted to domestic duties. Only male members are called for public meetings, where all crucial policy decisions are made.

3. Importance of Land

In general, the Nagas hold land as the primary gift from God, hence they are not expected to use it as a commodity for sale, because humans are merely its custodians. This is very close to the biblical understanding of land. The Old Testament teaches that the land belongs solely to YHWH. "You shall not sell the land in perpetuity, for the land is mine" (Lev. 25:23). We also see that the Psalmist in Psalm 24:1 declares: "The earth is the Lord's and the fullness thereof." The reference to "earth as the Lord's" is also referred to in the New Testament in that creation is the product of Christ (John 1:1–2), where Christ is identified as the creator of all things (Col. 1:16).[39] It is the village, clan and individual that use the land but the act of stewardship is within the wider understanding that the land belongs to the Supreme Being.

For the people of Chang, the most significant economic asset, as well as a source of social status, is land. Land and its boundaries are zealously guarded and any encroachment or disputes are strictly dealt with. The land system has its origin in the foundation of the village. Land is sacred for the Chang people. It occupies a central place in the tribal worldview. Rosy Baroi has rightly pointed out that, for Nagas in general, land is the source or origin, nourishment, support and identity.[40] It is not only sacred, the Nagas depend on it for their sustenance and thus their social, religious and economic systems are centred on the land. Land is their identity, so it is more than the means of production. Thereby, the struggle

[39] Samuel Richmond Saxena, "Tribal's and Ecology: A Theological Response," in *ATJ*, eds. Bishop D. K. Sahu et al., vol. 4, (2014), 39.

[40] Rosy Baroi, "The Land and the Tribal Identity: A Naga Womanist Quest for Identity," in *MJT* 3,4/1,2 (2013): 85.

for land rights is a struggle for identity and justice. It belongs to all, with equal rights and equal freedom to live on it.

It is the community that takes primary responsibility for the stewardship of land, so the gift of land is shared by all community members.[41] In this communitarian ownership, every person in the community has a share in it. The Chang chiefs did not have an exclusive monopoly on the land. Each village has its village boundaries marked by natural boundaries such as streams, ranges, etc.

The fact is that ownership of land remains the monopoly of the menfolk: women are denied the right to inherit, thereby uprooting them from their traditional earth-centered life and culture.[42] Thus, this section attempts to explore the importance of land and the system of land ownership to further ascertain how far Chang women are considered as equal partners because their identity and rights to citizenship are drawn from the land.

3.1. Types of Land Ownership

There are two types of land ownership - private land and clan land. Private land, as the term implies, belongs to families and access to this land is mainly through inheritance. Clan land is common land owned by the villagers for common purposes, such as village reserve forest, playground, grazing ground, etc. No person, other than members of the village, has the right of being the co-owner. In this case a person becomes a co-owner by virtue of being born in that village.

3.2. Pattern of Land Owning System

As with other Naga tribes, the Chang tribe has strict rules regarding the landholding system, guided by their customary laws. Every village has a strict boundary with the neighbouring villages. Each clan then occupies a defined area of land. When an outsider or a new member comes to settle in a village, he can choose which of the clans he would like to join. The Chang tribe is also a patriarchal society, so the practice of both communal and private land ownership follows male succession – i.e., only male has the right to inherit. The principle of patrilineal descent is strictly followed - that is, the father-son-brother line of inheritance. The man has complete control over property rights.

The question immediately raised, therefore, is how can the traditional communal ownership system purport to promote justice and protect the entire community from exploitation when women are denied the right to inherit land? The land ownership right is acquired by becoming a member of the community,

[41] Nirmal Minz, "Tribal Perspective on Ecology," in *The Tribal World View and Ecology*, eds. A. Wati Longchar and Yangkahao Vashum, Tribal Studies, (Jorhat: TSC, 1998), 4.

[42] Bhatla, expresses that in many developing countries, including those in South Asia, laws, policies, cultural and customary practices restrict women's ability to own or inherit property, and as a result it contribute to their vulnerability. Cf. Nandita Bhatla, et al., "Introduction," in *Property Ownership & Inheritance Rights of Women for Social Protection–The South Asia Experience*, eds. Pradeep Panda et al., (New Delhi: International Center for Research on Women, 2006), 4.

therefore, by denying women the right to ownership of land they are also denied membership rights of that community. Without a land right there is a question of identity as equal citizens. This practice further made women completely dependent on men, forcing them into an inferior, lowly status, deprived of opportunities.[43] Since, for Chang, land is an important asset that dictates identity and status, the system of oppression should not preserve it. Women should not be regarded as strangers who cannot inherit land.

4. Status and the Role of Chang Women

The term "status" refers to an individual's position in the social structure, thus the status of women is defined by their role and responsibilities in society. To write about the status of Chang women is rather a challenging endeavour, as there is no substantial written information available. Therefore, this research depends mainly on questionnaires, personal interviews and FGD. It also includes personal observations and some references from written sources that are available.

In order to reinforce the findings of this research work, the researcher sent questionnaires to both men and women, aged 20 upwards. The data-based findings are as follows:

Questionnaire Finding–Table No. 1

The questionnaire was sent to 250 people with a view of obtaining statistical data on the perception of the status of Chang women in society.[44] The question posed, and the four reply options that were used in the questionnaire, together with percentage responses from the 229 replies received were as follows.

1. Are women given equal leadership opportunity in any kind of organizations?

1. Yes.	(31.4%)
2. No.	(42%)*
3. Lack of self-confidence.	(17.9%)
4. Can't say.	(8.7%)

*Out of 229 respondents, 96 people (45 females and 51 males) opted for this category (i.e., 42%).

From these results, the study confirms women are not given an equal leadership opportunity in any kind of organization.

As everyone is assigned specific roles in society, so "role" is the determining factor. Unfortunately, however, the role of women is largely confined to the home and they are not assigned many major roles beyond it. Some claim that

[43] In an interview with Yimtsusangla, an advocate, she expresses that, from the very beginning women are made to depend on the male members in the family because of which they still lack confidence to take leadership. This is also the observation of the researcher (12 May 2014).

[44] The complete questionnaire is in Appendix—2.

Chang women enjoy special honour, respect and equality with men. There are arguments that atrocities against women are relatively unknown, and there are no problems of dowry, child marriage or caste distinction. Nevertheless, these alone cannot exclude the existence of gender inequality and discrimination that exists, in disguise, in various dimensions. In most families, women are not permitted to altercate with men and are not permitted to defend or assert their rights.[45] They are expected to be submissive, and, in part, this explains the relative absence of domestic violence in society. In order to be socially acceptable, a woman must conduct herself within the behavioural custom endorsed by patriarchal approval.

Talking about women in India, R. L. Hnuni, a prominent Indian biblical feminist scholar, states that women begin to suffer right from their childhood and that this multiplies as they grow towards maturity and attain motherhood. She also agrees that they own nothing in the household throughout their life.[46] In his article, Sao Tunyi asked the question, "Is there gender inequality in Nagaland?" To prove the answer right, he shared an experience he had in one of the villages in Nagaland. In his capacity as a member of a team studying infant and maternal mortality, he travelled to several villages in Nagaland, interacting with village council members. At a meeting held in one of the villages, 52 male members of the village council attended. On being asking the reason that there was only "male only" representation, the explanation given was that the Naga villages are run in accordance with Naga customary law, where women are not entitled to be enforcers of the law.[47] This is the pervasive male dominant attitude that prevails everywhere, both in rural and urban areas. These structures and systems need to change. The problems faced by Chang women on a daily basis are basically similar to those faced by women in different States in India. The Changs, being a male-dominated society espousing gender inequality, are the main cause of suppression of their status and freedom.

Christening of a Child

In human society, both male and female contribute equally. However, customs and traditions frequently fail to give women equal rights. Discrimination of women starts right from birth, as mentioned earlier. When a child is born certain norms are still observed, especially regarding the christening of a child. They differ, according to the sex of the child and are still practised today. For a male child, the prohibition period lasts for six days after birth and, for a female, five days. A boy child is named on the sixth day and a girl child on the fifth day. Once

[45] Interview with Ayang from Nakshou village on 9 May 2014. The same view was expressed by (Ms) Yongching from Tuensang village.

[46] R. L. Hnuni, *Vision for Women in India: Perspectives from the Bible, Church and Society* (Bangalore: Asian Trading Corporation, 2009), 60.

[47] Sao Tunyi, *Is there Gender Inequality in Nagaland*, http://morungexpress.com/is-there-gender-inequality-in-nagaland, in Editorial column December 10th 2015, (14 December 2015).

this prohibition period is over family members, along with the mother resume their daily activities. So, in the case of a boy child another day of rest was added.

Children's Day

Generally women were excluded from certain social events. For Chang, for example, Children's day is a festival celebrated during winter, which is celebrated under the trees.[48] This festival is marked by a procession of the elder sons of every family carrying items of food. Decorated stars are hung on the trees signifying the number of sons in the family. Female children are not permitted to participate. The food parcels are shared by all while the stars are kept hanging on the trees.[49]

Naknyulem

Naknyulem literally means "festival of victory over darkness." It is one of the major Chang festivals, which is celebrated during winter - usually in the second week of January.[50] On this occasion bread is made by using sticky rice, and distributed among the children. A boy child is given six pieces and a girl child, five. It is said that the number of pieces signify difference in the strength of male and female.

Again, in Chang society, the trunk of a tree signifies the male and the leaf signifies the female.[51] When the wind blows the weak leaves are blown away by the wind in whichever direction it is going. Likewise, every Chang woman is considered as a leaf that can be taken away in marriage by any other clan or community member. In exercising her right to speak, she would be condemned as ordinary and as useless as a "leaf." This is often the attitude of the menfolk, who always consider women as the weaker sex, right from childhood.

When the issue of the women's role arises, it is often argued that women - especially Naga women as a whole - have all the privileges.[52] However, this observation is not to be taken at face value. The only determining factor would be to examine their ground-level realities and actual living conditions. Equality with men includes sharing power in policy and decision making at various levels. The unbalanced gender relations in Chang society, as in other Naga tribes, is created by a rigid dichotomy between the private sphere represented by home, and the public sphere represented by the outside world of governance and decision-

---

[48] Although it is not commonly celebrated at present, but in olden days this festival was celebrated with much fervour.

[49] Kumar, *Society and Culture*, 10.

[50] "Naknyulum; conquest of "darkness by light," in *Nagaland Post,* an article issued by Chang Khulei Setshang, (Chang Tribal Council), July http://www.nagalandpost.com/PostMortem, (24 July 2015); Nyimangyang, "A Comparative Studies of the Feasts and Festivals of Chang Naga and Israelites," *BD Thesis.* Senate of Serampore College/University, 2000, 18.

[51] Interview with Nokching, Tuensang village on 24 May 2014.

[52] In an interview with K. N. Somba from Tuensang village, he expresses that Chang women have all the privileges, she enjoys equal status as men, but this is not true. Interviewed on 25 October 2015.

making. Male dominance is still prevalent in Chang society where the exclusion of women is evident in every aspect of life. Women perform the role of a wife, mother, child bearer, food producer, and household manager. They are assigned all the strenuous kinds of work in close proximity to earth's resources.

In ancient times, headhunting was carried out without the involvement of women but when the men were away hunting for heads day and night, it was the women who took care of all family matters. Feasting is not possible without the involvement of women in preparing meals. Their cooperation and support is vital, to ensure their husbands' status. Yet women have no right to the custody of their children or marital property upon divorce, and this leaves them in a very vulnerable state.

Women who are spinsters, widows and divorcees are called *latnyu* in Chang. They have the right to live in their father's house during their lifetime. If they decide to remain single, a house will be built for them alongside the clansmen. Their needs will be provided for by their late husbands' relatives. The costs and needed materials would be collected from among the deceased husband's clan members. If the house needed repairing, the clansmen would take a day off from their personal work to effect repairs. In this way, widows were under the protection of the men, who had been taught to protect and defend women from their childhood.

4.1. Marriage

Marriage plays an important role in the life of women. Put very briefly, in Chang society it is not only a couple uniting in matrimony, it can also be likened to the ancient Israelite society whereby two families and two clans are joined together, through marriage. Marriage with one's people is encouraged because it is believed that marrying into one's culture and tradition strengthens the village. More importantly, the woman's family can keep watch, to ensure her security and safety. For these reasons, exogamy is strictly followed in marriage. A woman who marries outside the village is considered "lost" and so violation of this tradition results in the woman being banished from her family and the community, and she would have to follow her husband.

4.2. Bride Price

The bride price was paid by the man to the bride's family as compensation for the loss of a worker because a woman plays a vital role in the family economy.[53] This, again, is a clear indication that women are considered as chattels since the respective family would have been compensated on the woman's departure to her spouse's house. Generally, women are given only movable gifts, depending on the family's wealth. Today very few parents, especially in urban areas, give gifts of equal value to children of both genders. They share their property equally with all

[53] This is still practiced in rural areas.

children without any distinction.[54] Anything given to a daughter on her marriage is essentially considered as gift to the woman.

Questionnaire Finding—Table No. 2

A questionnaire was sent to 250 people, of which 217 people (100 females and 117 males) responded. The questions, and the four options which were used in the questionnaire are as follows, together with the results of the findings:[55]

1. What are the things given to women as her inheritance during marriage?

1. Perishable item	(59%)
2. Land	(15.2%)
3. Both	(23.5%)
4. Can't say	(1.8%)

From these results, therefore, it is seen that women are given mainly perishable items at the time of their marriage.

4.3. Divorce

Divorce takes place generally on account of adultery, incompatibility, barrenness, abusive treatment, and misunderstanding within families. Divorce settlements are made according to traditional (customary) law. The ratio of things the wife brought with her and added to the marriage plays an important role during divorce – it is divided equally between husband and wife. However, the wife does not get custody of the children. In the case of divorce, the concerned parties will inform the families. In its initial stages, the family will try reconcile the couple. On failing to unite them, the respective families will inform the clan elders (known in Chang as *chempen)* who act as negotiators. The families, along with the clan elders from both parties will arrange the date and preside over the divorce proceedings. Reasons for the divorce will be heard from the couple. At the end of the hearing, if it is decided that one of the parties was at fault or had committed a mistake, then that party is denied any share of property they had acquired since the marriage.

4.4. Steps to Uplift Women's Status

In general, women are subordinated, degraded and made to depend on men, who often considered women to be inferior. Socially, women's status is low because she is occupied in unpaid and unacknowledged domestic work The birth of a daughter into the family was regarded as a calamity.

In order to support these findings of this project, the researcher sent questionnaires to both men and women aged 20 years and upwards. The people were asked what should be done in order to improve the status of women in society.

---

[54] An interview with Alepla (teacher) from Litim village on 4 May 2014.

[55] The complete questionnaire is in Appendix—2.

Questionnaire Finding—Table No. 3

The questionnaire was sent to 250 people and 188 people (89 female and 99 males) responded. The question and five options, together with the results, were as follows.[56]

1. What steps should be taken in order to uplift women status?

    1. Education: 37.2%
    2. Give awareness about their Rights: 26.1%
    3. Equal leadership opportunity: 21.8%
    4. Take good care of the domestic affairs: 12.8%
    5. Can't say: 2.1%

Therefore, these results show that women need to be given proper education, along with an awareness about their rights and equal leadership opportunities, in order to improve their status in society.

5. Different Roles Played by Women

Before the advent of Christianity, the neighbouring villages were hunting for each other's head. In order to protect themselves from enemies, men usually assume the role of guarding their village. On the other hand, women took responsibility for domestic affairs and agricultural work, along with raising children.[57] Today there is peace between neighbouring villages; head hunting has been abolished. However the distinction of work between men and women still exists, even though the situation has changed completely. The trend of those days - different gender roles - still prevails where women of all categories do all types of domestic work.[58] The gender role of the past is used to bind her to the traditional position in society. It is estimated that, in Nagaland, about 65.2% of women are engaged in agricultural work as cultivators,[59] as they are seen to be closer to mother earth. Women are also seen engaged in less organized sectors of work such as daily wage labourers, vegetable and processed food vendors, along with traditional work such as weaving, cooking, and sewing.[60]

---

[56] The complete questionnaire is in appendix—2.

[57] Gender roles are socially constructed norm and not biologically determined. Cf. Omega Bula, "Threat to Women's Rights and Dignity: Tourism and Gender in Africa," in *Deconstructing Tourism Who Benefits? A Theological Reading from the Global South*, series No. 6. eds. Caesar, D'Mello, Wati Longchar, and Philip Mathew, (Taiwan: PTCA and SCEPTRE Kolkata, 2014), 118.

[58] Writing about Angami Naga women, Aphuno Chase Roy, also states that a war culture has promoted a patriarchal society. Cf. Aphuno Chase Roy, *Women in Transition: Angami Naga Women from 1878 to the Present* (Kohima: ACLS 2004), 32.

[59] "20 years since the Beijing Declaration, where do we stand?" *The Morung Express* http://www.morungexpress.com/express_review (December 2015).

[60] Z. K. Pahrii, "Naga Women Vegetable Vendors in Nagaland," in *Sandeshbharika: Women and Environment*, (2015), 21–5.

5.1. The Role of Women in Politics

In wider Nagaland, there is not one woman legislator in the 60 member state legislative Assembly. It is a matter of great concern that even after more than 56 years of statehood, the voice of half of the population is not represented in decision-making bodies. Their contribution in the field of politics is seen only as voters. They are unable to be elected in male dominated elections.[61] It is to be appreciated that, during the last Nagaland general election in 2014, two women contested seats through their own initiations. Even though they were not elected, the steps they have taken is historic. Since all parties are dominated by male leadership, preference is given to the male candidates. As clearly expressed by Moanaro Jamir, traditional attitudes continue to influence the involvement of women in politics, because politics are viewed as an area where only men can become actively involved.[62]

In village administration, all forms of leadership are undertaken by men, whether or not they are literate. At present, a minimal number of seats have been reserved for women. The Chang villages are always headed by male leaders (known as "village Chairman"). Not one woman was given this particular leadership opportunity as they are always regarded as being incompetent.

The Ao tribe is one of the major tribes in Nagaland. In this society as well, the highest administrative power was held by the village council and women were not given any role. The patriarchal society does not provide any place for women to exercise their leadership ability, and were even denied membership in any decision-making bodies. It is strongly held that important decision making is not the proper role of women, who, in this respect, are certainly regarded as inferior to men.[63]

In an interview with K. N. Somba, (a prominent senior citizen from Tuensang village) regarding women's leadership in society, he confirms although women are not given leadership responsibility in village administration and political realm, they are given roles and are active in every other aspect.[64] This clearly represents female subjugation, because all major decisions are taken there: the male dominated society thus restricts women from taking part as equal participants. These days, in political organizations, there is only a token representation of women.

---

[61] Toshimenla Jamir, "Engendering Public Space in Naga Society: Tradition and Modernity," in *Indian Folklife*, No. 33 (2009), 20, http://www.indianfolklore.org/journals/index.php/IFL/article/view/108, (11 November 2014).

[62] M. Imchen Jamir, "Role of the Ao Women in Church and Society," in *IJT* No. 37 (1995): 48.

[63] Jamir, "Role of the Ao Women," 47– 8.

[64] Interview with K. N. Somba, Tuensang village (25 October 2015).

Questionnaire Finding—Table No. 4

A questionnaire addressing the issue of women's leadership was sent to 250 people, of which 205 people responded. The question, the three options and the results of that survey are as follows.[65]

1. Do you believe there will be any advancement in the society when there are more women in leadership?

1. Yes:	60%
2. No	24.4%
3. Can't say	15.6%

This result seems to indicate that people believe women are capable of taking on leadership rules and, in general, they also believe in the advancement of society under their leadership.

5.2. Role of Women in the Church

Chang churches today still remains male-dominated in terms of its leadership and decision making.[66] It continues to marginalize and ignore women through their interpretation of the Bible, which gives men dominance. The subordinate role played by women in the Church is reflected in the role allowed them by the men who control the church.[67]

The *Chang Baptist Lashuong Thangyen* ("CBLT"), brings all the Chang churches together.[68] The Executive secretary is elected for a term of five years and can be re-elected for a further five year term.[69] To date, his position has always been filled by men.

There is a department for women in CBLT (with a female secretary who also acts as the head of the office), and an evangelist. This is one arena where women play leading roles. This office brings all the Chang Baptist women together. All the annual events are proposed by the *Chang Baptist Thangyen Sao*, ("CBTS") and the women's department in the local churches carries out the various responsibilities

[65] The complete questionnaire is in Appendix—2.

[66] In an interview with Achila, one of the prominent senior woman pastors, rightly points out that, no matter how educated, spiritual and experienced women are, they are not given the rightful place in the church (17 May 2014).

[67] Limatula Longkumer states that, Christian theology contributes towards women's subordination and exclusion in ecclesial ministry. In formulating feminist methodology, she highlights the importance of deconstruction. She clearly states: "Critiquing of and deconstructing existing male biased Christian Theology is the task of feminist theology." The feminist theologian has the task to deconstruct the established theories and methods that have been used to exclude and oppressed women in the church. Limatula Longkumer, *Women in Theological Education: Pedagogical Issues* (Bangalore: BTESSC, 2012), 94–5.

[68] Chang Baptist Churches Association.

[69] Interview with L. Ongmang former Executive Secretary, CBLT, (10 January 2016).

assigned to the local churches by CBTS.[70] But, all the annual events must first be approved by the general committee, dominated by men, and the committee members have the right to accept or reject them. It is time the churches take up the cause of the empowerment of women and equal acceptance in society. As stated by Evangeline Rajkumar, there are many women who have excelled in roles of leadership, yet the Indian Church is also a patriarchal church, so women are denied leadership roles.[71]

Today in Chang society, there are many qualified theologically trained women who are competent of taking on leadership responsibilities, and yet, but as men dominate leadership roles, women are not given their rightful place within them. There are only two ordained women in Chang churches. It should be noted here that, on 14 July 2014, the Church of England voted to allow women bishops.[72] It was indeed a historic decision, which overturned centuries of tradition in a church that has been deeply divided over the issue, and finally the decision has been taken. Another historic development was the consecration, on 29 September 2013, of Eggoni Pushpa Lalitha, from the Church of South India Diocese as the first woman bishop of India.[73]

When the issue of women's leadership in the church is discussed, scripture is often used by men to justify their claim, for example, 1 Corinthians 11:3–9; 14:34–35 but no effort is made to understand its historical context.[74] Other important factors that limit women's leadership role in the Church are cultural and traditional – basically that only men assume leadership roles as dictated by cultural norms. This patriarchal nature continues to influence decisions regarding the appointment of women in positions of leadership.

5.3. Role of Women in the Domestic Economy

Women have so many impediments that bind her to hearth and home. They are mostly confined within the four walls of the home and men are usually engaged outside it. For Chang women, agricultural activity is the main outdoor occupation. Certain occupations – for example, rearing livestock, growing orchids, weaving, and selling vegetables or finished products - along with child rearing and education are exclusively assigned to women. Weaving, which is exclusively the domain of women, contributes extensively to the family's economic growth. Children's education, management of the household, and so many other needs

---

[70] Chang Baptist Women Association.

[71] Evangeline Anderson Rajkumar, "Practicing Gender Justice as a Faith Mandate in India," in *SWC* 13/1 (January 1, 2007): 44.

[72] Stephen Castle, "Church of England Votes to accept Women as Bishops," *The New York Times* 14/14, http://www.nytimes.com/2014/07/15/world/europe (14 July 2014).

[73] Vasudha Venugopal, "CSI appoints woman as bishop," in *The Hindu,* http://www.thehindu.com/news (28 September 2013).

[74] Most of the pastors do not have proper theological background.

are met through this occupation. In fact, women contribute more because while they work equally with men in the field, they also have to work at home where men generally do not help. Domestic labour is a perishable commodity, and is one which is not recognized or protected by laws – it comes under the domain of women.[75] Basically, men control community resources and social systems while women are in charge of the family, the domestic economy and production. Generally, women have to work longer hours and travel longer distances for food, fuel, fodder, and drinking water. This increased work burden impacts not only on women's physical and emotional health but it also affects children's health and education.

One of the important issues that needs to be challenged is the division of labour, which is socially constructed. As rightly pointed out by Khatoli Khala, the gender division of labour is not a biological mechanism, it it is generated by society and culture.[76] This is an issue faced not only in rural areas but even in urban areas where all domestic work is relegated to women, irrespective of their status in the world outside her home. There still exists a stereotype attitude of the male as the breadwinner, but this is often far from the truth. The working woman's situation is even worse. No matter what position she holds in the workplace, when it comes to the family she is expected to carry out all kinds of household chores after a tiring day's work. Above that, sometimes she is subjected to filthy verbal and heinous physical abuse. It is imperative that we give this serious thought, and focus our attention on the empowerment of women. They have an active role to play in society in all spheres. The role of the male is to ensure that the female has an equal voice within the family and in society at large. Generally, women perform all agricultural operations, therefore, given the importance of women in this field, provision of education must be a priority to enable her to make critical decisions. Due to the lack of proper education, women are less aware of their rights. If women are given better education, there can be a shift from subsistence living to a market oriented economy. Irrespective of gender, everyone should have equal access to resources and opportunities. There is a wide gap between men and women in society with men having more liberty than women. This is even more frustrating where property is concerned, and the drudgery that women farmers experience. In spite of being primary food producers, women continue to enjoy no economic gain, due to the lack of land ownership rights. Women. especially farmers, are unable to access capital or credit facilities from the banks.

---

[75] Rakesh K. Singh and Renuka Ramanujam, eds., "Women's Link," in *Social Action Trust*, Women, Work and Economy, vol. 20 (December 2014), 1.

[76] Khatoli Khala, *Women and Agriculture in Nagaland: A Gender Study of Sumi Customary Law and Custom* (Kohima: N.V. Press, 2012), 60–1.

6. Pattern of Wages

In 1976 the Indian government passed an important law on wages, declaring equal pay for equal work for both genders.[77] But, for the same amount of work done, females are generally paid less and are exploited on various grounds. To demonstrate this, the Wage Pattern in certain villages was studied. The villages selected for this survey covered all the five ranges under Tuensang district, Chang tribe. An analysis showed that, of the ten villages surveyed, there was a maximum Rs 50 differential in favour of men viz: Chingmei, Chendang, Hakchang, Kejok, Buthenbou and Khudei. Three paid equal wages Noksen, Longra and Helipong. Interestingly Tuensang village (only) paid women a higher rate of Rs 200 as opposed to Rs 150 for men.

This data was collected from a sample of 10 selected villages, with selected respondents who were personally interviewed during the field research. The researcher considers the primary data gives better quantitative results as opposed to those of the official survey and the village council's record. These sample daily wage pattern gives a clear indication of wage discrimination against women in the majority of cases. Out of the ten villages surveyed, only three villages practice equal payment for both men and women, and the women labourers in six villages are paid less than men labourers even though they do same kind of work. The village male administrative body decides the wages and the women have no voice to disagree since the decision is governed by customary law. The legal provision of Article 39 (d) of the Constitution is that men and women should be paid equally for the same kind of work, but this is far from what happens in practice for Chang women.

7. Impact of Christianity on Women

As Christianity began to penetrate the Naga society, it ushered unparalleled waves of change in the belief system and in cultural practices. With the new religion was brought modern education. The conversion of Chang from their traditional belief of Animism to Christianity brought great change in the people's outlook. Even though many indigenous practices ceased, and new forms of culture were introduced, some customary practices still prevail among the Chang people. Christianity is conveniently blended with traditional customs and tradition. The church continues to be male-dominated institution. However, in the secular sphere, the concept of women's emancipation has received much attention. One cannot deny the impact Christianity has made. The village social institution for men, *Morung* was replaced by modern schools for both male and female, hospitals were founded, the practice of headhunting was eradicated, and people began to abstain from consumption of alcohol (local rice beer). Despite that, however, the advent of Christianity has not changed most of the religious laws. The customary

[77] Lucy Zehol, *Women in Naga Society* (New Delhi: Regency Publications, 1998), 8.

social practices limiting women's freedom still exist and continue to regulate the daily activities people's lives. In this connection, the following section highlights both international and national human rights laws that safeguard women's rights.

8. Women's Rights Law

8.1. International Human Rights Law

The International Bill of Human Rights laid down a comprehensive set of rights applicable to everyone, including women.[78] In spite of that, additional bills for protecting women's rights were deemed necessary to sufficiently guarantee protection of their rights. Thereafter, women's rights have been strengthened by various declarations and conventions formulated in the UN. The UN established a commission on the status of women in 1946. One of the most important declarations on which gender equality is stipulated, is the Convention on the Elimination of all Forms of Discrimination Against Women (CEDAW), adopted by the UN General Assembly in 1979, and put into effect in 1981.[79] CEDAW identifies many areas where there has been discrimination against women regarding their political and legal rights, marriage and the family, and unemployment.[80] In relation to women's property, inheritance rights, CEDAW Article 16 (1) (h) ensures: "The same rights for both spouses in respect of the ownership, acquisition, enjoyment and disposition of property."[81] Notwithstanding the provision, Governments in South Asia have failed to fulfil their duty to secure protection for women. As a result, women become refugees, or are internally displaced without access to a protection mechanism.[82] Women's insecurity in South Asia is compounded by cultural and societal situations where they still occupy a subservient position to men. Accordingly, this provision on women's rights is far from implementation.

---

[78] The International Bill of Human Rights is a term used to refer collectively to three instruments: the Universal Declaration of Human Rights, the International Covenant on Economic, Social and Cultural Rights and the International Covenant on Civil and Political Rights and its two optional protocols. Cf. Yolande Sadie, "Women's Rights in the Islamic World: An Overview of Twenty-Six Countries," in *JIS* No. 20 (2000): 63.

[79] Sally Engle Merry, "Gender Justice and CEDAW: The Convention on the Elimination of All Forms of Discrimination against Women," in *Hawwa* 9/1–2 (2011), 49–50.

[80] Merry, "Gender Justice and CEDAW," 50.

[81] "Women's Equal Property and Land Rights hold key to reversing toll of poverty and HIV/AIDS in Swaziland: A Human Rights Report and Proposed Legislation," in https://www.law.georgetown.edu/academics/law-journals/gjil/upload/1-WomensEqualProperty.pdf, 385.

[82] Oishik Sircar, "Can the Women Flee?–Gender-Based Persecution, Forced Migration, and Asylum Law in South Asia," in *Gender, Conflict and Migration* ed. Navnita Chadha Behera, (New Delhi: SAGE Publications Private Ltd, 2006), 263.

8.2. Constitution of India on Women Rights

The Indian Constitution ensures protection for women. It grants women and men equality in law and prohibits any kind of discrimination based on gender. Article 14 of the Indian Constitution guarantees equality before the law. Article 51 renounces "practices derogatory to the dignity of women."[83] Article 39(d) of the Constitution rules that the State shall, in particular, direct its policy towards securing equal pay for equal work, regardless of gender.[84] In 1976, the Government passed the "Same Payment Act" and amended it in 1987. The law now makes it mandatory for employers to pay equal wages to both men and women workers and prohibits the discrimination of women in matters of recruitment, training, promotion and transfer. The amended Act also provides for stricter punishment for violation of this mandate.[85] The question is how far the constitutional rights safeguard women's rights.

Article 371 (A) of the Indian Constitution

In 1947, when the Indian Government assumed administration of the Nagas, the existing Naga law was protected by adding Article 371(A) of the Indian Constitution.[86] For several centuries, Nagas had protected their land and resources as their birthright, as enshrined by Article 371(A). Nagas' rights over land and resources were firmly established as absolute rights as this clause serves to grant Nagaland sovereign-like status. Article 371 (A) (1) reads as follows:

(a) (iii) The Constitution of India 1949, gives "special provision for the administration of civil and criminal justice involving decisions according to Naga customary law."[87]

The women's legal system differs from country to country. These are amended from time to time, to keep pace with changes in society and respond to various other influences. Most constitutions prohibit sex discrimination, to name few: the Constitutions of Brazil, Article 5 (1), Burkina Faso 1 (3), Itaty 3 (1), Mexico Article 4, Philippines 11 (14), South Africa in Provision 1 and section 9, India 14, 15.[88] Despite the promising Constitution of India to make it a just and equitable society where both men and women enjoy equal status, the reality is disappointing, even after so many years of Indian Independence.

---

[83] Article 18, Universal Declaration of Human Rights cited by Tehmina Arora, "Religion, Law and Actualities in India Unequal children of the Same God," in *Side by Side: Gender from a Christian Perspective* ed. Beulah Wood, (Bangalore: SAIACS Press, 2007), 211.

[84] Paras Diwan, and Peeyushi Diwan, *Women and Legal Protection* (New Delhi: Deep and Deep Publication, 1994), 12.

[85] Paras, and Peeyushi, *Women and Legal*, 12.

[86] Khala, *Women and Agriculture*, 14.

[87] Customary Law will be studied in detail in the following section.

[88] Lorenzo Cotula, *Gender and Law: Women's Rights in Agriculture* (Rome: Food and Agriculture Organization of the United Nations, 2002), 6.

Though constitution grants equality and empowerment to women, when it comes to implementation from the grass roots to the topmost structure of the administration, women are confronted by problems caused by patriarchy. In addition, besides prohibiting discrimination, the Indian Constitutions also mention affirmative action clause (Article 15 {3}), India, being signatory to all major human rights instruments of the United Nations. Despite this, however, the communities in India continue to treat men and women with obvious bias.

9. Customary Law

Lorenzo Cotula defines Customary Law as "a body of rules founding its legitimacy in tradition, that is, in its claim to have applied from time immemorial."[89] Law is very important in studying the status of women in the society, and redefining is also important. All the tribes in Nagaland have their own customary laws which had existed for several centuries gaining strength to strength. It is rightly said that, Naga Customary laws are made by the Patriarchy, of the Patriarchy and for the Patriarchy.[90] In her attempt to write on the customary law of Chakhesang Naga women, Adino Vitso states that, "custom is the major source of law that regulates human behaviour in early societies in the absence of written law."[91] She further claims that, the origin of customs lies in habit. Behaviour which is a habit adopted by the people becomes a custom.[92] Then that custom becomes accepted and subsequently becomes law. She concludes custom is the oldest form of unwritten law, established by usage.[93] Over time, this has been institutionalized by the village council, under the leadership of the chieftain or the council chairman. The village council is a democratic, decision-making institution. It means the custom has now become part of the village's customary law. The customary law of Chang Naga has been shaped by agrarian structure because the life of the people mainly revolves around agricultural practices, and so the different activities carried out—habits becoming customs—were based on agricultural relations. Thus, customary law is based upon the habitual conduct of a given society. It must be studied in contrast to written constitutional laws passed by legislative bodies or organizations. It is open to amendment with the change of time and society. Today in most villages, the age-old customary laws are considered the law of the land, and the only way to maintain discipline and harmony. In fact, every civilized society should uphold the law and customs, as it offers a system of rules that secure the settlement of disputes without recourse to violence.

---

[89] Cotula, *Gender and Law*, 14.

[90] Elijah Chara, *Justice for Naga Women and the Patriarchy* in http://www.nagalandpost.com/PostMortem/PostMortem march 9/15.

[91] Vitso, *Customary Law and Women*, 2.

[92] Vitso, *Customary Law and Women*, 2.

[93] Vitso, *Customary Law and Women*, 3.

Prior to the British regime, the Naga Hills had their own laws to deal with criminal and other disputes. This pattern continued uninterrupted until the advent of British administration. The British administered Naga Hills as the frontier district of Assam from 1881 until they transferred it to the Indian Government in 1947. The British administration concentrated on maintenance of law and order in the border district. As a result the existing native customs and practices were left undisturbed.[94] Nagas were given the freedom to rule and administer their villages according to their customs and traditions. This policy continued, even after independence.

Custom is not law, but it controls the code of conduct for the members of a society and becomes the binding force of that society. The law has its source from human needs. The traditional rules were important in regulating the life of the people and maintaining social order. In general, customary laws are as old as the tribe itself. Any action was based on a natural justice. But today, sadly, customary laws are used to justify any arbitrary action. How long can the Nagas - particularly Chang – keep to the laws that are irrelevant to them in the present context? We need to re-examine the present patriarchal laws urgently, and build a consensus that makes a reality of gender-friendly behaviour at every level.

10. Inheritance Rights of Women

An inheritance right for women is important, especially for women trapped in unhappy and abusive marriages. Because their access to land and other resources are limited, they have limited choice other than to remain with the abuser.

As with women in all other patriarchal societies, Chang women do not have the right of land ownership.[95] Male members of the family alone have that right.[96] Father is the absolute owner of all property in his possession, both ancestral and acquired. Whether rich or poor, properties like a house, land, and a field are shared equally among sons. Daughters are denied the right to inherit the land, more particularly ancestral land. Fathers/brothers follow custom, especially when it relates to clan or ancestral land.[97] As Eyingbeni Humtsoe rightly states, denying

[94] Piketo Sema, *British Policy and Administration in Nagaland: 1881-1947* (Delhi: Scholar Publishing House, 1992).

[95] Nokchingsomba from Sipongsang village was interviewed regarding Chang women's inheritance rights. He states that, in terms of property inheritance rights women are in a disadvantaged position because the practice of inheritance rights passes through men and not women.

[96] In an interview with L. Chaba, on the issue of women's inheritance rights, he strongly states that he would never support women's inheritance rights. The reason he gives was "Chang women are considered as leaves." He further states that customary law does not permit women to inherit property. Such is the attitude of many educated men in the Chang society. His voice represents the majority of the Chang men who have the same attitude towards women (30 October 2015).

[97] An interview with Yimtsusangla Chang, Advocate, Tuensang District on 12 May 2014.

women the right to inherit ancestral land implies that they are of negligible importance to the village and tribe.[98]

The practice of passing inheritance through the male line is found in almost all the tribes in Nagaland.[99] If the parents are considerably wealthy and if they so wish they give landed property to daughters provided that the property has been acquired by the parents and does not belong to the clan or ancestral family. The reason for such an inheritance system was that, the society is a patriarchal one and when women marry they live in their husband's house and thus everything they own belongs to the husband's family.[100] In order to keep land ownership intact, within the same family and clan, daughters are deprived of their constitutional rights and are denied the possibility of inheriting ancestral land because of customary law, despite the fact that customary law contravenes the Indian Constitution relating to women's rights. The point to be made here is that, both men and women should have the customary right to land ownership. The land can be inherited through the right channel. A "Will" can be drawn up if the need arises for the land to remain within a particular family or clan.

A huge amount of land (ancestral property) is owned by the clan and, to date, there is no record of it having been handed on, in part or in whole, to a daughter. As stated previously, this is in order to keep land within the clan into which the woman was born. The only exception to this has been when an exceptionally rich family has given their land to their daughters on marriage. In those circumstances that plot of land would then belong to her newly established family and would never revert. She, along with her husband and children would have the right to ownership.[101]

However, the trend of exclusive male rights is starting to change in a few families, especially in urban areas. In an interview on this subject, Koma Sipong asserts, "In the past women were not given landed property, but that is no longer applicable. That system has long ben outlived and so, in today's context, land should be shared equally between daughters and sons."[102]

The most important thing that alienates women from owning land is customary law. It denies women's ownership of land, (a man-made separation from mother earth) and thereby prevents them from a direct involvement in the management and restoration of the mother earth. Women should be legally

---

[98] Eyingbeni Humtsoe, "Beyond the Kitchen and the Pew: Naga Women and Leadership Roles," in *Nagas Today: Indigeneous Discourse* eds. Zuchamo Yanthan et al., (New Delhi: Naga Students' Union, Delhi Publication, 2010), 93–4.

[99] Asangla, "Naga Women or Women in Nagaland?" 85.

[100] Interview with Y. Akala (on 29 October 2015), and Senti (14 May 2014). Akala further states that this kind of narrow understanding is not applicable anymore, therefore, she strongly claims that women should be given all the rights that are entitled to men.

[101] Interview with Akhala of Bhumpak Village (9 May 2014).

[102] Interview with A. Koma Sipong, Tuensang town (3 May 2014).

entitled to inherit property. The concept that the woman's place is in her parents' home is only a temporary one and that in marriage she assumes the identity of her husband has resulted in the unequal treatment of sons and daughters.[103]

Another important issue on a widow's property rights is that it greatly depends on where she takes shelter. If she continues to stay in the house, even after the death of her husband, she has complete control over the family's property. If she decides to remarry at her own wish, the property will be given to the children, and in absence of children, her deceased husband's kinsmen will have the ownership right.[104]

For decades, women have lacked awareness concerning their legal rights. For this reason no changes were made in the customary law because the policy was in the hands of male leaders. Such act of deliberate female seclusion meant equality was denied to women. Only when women are given space in the traditional decision-making bodies, can there be justice and equality. Independent ownership of land is one of the matters of vital importance that will help to promote the well-being and empowerment of women.[105]

Focus Group Discussion Finding

In order to further support this analysis, the researcher also used FGD, whose findings on the issue of "Inheritance Rights of Women" are repeated here. FGD played a major role in gathering the perspectives of communities about women's property ownership rights. There were 10 Focus Groups, with participants drawn from a wide age range and the majority being married. The groups were questioned on their observations about women's inheritance rights and how they might respond to the issue when their daughters were refused inheritance rights. For this research, each group met on different occasions to focus on the topic, "Inheritance Rights of Women,"[106] with particular reference to the following questions:

1. Why are women denied the right to inherit land?
2. What will be the consequence if women are given inheritance rights?
3. On what grounds are women denied inheritance rights?
4. Why cannot daughters have the same rights as sons?

These questions were discussed, in detail, by the groups. They each made an exhaustive exploration of these issues and there was an exchange of ideas, as they

---

[103] Humtsoe, "Beyond the Kitchen," 94.

[104] Interview with M. Y. Chusa (11th May 2014), the same opinion has been expressed by H. Sao from Kejok village (15 June 2015).

[105] Bina Agarwal, *A Field of One's Own Gender and Land Rights in South Asia*, (Cambridge: Cambridge University Press, 1994), in https://www.google.co.in/.

[106] It is impossible to bring out all the details of the discussions due to limited space however, important issues discussed here are highlighted.

commented to each member's point of view and the issues raised were confirmed, reinforced or contradicted, as they were raised. The result of the discussions is useful as it enables us to study the social functions of the community. It also informs about the attitude towards women in general.

Every group opined that if ancestral land is given to women then it will be lost because whatever she inherits will be inherited, in turn, on marriage, by her husband. In this connection, a proposal was made that since ancestral land is not to be sold by anyone therefore, if women inherit, then they must immediately make a "WILL," (a legal document) citing that when she dies ownership of the property will revert to the rightful lineage so the clan/ancestral land remains intact (ie with the particular clan).

The majority of the members expressed the view that, in this 21st century everyone, irrespective of their sex, should be given due respect and equal importance and that justice should not be denied to any individual on the basis of their gender. Denying a woman her inheritance rights was the main cause of her degradation in society because she is denied her rights to be independent.

The consensus was that today, women's economic vulnerability is the main cause of violence and insecurity.[107] The focus group strongly suggested that women's access and control over land, housing and property is vital for her everyday survival, economic security and physical, as well as psychological, safety. Thus, the matters of ownership, access and control over immovable assets by women emerged as a significant area that needs to be integrated into the community's law and custom.

11. Critique on Chang Customary Law

Customary law, which is handled by male leadership allows no space for women to exercise any power on this issue of land inheritance.[108] There are legal biases in the system for which reform is needed, especially in the case of inheritance law. Existing practices are defended as being part of tradition and seen as being legitimate since it has been practiced for centuries. In general, Chang women have no property rights (known as *phet-si-ek)* other than anything that might be given on marriage. As a result they are stripped of their dignity and self-worth and are forced to depend on relatives for economic and social security.

In her article, "Ao Naga Customary law," Imsopangla emphatically confirms that the Naga customary laws of inheritance still control the practice of land

[107] This is also the observation of the researcher.

[108] Sipong was interviewed regarding women's inheritance rights, and he strongly responded that he is against the women's inheritance rights because the customary law does not permit women to inherit land.

ownership. Consequently, she calls for equal rights for both men and women because land plays an important role that dictates a person's identity and status.[109]

One woman interviewee confirmed she had been disinherited from land ownership. She stated that providing a daughter with land or other property was viewed by male members of the family as a loss to the family once she married.[110] She said that socially constructed gender differences continue to be the chief source of women's oppression, with various forms of social identity and social structures being used against them.

In a context where identity is basically attached to the land, it is necessary for Chang women to claim their inheritance rights in order to re-define her identity and to do this, the customary law should be amended. That law was developed and enforced during the initial development of a tribe, to establish themselves as people with their own identity and dominance. Hence, it was important for the people to hold and maintain their claim of ownership over their land. But, in today's context, the issue is no longer applicable as each tribe has already established their ownership and dominance over their land. This same view has been expressed by Rosy Baroi.[111]

In earlier days, buying and selling land was strictly prohibited because of the concept that the land belongs to God, but today buying and selling land is widespread, especially in urban areas. The case here is that, if the need for establishing ownership and dominance has been met, and with the practice of selling and buying land so well established, so also the daughters should be given the right to inherit immovable property - along with the sons. Therefore, customary law should be amended according to present day needs.[112]

There is an instance in Tanzania where a women inherited clan land and the issue was settled in the court in her favour. In that case, a discriminatory customary land tenure rule was overthrown with the support of the Constitution and the international Human Rights Law. The facts as given in court were that, a Haya woman inherited land from her father, and she sold it to someone who was not from her clan. On hearing the news the male clan members brought the issue citing that women could not sell land under Haya customary law. Based on the principal of non-discrimination on the grounds of gender, as stated in article 13 (4) of the Bill of Rights (which was formally approved and invested with legal authority by Tanzania), the court stated that she could sell land on the same

---

[109] Imsopangla, "A Liberative Theology of Inheritance: A Critique of the Ao Naga Customary Law of Inheritance," in *Side by Side: Naga Women Doing Theology in Search of Justice and Partnership* eds. Limatula Longkumer, Talijungla Longkumer, (Kolkata: CCA-EGY Unit & Naga Women Theological Forum, 2013), 52.

[110] Interview with disinherited woman from Tuensang Town (name withheld for privacy reason, on 4 June 2014).

[111] Baroi, "Land and the Tribal Identity," 94.

[112] Finding of FGD.

conditions as men. The court therefore, pronounced that the sale of the land was valid.[113]

As mentioned above, even though the Indian Constitution has provided equal rights and opportunities for both genders, Chang society, particularly, is marked by inequalities. Temsula, chairperson of NSCW, expresses the need to look at the present social scene, which is marked by inequalities that are inherent in the traditional system relating to the social and economic status of women, especially in the case where customary law prohibits women's rights to inherit land.[114] There is an urgent need to reform the law relating to inheritance rights for women because women suffer unduly, due to legal biases in the system.

Akala Ao, rightly claims that there are four major factors that have contibuted to the Naga women's current status. They are: Naga Customary laws, Christianity, British rule and the creation of the Nagaland State within the Indian Republic.[115] She states that Christianity and British rule brought positive changes to the Naga women to a certain extent, but they failed to challenge injustices of patriarchy imbedded in the Naga customary law relating to women. She concludes that, none of the four factors could bring legal, systematic and moral changes and transform the oppressive patriarchal structure.[116] The compilations of customary rules were often created by male elders, and thus followed male-biased interpretations. Therefore, it can be seen that those rules often work to the disadvantage of women. This affects women's rights, particularly on the matter of inheritance rights.

Questionnaire Findings

A questionnaire was sent to 250 people, of which 199 people responded (96 females and 103 males) The question, options which were used in the questionnaire – and the results - are as follows.[117]

1. Are women given their constitutional right to inherit immovable property?

1. Yes	13.1%
2. No, because customary law does not permit	81.4%
3. Can't say	3.5%
4. Other factors	2.0%

[113] Cotula, *Gender and Law*, 47–8.

[114] NSCW Organizes Seminar on Legal Rights of Women in Wokha, http://www.nagalandpost.com (26 Feb. 2014). Cf. Mar Imsong, *God-Land-People: An Ethnic Naga Identity* (Dimapur: Heritage Publishing house, 2011), 169.

[115] Akala Ao, "Land and Tribal Women: A Cry for Gender Just Society," (paper presented at the Seminar on Significance of Land and its Resources Vis-a-vis Tribal Identity, Organized by the Clark Centre for Peace Research and Action, (Aolijen, Mokokchung, November 13-14, 2014), 4. Aolijen, Mokokchung, November 13-14.

[116] Akala Ao, "Land and Tribal Women," 5.

[117] The complete questionnaire is in appendix—2.

This result clearly shows that women are denied the constitutional right to inherit land because of traditional customary practices.

It is ironical that, when it comes to women's inheritance rights, the age-old practice is re-enforced. The menfolk always stick to the customary laws for every petty issue instead of rationalizing outdated and obsolete laws, which are becoming increasingly irrelevant to modern society. It is time to realize that their allegiance to those outdated practices is causing much harm to half the population (women formed almost half of the Chang population and play a vital role in it, both at home and in society generally). Times have changed: there was a time when customary laws were relevant, but today that is no longer the case. Changes in the laws are imperative, to update it and bring it in line with current times - conforming it to the changing needs of today's society.

Customary laws lack the mechanism to address modern issues such as rape, domestic violence, kidnapping, as they do not include gender specific concerns. This, perhaps, at best can be construed as a reflection of a Chang male mentality that places women under their direct protection, devoid of personal authority which was applicable only in the past. Women can no longer be treated merely as subjects to be protected or objects to be ruled over. Their personality and freedom as human beings needs to be respected and they need to be empowered by society so as to live within that society with dignity. It is very important, therefore, to promote a culture of equality in all areas between the genders.

Women's suppression under the Chang legal system of customary law is re-enforced by Article 371 "A" of the Indian Act of Constitution of 1962 by recognizing that the Naga customary law, which is applied to all the tribes in Nagaland, is always quoted, to justify gender discrimination, claiming that Nagaland is governed by that law.[118] Denying women the right to inherit land is equivalent to taking her life away, denying her human rights, and her identity as full human being. Patriarchal culture, tradition and social values are naively accepted as social, cultural and normative values in church and society and this has a direct impact on how women and their leadership is conceived, as well as how they are accepted in society.[119] This Article denigrates discrimination between male and female. Discrimination is inconsistent with the fundamental rights embodied in the Indian Constitution. It also violates the principles of Human Rights as perceived by the United Nations. Hence, there is an urgent

[118] The Article reads "Notwithstanding anything in this Constitution—(a) no Act of Parliament in respect of—(i) religious or social practices of the Nagas, (ii) Naga customary law and procedure, (iii) administration of civil and criminal justice involving decisions according to Naga customary law, (iv) ownership and transfer of land and its resources, shall apply to the State of Nagaland unless the Legislative Assembly of Nagaland by a resolution so decides."

[119] Discussing about women in North East India, Narola Imchen, clearly delineates three factors that subordinate women in leadership roles: Misinterpretation of the Scripture, traditional attitudes and cultural context. Cf. Imchen, Narola, *Women in the History of Christianity* (Jorhat, Assam: Tribal Development and Communication Centre, 2014), 190–1.

need to re-examine the customs and cultural practices currently in force, as they have such a detrimental impact on people's life. The laws of the land need amending, to ensure that they uphold equality, irrespective of gender.

12. Act of the Daughters of Zelophehad: A Paradigm for Chang Women

Having observed women's property inheritance law in the Old Testament in the light of AWA, the question arises, "How should we use the Bible to address this social issue?" Although, the biblical laws are embedded in the history and culture of that time, yet they provide us with criteria for evaluating how Scripture should be applied to our lives and culture.

The authority of the Bible, as God's word, transcends the culture and history of the time in which it was written. In the Old Testament, laws were made to protect women and slaves (Exod. 21:22). It also records that there is no-one above the law. The prophetic movements in Israel and Judah condemn the people in power, including the kings (2 Sam. 12). It was required to judge all cultures in relation to how justice was to be executed (Mic. 6:8). It has its foundation on the basis that all people are equal in the sight of God.[120]

In Old Testament times, inheritance was handed down through the male line. However, there are clear instances where women inherited ancestral land as well as private land. In fact, the right to inherit was sanctioned by God through Moses, as evident in Numbers 27:1–11. The act of the daughters of Zelophehad who claimed the ancestral land during the Israelite settlement period should be emulated. In this case, Numbers 27:1–11 is the best example of daughters inheriting ancestral land. Moses granted their petition. Hence, this biblical text is to proof that human beings are not to be bound by the laws all the time – that laws are made to enable people to live a meaningful life. But, if there are laws which are discriminatory and are unjust then there should be a way to rectify them. This is what the story of the daughters of Zelophehad says to us., This text is a constructive example for those daughters whose rights are being denied. In the same manner, the leaders should seek God's guidance in their policy making as Moses, who inquired from *YHWH* concerning the case brought by the five daughters. God's justice was extended to the daughters of Israel, so also the justice of God should be extended to Chang women.

Since the law was designed to regulate the life of the people, it was necessary for those statutes to evolve as the social situation of the people changes. Since laws are made for the welfare of the people, so they are to be changed and amended as the situation demands. This is the evidence that supports amendment of the present customary law on the issue of women's inheritance rights. The biblical law permits women to inherit ancestral land with the condition that the land should not be transferred to another tribe in their marriage. Even in the context of Chang Naga women, a "WILL" can be made so that the ancestral land does not transfer

[120] David Mark Ball, "Gender: Bible, Language and culture," in *Side By Side: Gender*, 85.

to another clan. If other male members have the right to sell, she, too must be given the right to do so. The daughters of Zelophehad were permitted to inherit the clan's land but the Chang women do not have that same right. Chang women should also draw inspiration from the acts of the daughters of Zelophehad, to move forward and claim the denied rights.

CONCLUSION

The above studies clearly show that there is inequality and sex-based discrimination so far as land ownership is concerned. It is the single most critical contributor to violations of the economic, social and cultural rights of Chang women, who suffer from oppression at many levels - economically, politically and culturally. They experience a lack of full humanity. It is customary law that has largely been a deciding factor regarding for the role and status of women.

The dichotomy of spheres based on sex was necessary in the early stage of the village formation as there were frequent raids and wars. However, the system has long outlived its usefulness and it is no longer relevant in the contemporary era. Therefore, women should be seen as an equal partner with men in all spheres of life.

Despite all these hurdles, many women could improve their social standing, from the second-class level enforced on them in a male dominated society. This is evidenced by the rise in literacy rates and active participation in fields that were originally beyond the scope of women. This is an indication that, against all odds, women are progressing towards an improved lifestyle that is full of promise.

Every Chang woman derives her identity from a village where all share the common heritage of customary laws. Despite the fact individuals have made great strides in almost every field. However, the customary laws continue to suppress women's rights. This suppression is enforced by denying them the right to be a legitimate member and participate in the clan's forum, village council, and citizens' meetings. There is a strict rule for the land holding system, whereby the patrilineal system is followed. It is time women are considered equal partners in every decision-making body. They should be encouraged to exercise their rights and assume equal participation.

There have been so many provisions, laws and policies of development services and opportunities for women. But, those constitutional rights and opportunities that ensure the protection of women are overshadowed by patriarchal customary laws. As long as the customary laws and traditional male, power-based structure remains unaltered, there will be no substantial change for women in Chang society. Social reform movements that are properly accompanied by legal reform could transform society. A lot still needs to be done in order to bring about equality in society. All these widespread exclusions of women dictated by patriarchal customary laws and practices should be completely abolished.

Like the daughters of Zelophehad, Chang women themselves should be able to take initiatives in claiming their rights that are denied. They need to break themselves free from the stereotypical image of home-maker. In order to retain their identity as children of mother earth, Chang women should unite and claim their rights, which are based on God, who is the ultimate owner and who gives, equally, irrespective of gender.

General Conclusion

The consequences of the action of the daughters of Zelophehad in seeking to inherit their father's land as described in Numbers 27:1–11 and the implications of this action for Chang women has been investigated. The Chang tribe is strongly patriarchal, and women are kept in a subordinate position in many matters. The action of the daughters of Zelophehad went totally against the patriarchal laws of the Israelites. The researcher wishes to relate this act to the current situation of the Chang women.

Throughout this investigation, the researcher has sought to reconstruct the ways in which ancient Israelite women are represented in biblical texts with reference to its representation in other non-Israelite West Asian sources. This investigation has covered status and role of ancient Israelite women by examining in detail the role of women in society, kinship structure, family and clan relationships, their status at law and in the tribal economy, their place in religious practices, marriage, and inheritance. Social scientific analysis of the Bible has helped to recover important aspects of gender in antiquity. Sources from archaeology, epigraphy along with Hebrew Bible inform about women's activities. Cross-cultural anthropological studies of the Hebrew Bible demonstrate the significant interdependence among early Israelite women and men. Kinship studies disclosed that ancient Israelite family was composed of a related nuclear families descended from the same lineage that includes up to three generations. In this structure, family was the cornerstone of Israelite society and each member in this family contributed equally to the household economy.

There was no hierarchical domination of female by male during the Iron Age I period. Closer reading and reading behind the texts, also informed by extra-biblical sources reveals the dominant contributions made by women. They enjoyed high status in the domestic realm exercising both power and authority. Women enjoyed dynamic participation in private family decisions, and this meant that as family was the most important social unit where women exercised significant power.

The issue of land and the ancient Israelites' relationship to it has been examined. The Old Testament is largely a story of the people's relationship to

YHWH through the land—the interrelationship between God, the land, Israel and *Torah*. The land has a theological significance. The land is owned by YHWH, and it is a divine gift to the Israelites. It offers them a secure home. Central to land is the *Torah* which consists of guidelines for land management, and it is part of YHWH's covenant with the Israelites. Their survival in the land is conditioned on faithfulness to the covenantal responsibilities. When the people violate their relationship with God, they pollute the sacred land and the consequence for breaking the covenantal laws is depopulation and desolation. Land is allotted to each tribe through lot and it should not be transferred to other tribe. Each family guarded its property carefully and each estate was defined by boundaries which were not to be removed.

There are land rest laws namely, Sabbath and Jubilee. Every seventh and fiftieth year, the Israelites are to allow their land to lie fallow so that the poor, strangers and wild animals can eat whatever crop is left. The land that is sold due to poverty could be redeemed by his nearest kinsmen. If there are no kinsmen to redeem the land, on the fiftieth year it reverts to the rightful owner. This also prevents accumulation of land in the hands of few rich people. We see that life in Israel is ordered by YHWH so that both the strong and the weak may live together peacefully. The law of succession and inheritance was designed by YHWH to ensure that the people would continue to enjoy their inheritance in the land. Their relationship with YHWH and their faith have rooted them in the land YHWH gave them.

AWA sources have contributed immensely to the understanding of biblical narratives. There is uniqueness in all the three ancient civilizations, that is, Israel, Mesopotamia and Egypt, yet the individual cultures of each society were not isolated from each other, but were subject to mutual influences. In all these three societies, the custom of giving pride price and dowry in marriage was practiced. Women have control over the dowry that she brought in marriage.

The foregone study unfolds two pictures about women: Firstly, women can own property; and secondly, they can act as a person in the judicial sense of the word. They had full rights to the extent of buying, selling and mortgaging. It is also true that, in most cases women appearing in the context of inheritance are related to men in one way or another, either as wives, widows or daughters. The inheritance laws aim basically at keeping the immovable property within the family. Generally wives could inherit property, but they are mostly managers of the holdings. On the contrary, evidence from Mesopotamia and Egypt shows mothers handing over real estates to the adopted daughters which the biblical authors have not mentioned.

Women are portrayed in the Bible as in a defenceless situation, robbed of their worth. Nevertheless, not all the Israelite women were in a vulnerable state and completely dependent on the male members of their family. The study of the six passages from the Old Testament (in chap. three), that dealt with women with property inheritance rights bear witness to ancient Israelite women in possession of wealth and property. They were afforded a degree of material security.

The daughters of Zelophehad represent the powerless section of people standing up for what is right. The arena where they stood is a sacred place. In the entire Old Testament narrative, they are the only women who stood at the entrance to the tent of meeting and made an astonishing demand using the word, "Give to us." They stand out as people who challenged the existing gender–biased law, and ensured that they change for the benefit of women. The opening speech by Zelophehad's daughters made outstanding claims in order to underscore their point. They refer twice to their father's death, to the fact that he had no son and to the evidence that he was not in the rebellious gathering of Korah. The importance of changing the legal concepts of women's place in society is considered and granted. The narrative makes a remarkable statement about the dignity and value of Israelite women.

Reading the Zelophehad's daughters' narrative in the light of the AWA and in the wider context of the Pentateuch revealed so many facts that are not mentioned in the Bible. Their case disclosed the fact that the Mosaic Law codes were not a closed law. The important issues accumulated through living experience of the laws were accorded new authority. Their names appear as district names, they are listed in the census list, and their names are stated thrice in the biblical account. This clearly confirms that they are real historical women who inherited the territory in Northern Manasseh.

As it has been studied, there are scholars who conclude that, the narrative is about the preservation of the father's name, that they challenged patriarchal policies for the benefit of male, "the continuation of the father's name." But, given the androcentric world in which they lived, it is argued that they have been wise enough to focus their presentation of the case on the preservation of their father's name. Indeed, their clever approach to problem-solving is admirable for its honesty and confidence.

The current position of Chang women has been reviewed. Every Chang individual derives their identity from a village where all share the common heritage of customary laws. The customary laws continue to suppress her rights by denying her to be a legitimate member and participation in clan's forum, village council, and citizen meeting.

The land gives the people of Chang economic security and social status. Chang as a patriarchal society, father has complete control over the family. A son could be dependent even though he is grown old as long as his parents are alive, but he could be independent after his parents are dead. They have the autonomous share in the family property. However, female do not have this rights. This sex-based discrimination with regard to land ownership is one of the single most critical contributors to violations of the economic, social and cultural rights of

Chang women. They experience a lack of full humanity. By and large, customary law has been a deciding factor for the role and status of women.

The UN has shown concern for women empowerment, and Indian constitution bequests women identical rights and prospects. This legislation in India not only removes the discrimination against women but also empowers the women. Yet, this constitutionally assured elementary right to property has been a failure. The existence of these laws written down in the books alone without implementation is the major problem in India. The implementation of these legislations in actual sense is unavoidable to remove the discrimination in the society.

Legislation regarding domestic violence tends to address only physical violence, but denying her property inheritance rights is also an economic violence perpetrated on women which is also a domestic violence. This economic abuse needs to be addressed

The constitutional rights and opportunities that ensure protection of women are overshadowed by patriarchal customary laws. The conclusion reached as a result of questionnaires, interviews and focus group discussions is that, Chang women need to move forward and stand up for their rights. To do this, education is essential, as it will lead her to get access to information about her fundamental rights.

This leads to the conclusion that, the leadership principle was operative in the homes of ancient Israel and in that domain women played active roles. Insights from extra biblical sources along with biblical evidences have revealed that women along with their engagement with childcare, production, and reproduction, actively involved in the endeavour to survive. They enjoyed substantial amount of autonomy and freedom where she could also own goods and immovable property. Women in ancient Israelite society did have inheritance rights sanctioned by God.

Chang Naga women are wrongly repressed and denied their 21st century rights through the practices of customary laws and a patriarchal system that refuses to allow them any freedom. The customary laws that deny women's ownership of land is a painful man-made separation of women from the mother earth. The story of five daughters should be used as an example to challenge anything that limits their capabilities. The five daughters show us that without land inheritance rights there is no identity. They represent intelligent, courage and responsible. The unjust system and structures that systematically discriminate and exclude women should be analysed and restructured so that women can also live with dignity and self-respect.

Like the daughters of Zelophehad, Chang women themselves should be able to take initiatives in claiming their rights. The daughters' determination to achieve their goal despite the odds should inspire Chang women who are experiencing powerlessness and injustice based on gender. Chang women need to break themselves free from the stereotypical image of a home maker which still remained largely unchanged. As long as these remain unaltered, there will not be any substantial change in Chang society. A lot still needs to be done in order to bring about equality in society. It is time that Chang women unite and claim their rights to land inheritance so that they can retain their identity as children of the earth because land is an important asset dictating identity and status.

This study of the story of the daughters of Zelophehad has inspired me to believe that God is on the side of disenfranchised women. However, they have to stand up and fight for their rights. My hope is that Chang Naga women and all women facing similar injustice and inequality will find inspiration in the insights of this study. I also hope that preachers and teachers of the Bible will draw fresh insights from this work to take the fight of women to the pulpits and legal institutions to restore what rightfully belong to women.

Appendix—1

(- of Chapter five)

Indian Map

Source-Appendix 1: "Tuensang District Map," Maps of India.com
http://www.mapsofindia.com/maps/nagaland/districts/tuensang.html
(30 August 2016)

Appendix—2

Questionnaire

Dear Revd/Dr/Mr/Ms. ....

The intention of this survey is to understand the status of women in Chang society with special emphasis on her right to inherit both movable and immovable properties. I would appreciate if you could kindly provide your honest opinions on the proposed questions. Your response will be used only for this research purpose and your identity will be kept confidential.

Sincerely,

Nyimangyang Chang,
Union Biblical Seminary
Bibvewadi, Pune-37
Maharashtra
E-Mail-nyimang5@gmail.com

....

Personal information

Name:................................

Occupation:.........................

Female/Male

Married/Unmarried

Age (a) 20–35 (b) 36–41, (c) 55 & above

Place.......................................

Church ....

---

1. Are women given equal leadership opportunity in any kind of organizations?
    1. Yes.
    2. No.
    3. Lack of self-confidence.
    4. Can't Say.
2. What are the things given to women as her inheritance during marriage?
    1. Perishable item
    2. Land
    3. Both
    4. Can't say
3. What steps should be taken in order to uplift women status?
    1. Education
    2. Give Awareness about their Rights
    3. Equal Leadership Opportunity
    4. Take good care of the domestic affairs
    5. Can't say
4. Do you believe there will be any advancement in the society when there are more women in leadership?
    1. Yes
    2. No
    3. Can't say
5. Are women given her constitutional right to inherit immovable property?
    1. Yes
    2. No, because customary law does not permit
    3. Can't say
    4. Other factors

Bibliography

Aaron, David H. "The Ruse of Zelophehad's Daughters." *HUCA* 80 (January 1, 2009): 1–38.

Abegg (Jr) M.G. "גדל." *NIDOTTE.* Vol. 1. Edited by Willem A. VanGemeren, et al. Cumbria: Paternoster Press, 1997, 823–7.

Ackerman, Susan. "Digging up Deborah: Recent Hebrew Bible Scholarship on Gender and the Contribution of Archaeology." *NEA* 66/4 (December 2003): 172–84.

______. *Warrior, Dancer, Seductress, Queen: Women in Judges and Biblical Israel.* New York: Yale University Press, 1998.

Adler, Rachel. *Engendering Judaism: An Inclusive Theology and Ethics.* 1st ed. Illinois, USA: Varda Books, 1999.

Ahlstrom, G.W. *Royal Administration and National Religion in Ancient Palestine.* Studies in the History of the ANE Series. Leiden: E.J. Brill, 1982.

Albertz, Rainer. "A Pentateuchal Redaction in the Book of Numbers? The Late Priestly Layers of Numbers 25–36." *ZAW* 125/2 (2013): 220–33.

Alexander, Anna Vareed. *Biblical Women: Our Foremothers Women's Perspective.* Edited by Faria, Stella et al. Indore: Satprachar Press, 1997.

Allen, Ronald B."'Numbers." *The Expositor's Bible Commentary.* Abridged edition. Vol. 1. Edited by Kenneth L. Barker, and John R. Kohlenberger III. Grand Rapids, Michigan: Zondervan, 1994, 171–235.

______."Numbers." *The Expositor's Bible Commentary with the New International Version of the Holy Bible.* Vol. 2. Edited by Frank E. Gaebelein et al. First Grove Weidenfeld Evergreen Edition. Grand Rapids, Michigan: Zondervan Corporation, 1990, 657–1008.

Allen, Troy D. "Problems in Egyptology: Ancient Egyptian kinship." *JBS*, 31/2 (November 2000): 139–48.

Alt, Albrecht. *Essays on Old Testament History and Religion*. Trans. R.A. Wilson. Garden City, New York: Doubleday, 1967.

Altmann, Alexander, ed. *Biblical and Other Studies*. Cambridge: Harvard University Press, 1963.

Amiamadu, Amadi. "A Functional Equivalence Translation of the Zelophehad Narrative in Numbers 27:1–11." *Scriptura*, 93 (2006): 293–304.

Anderson, Cheryl B. Women, Ideology, and Violence: Critical Theory and the Construction of Gender in the Book of the Covenant and the Deuteronomic Law. London: T&T Clark, 2006.

Anderson, Bernhard W., Steven Bishop, and Judith Newman. *Understanding the Old Testament*. 5th ed. Upper Saddle River, New Jersey: Pearson Prentice Hall, 2007.

Anderson, Bernhard W. *Understanding the Old Testament*. Eaglewood Cliffs, New Jersey: Prencetice-Hall, INC., 1961.

Arnold, Bill T. *Who Were the Babylonians?* SBLABS. Atlanta: SBL, 2004.

Bach, Alice ed. *Women in the Hebrew Bible: A Reader*. New York: Routledge, 1998.

Bareh, H. M. *Encyclopaedia of North-East India*. Vol. 6. Nagaland, 2001.

Baroi, Rosy. "The Land and the Tribal Identity: A Naga Womenist Quest for Identity." Edited by Atula Ao and Arjuna Rao. *MJT* 3,4,/1,2 (December 2013): 82–100.

Barr, James. *History and Ideology in the Old Testament: Biblical Studies at the End of a Millennium*. Oxford, England: Oxford University Press, 2000.

Barth, Christoph. *God with us: A Theological Introduction to the Old Testament*. Edited by Geoffrey W. Bromiley. Grand Rapids: William B. Eerdmans Publishing Company, 1991.

Barton, John (ed). *The Cambridge Companion to Biblical Interpretation*. Cambridge Companions to Religion. Cambridge, England: Cambridge University Press, 1998.

______, (ed). *The Biblical World*. Vol. 1. New York: Routledge, 2002.

Bartor, Assnat. "The Representation of Speech in the Casuistic Laws of the Pentateuch: The Phenomenon of Combined Discourse." *JBL* 126/2 (2007): 231–49.

Beal, Lissa Wray. *1 & 2 Kings*. Apollos Old Testament Commentary. Vol. 9. Illinois: IVP Academic, 2014.

Beattie, Derek Robert George. "Book of Ruth as Evidence for Israelite Legal Practice." *VT* 24/3. (July 1974): 251–67.

Behera, Navnita Chadha, ed. *Gender, Conflict and Migration*. Women and Migration in Asia Vol. 3. New Delhi: SAGE Publications Private Ltd, 2006.

Bellis, Alice Ogden. *Helpmates, Harlots, and Heroes: Women's Stories in the Hebrew Bible* 2nd ed. Louisville: Westminster John Knox Press, 2007.

Ben-Barak, Zafrira. *Inheritance by Daughters in Israel and the Ancient Near East: A Social, Legal and Ideological Revolution*. Michigan: Archaeological Center Publications, 2006.

Bendor, Shunya. *The Social Structure of Ancient Israel: The Institution of the Family* (בית־אב) *from the Settlement to the end of the Monarchy*. Jerusalem Biblical Studies. Jerusalem: Simor, 1996.

Bertman, Stephen. *Handbook to Life in Ancient Mesopotamia*. New York: Facts on file, 2003.

______. "Women in the Ancient Mediterranean World: Ancient Israel." *BR* 39 (1994): 31–45.

Bidmead, Julye. "Legal status: Ancient Near East." *The Oxford Encyclopedia of the Bible and Gender Studies*. Vol. 1 (ASI–MUJ). Edited by Julia M. O'Brien et al. New York: Oxford University Press, 2014, 403–8.

Bird, Phyllis A. "Women in the Ancient Mediterranean World: Ancient Israel." *BR* 39 (1994): 31–45.

Blenkinsopp, Joseph. "Deuteronomy." *The New Jerome Biblical Commentary*. Edited by Raymond E. Brown, et at. Bangalore: TPI, 1990, 94–109.

______. *Isaiah 1–39*. Edited by William Foxwell Albright et al. Vol. 19. AB. New York: Doubleday, 2000.

Block, Daniel I. "Judges." *Zondervan Illustrated Bible Backgrounds Commentary: Joshua, Judges, Ruth, 1 & 2 Samuel*. Vol. 2. Edited by John H. Walton, Grand Rapids, Michigan: Zondervan, 2009, 94–241.

Bloch-Smith, Elizabeth, and Beth Alpert Nakhai. "A Landscape Comes to Life: The Iron I Period." *NEA* 62/2 (June 1999): 62.

Bordreuil, Pierre, Felice Israel, and Dennis Pardee. "King's Command and Widow's Plea: Two New Hebrew Ostraca of the Biblical Period." *NEA* 61/1 (March 1998): 1-13.

Borowski, Oded. *Daily Life in Biblical Times*. Atlanta: SBL, 2003.

Botta, Alejandro F., and Pablo R. Andinach, eds. *The Bible and the Hermeneutics of Liberation*. 59. Atlanta: SBL, 2009.

Branch, Robin Gallaher. "Eleazer." *DOTP.* Edited by Desmond Alexander, and David W. Baker 2003, 214–21.

Bray, Jason S. *Sacred Dan: Religious Tradition And Cultic Practice in Judges 17–18*. London: T&T Clark, 2006.

Brenner, Athalya, ed. *A Feminist Companion to Exodus to Deuteronomy*. The Feminist Companion to the Bible Series 6. Sheffield: Sheffield Academic Press, 1994.

Brenner, Athalya, and Carole R. Fontaine, eds. *A Feminist Companion to Reading the Bible: Approaches, Methods and Strategies*. Sheffield: Sheffield Academic Press, 1997.

Bright, John. "The Apodictic Prohibition: Some Observations." *JBL* 92/2 (June 1973): 185–204.

Broida, Marian. *Ancient Israelites and their Neighbors: An Activity Guide*. Illinois: Chicago Review Press, 2003.

Brown, Francis, S. R. Driver, and Charles A. Briggs. "שְׁאֵר." *The New Brown-Driver-Briggs-Gesenius Hebrew and English Lexicon: With an Appendix Containing Biblical Aramaic*. Peabody, Massachusetts: Hendrickson Publishers, 1979.

Brueggemann, Walter. *The Land: Place as Gift, Promise, and Challenge to Biblical Faith*. 2nd ed. Minneapolis: Fortress, 2002.

______. "Reflections on Biblical Understandings of Property." *IRM* 64/256 (October 1975): 354–61.

______. "The God of Joshua . . . Give or Take the Land." *Int* 66/2 (April 1, 2012): 164–75.

Buchanan, Gray George. *A Critical and Exegetical Commentary on Numbers*. Edited by Samuel Rolles Driver et al. 3rd edition. ICC. Edinburgh: T & T Clark, George Street, 1956.

Budd, Philip J. "Numbers." *WBC*. Vol. 5. Edited by David A. Hubbard et al. Texas: Word Books, Publisher, 1984.

Bullock, C. Hassell. *An Introduction to the Old Testament Poetic Books*. Chicago: Moody Press, 2007.

Burnside, Jonathan. "'What Shall We Do with the Sabbath-Gatherer?' A Narrative Approach to a 'Hard Case' in Biblical Law (Numbers 15:32–36)." *VT* 60/1. (January 1, 2010): 45–62.

Bush W. Frederic. "Ruth." *WBC, Ruth/Esther*. Vol. 9. Edited by David A. Hubbard et al. Dallas Texas: Word Books, Publisher, 1996, 1–268.

Camp, Claudia V. *Wisdom and the Feminine in the Book of Proverbs*. Bible and Literature. Sheffield: Almond Press, 1985.

Campbell (Jr), Edward F. *Ruth: A New Translation with Introduction, Notes, and Commentary*. 4th ed. Vol. 7. AB. Garden City, New York: Doubleday & Company, 1978.

C.F. Burney. *The Book of Judges, with Introduction and Notes, and Notes on the Hebrew Text of the Books of Kings, with an Introduction and Appendix*. Edited by Harry M. Orlinsky. New York: KTAV Publishing House, 1970.

Caragounis, Chrys C. "בת." *NIDOTTE*. Vol. 1. Edited by Willem A. VanGemeren, et al. Cumbria: Paternoster Press, 1997, 779–81.

Carpenter, Eugene. "עדה." *NIDOTTE*. Vol. 3. Edited by Willem A. VanGemeren et al. Cumbria: Paternoster Press, 326–8.

______. "נרע." *NIDOTTE*. Vol. 1. Edited by Willem A. VanGemeren, et al. Cumbria: Paternoster Press, 1997, 895–6.

Carr, David M. *An Introduction to the Old Testament: Sacred Texts and Imperial Contexts of the Hebrew Bible*. West Sussex, UK: Wiley-Blackwell, 2010.

Casperson, Lee W. "Sabbatical, Jubilee, and the Temple of Solomon." *VT* 53/3 (2003): 283–96.

Ceresko, Anthony R. *Introduction to Old Testament Wisdom: A Spirituality for Liberation*. Mumbai: St Paul Press, 2000.

______. *The Old Testament: A Liberation Perspective*. Mumbai: St Paul Press, 1992.

Chang, Impongsoted. *LilangkhalaKhun: The Chang Naga Women Headgear*. Dimapur, Nagaland: Impongsoted Chang, 2014.

Charpin, Dominique. *Writing, Law, and Kingship in Old Babylonian Mesopotamia*. Trans. Jane Marie Todd. Chicago: University Of Chicago Press, 2010.

Chavalas, Mark W. and K. Lawson Younger (Jr), eds. *Mesopotamia and the Bible: Comparative Explorations*. JSOTSup. Series 341. New York: T & T Clark International, 2003.

Chianeque, Luciano C. and Samuel Ngewa. "Deuteronomy." *Africa Bible Commentary*. Edited by Tokunboh Adeyamo et al. Nairobi, Kenya: WordAlive Publishers Zondervan, 2006, 208–54.

Childs, Brevard Springs. *Biblical Theology of the Old and New Testaments: Theological Reflection on the Christian Bible*. Minneapolis: Augsburg Fortress; SCM Press, 1992.

Claassens, Juliana. "'Give us a Portion Among our Father's Brothers': The Daughters of Zelophehad, Land, and the Quest for Human Dignity." *JSOT* 37/3 (March 2013): 319–37.

Clines, David J. A. et al. eds. "ארץ." *The Dictionary of Classical Hebrew*. Vol. 1,(a). Sheffield: Sheffield Academic Press, 1993, 384–97.

______. "ארמא." *The Dictionary of Classical Hebrew*. Vol. 1,(a). Sheffield: Sheffield Academic Press, 1993, 130–2.

______. "עמד." *The Dictionary of Classical Hebrew*. Vol. 1,(a). Sheffield: Sheffield Academic Press, 1993, 463–75.

______. "*Job 1–20*." *WBC*. Vol. 17. Waco, Texas: Word Books Publishers, 1989.

Cogan, Mordechai, and Tadmor. *2 Kings: A New Translation with Introduction and Commentary*. Vol. 2. AB. USA: Doubleday & Company, INC., 1988.

Collins, Billie Jean. *The Hittites and Their World*. Edited by Andrew G. Vaughn. Archaeology and Biblical Studies No. 7. Atlanta: SBL, 2007.

Collins, John Joseph. *The Bible after Babel: Historical Criticism in a Postmodern Age*. Grand Rapids: Michigan: William B. Eerdmans Publishing Company, 2005.

Cotula, Lorenzo. *Gender and Law: Women's Rights in Agriculture*. Rome: Food and Agriculture Organization of the United Nations, 2002.

Craigie, Peter C. *Ugarit and the Old Testament*. Grand Rapids: Eerdmans, 1983. Craigie, P. C. "The Poetry of Ugarit and Israel." *TB*, 1971: 3–31.

Creach, Jerome F D. "Joshua 13–21 and the Politics of Land Division." *Int* 66/2 (April 2012): 153–63.

Crenshaw, James L. "Job." *OBC*. Edited by John Barton and John Muddiman. Great Clarendon: Oxford University Press, 2007, 331–55.

______. *Old Testament Wisdom: An Introduction*. Rev. Sub ed. Atlanta: John Knox Press, 1998.

Day, Linda and Carolyn Presslereds. *Engaging the Bible in a Gendered World:An Introduction to Feminist Biblical Interpretation in honor of Katharine Doob Sakenfeld*. London: Westminster John Knox, 2006.

Delitzsch, F.F. *Biblical Commentary on the Book of Job*. Vol. 2. Trans. Francis Bolton. Grand Rapids, Michigan: Wm. B. Eerdmans Publishing Company, 1961.

Dell, Katharine J. *The Book of Proverbs in Social and Theological Context*. Cambridge: Cambridge University Press, 2006.

Dentan, R.C. "Book of Numbers." *The Interpreter's Dictionary of the Bible: Illustrated Encyclopedia Identifying and Explaining all Proper names and Significant terms*, (K–P). Edited by George Arthur Buttrick et al. Nashville: Abingdon Press, 1962, 567–71.

Derby, Josiah. "The Daughters of Zelophehad Revisited." *JBQ* 25/3, September 1997, 169–71.

deSilva, David A. "Rhetorical Criticism." *The Oxford Encyclopedia of Biblical Interpretation*. Vol. 2. Edited by Steven L. Mckenzie et.al. New York: Oxford University Press, 2013, 273–83.

Dever, William G. *Who were the Early Israelites and where did they come from*. Grand Rapids: William B. Eerdmanns Publishing Company, 2000.

Diamant, Anita. *The New Jewish Wedding*. New York: Simon and Schuster, 1985.

Dietrich, Walter. "1 and 2 Kings." *OBC*. Edited by John Barton and John Muddiman. Great Clarendon: Oxford University Press, 2007, 232–66.

______. *The Early Monarchy in Israel: The Tenth Century B.C.E.* Translated by Joachim Vette. Vol. 3. Biblical Encyclopaedia. Atlanta: SBL, 2007.

Diffey, Daniel S. "The Royal Promise in Genesis: The Often Underestimated Importance of Genesis 17:6, 17:16 and 35:11." *TB* 62/2 (2011): 313–9.

Diwan, Paras, and Peeyushi Diwan. *Women and Legal Protection*. New Delhi: Deep and Deep Publication, 1994.

D'Mello, Caesar, Wati Longchar, and Philip Mathew, eds. *Deconstructing Tourism Who Benefits?: A Theological Reading from the Global South*. Series 6. Taiwan: PTCA and SCEPTRE (Kolkata), 2014.

Drane, John W. *Introducing the Old Testament*. 3rd edition. Oxford: Lion Hudson, 2011.

Drinkard, Joel F. "The History and Archaeology of the Book of Joshua and the Conquest/Settlement Period." *R&E* 95/2 (1998): 171–88.

Duguid, Iain M. *Numbers: God's Presence in the Wilderness*. Edited by R. Kent Hughes. Wheaton, Illinoise: Crossway Books, 2006.

Dumbrell, William J. *The Faith of Israel: A Theological Survey of the Old Testament*. 2nd ed. Leicester: Baker Books, 2002.

Ebeling, Jennie R. *Women's Lives in Biblical Times*. Auckland, New Zealand: T&T Clark International, 2010.

Edersheim, Alfred. *Bible History: Old Testament*. New Updated Edition. Peabody, Massachusetts: Hendrickson Publishers, 1995.

Edzard, Dietz Otto. *Gudea and His Dynasty*. Vol. 3/1. Toronto: University of Toronto Press, 1997.

Eichrodt, Walther. *Theology of the Old Testament,* Vol. 1. Trans. J. A. Baker. Philadelphia: Westminster Press, 1961.

Ellens, Deborah L. *Women in the Sex Texts of Leviticus and Deuteronomy: A Comparative Conceptual Analysis*. Library of Hebrew Bible/OT Studies. New York: T & T Clark, 2008.

Ellens, J. Herold et al., eds. *God's Word for Our World*. London: T&T Clark International, 2004.

Ellickson, Robert, and Charles Thorland. "Ancient Land Law: Mesopotamia, Egypt, Israel." *C-KLR* 71/1 (October 1, 1995): 321–411.

Ellis, Maria De Jong. *Essays on the Ancient Near East: In Memory of Jacob Joel Finkelstein*. Memoirs of the Connecticut Academy of Arts and Sciences. Hamden, Connecticut: Archon Books, 1977.

Enns, Peter. "משפט." *NIDOTTE*. Vol. 2. Edited by Willem A. VanGemeren, et al. Grand Rapids: Zondervan, 1997, 1142–4.

Erickson, Paul A., and Liam D. Murphy, eds. *A History of Anthropological Theory,* 2nd edition. Canada: Broadview Press, 2003.

Evelyn and Frank Stagg. *Women in the World of Jesus*. Philadelphia: Westminster Press, 1978.

Exum, J. Cheryl. "Feminist Criticism: Whose Interests are Being Served?" *Judges and Method*, 1995, 65–90.

______. *Fragmented Women: Feminist (Sub)versions of Biblical Narratives*. Sheffield: JSOT Press; TPI, 1993.

______. *Plotted, Shot, and Painted: Cultural Representations of Biblical Women.* Sheffield: Sheffield Academic Press, 1996.

Fabry, H.–J. "מַטֶּה" in *TDOT.* Vol. 8. Editors. Botterweck, Ringgren, Fabry. Grand Rapids, Michigan: William B. Eerdmans Publishing Company, 1997; 241-9.

Fairservis (Jr), Walter A. *Mesopotamia, the Civilization that Rose out of Clay.* New York: The Macmillan Company, 1964.

Faust, Avraham. *The Archaeology of Israelite Society in Iron Age II.* Trans. Ruth Ludlum. Winona Lake, Indiana: Eisenbrauns, 2012.

Fee, Gordon D., and Robert L. Hubbard Jr, eds. *The Eerdmans Companion to the Bible.* Grand Rapids, Michigan: William B. Eerdmans Publishing Company, 2011.

Fewell, Danna Nolan et al. eds. *Reading Between Texts: Intertextuality and the Hebrew Bible.* Kentucky: Westminster/John Knox Press, 1992.

Finkelstein, Israel and Amihai Mazar. *The Quest For the Historical Israel: Debating Archaeology and the History of Early Israel.* Boston: BRILL, 2007.

Finkelstein, Israel, and Neil Asher Silberman. *The Bible Unearthed: Archaeology's New Vision of Ancient Israel and the Origin of its Sacred Texts.* New York: Simon and Schuster, 2002.

Fiorenza, Elisabeth Schussler, ed. *Searching the Scriptures: A Feminist Commentary.* Vol. 1. New York: The Crossroad Publishing Company, 1994.

______. "Rhetorical-Hermeneutical Criticism." *The Oxford Encyclopedia of the Bible and Gender Studies.* Vol. 2 (PAT–WOM). Edited by Julia M. O'Brien et al. New York: Oxford University Press, 2014, 247–55.

Fischer, Irmtraud, Mercedes Navarro Puerto, and Jorunn Okland. *Torah. The Bible and Woman: An Encyclopedia of Exegesis and Cultural History*—Hebrew Bible/Old Testament. Atlanta: SBL, 2011.

Fishbane, Michael A. *Biblical Interpretation in Ancient Israel.* New York: Clarendon Press, 1985.

Flack, Elmer E. "Flashes of New Knowledge: Recent Study and the Book of Numbers." *Interpretation* 13/1 (January 1959): 3–23.

Fleishman, Joseph. "A Daughter's Demand and a Father's Compliance: The Legal Background to Achsah's Claim and Caleb's Agreement (Joshua 15:16–19; Judges 1:12-15)." *ZAW* 118/3 (2006): 354–73.

Flint, Peter W, and Andrea E. Alvarez. "The Preliminary edition of the first Numbers Scroll from Nahal Hever." *BBR* 9 (1999): 137–43.

Fontaine, Carole. *Smooth Words: Women, Proverbs and Performance in Biblical Wisdom* JSOTSup Series356. New York: Sheffield Academic Press, 2002.

Fretheim, Terence E. "Numbers." *OBC* . Edited by John Barton and John Muddiman. Great Clarendon: Oxford University Press, 2001, 110–34.

Frymer-Kensky, Tikva. *Reading the Women of the Bible: A New Interpretation of their Stories*. New York: Schocken, 2004.

______. *In the Wake of the Goddesses: Women, Culture, and the Biblical Transformation of Pagan Myth*. New York: Free Press, 1992.

Fuchs, Esther. *Sexual Politics in the Biblical Narrative: Reading the Hebrew Bible as a Woman*. Sheffield: Sheffield Academic Press, 2000.

______. "The Literary Characterization of Mothers and Sexual Politics in the Hebrew Bible." *Semeia* 46, 1989: 151–66.

Galpaz-Feller, Pnina. "The Widow in the Bible and in Ancient Egypt." *ZAW* 120/2 (2008): 231–53.

Gane, R.E., Milgrom, J. "קָרַב." *TDOT*. Vol. XIII. Edite by G. Johannes Botterweck, Helmer Ringgren, and Heinz–Josef Fabry. Trans. David E. Green. Grand Rapids: William B. Eerdmans Publishing Company, 2004, 134–48.

Geller, Markham J. "New Sources for the Origins of the Rabbinic Ketubah." *HUCA* 49 (January 1, 1978): 227–45.

George, Alexi E. "Leviticus." *South Asia Bible Commentary: A One-Volume Commentary on the Whole Bible*. Edited by Brian Wintle et al. Rajasthan, India: Open Door Publications, 2015, 135–70.

Gevaryahu, Gilad J. "The Root גרע in the Bible: The Case of the Daughters of Zelophehad and beyond." *JBQ* 41/2 (April 1, 2013): 107–12.

Goddard, Burton L. "Law." *New International Bible Dictionary*. Edited by J. D. Douglas et at. Grand Rapids, Michigan: Zondervan Publishing House, 1987, 583–7.

Goh, Samuel T S. "Ruth as a Superior Woman of חיל?: A Comparison between Ruth and the 'Capable' Woman in Proverbs 31:10–31." *JSOT* 38/4 (June 2014): 487–500.

Goldingay, John. *Old Testament Theology. Israel's Faith*. Vol. 2. Downers Grove, Illinois: InterVarsity; Paternoster, 2006.

______.*Old Testament Theology: Israel's Life* Vol. 3. Downers Grove: IVP Academic, 2009.

Gordon, Cyrus Herzl. "Biblical Customs and the Nuzu Tablets." *BA* 3/1 (February 1940): 1–12.

Gottwald, Norman K. "Sociology: Ancient Israel." *The ABD,* (Si–Z). Vol. 6. Edited by David Noel Freedman et al. New York: Doubleday, 1992, 79–89.

______. *The Tribes of Yahweh: A Sociology of the Religion of Liberated Israel, 1250–1050 B.C.E.* Maryknoll: Orbis Books, 1981.

Gottwald, Norman K., and Richard A. Horsley, eds. *The Bible and Liberation: Political and Social Hermeneutics*. Rev Sub edition. Maryknoll, New York: Orbis Books, 1993.

Gowan, Donald E. "Wealth and Poverty in the Old Testament: The Case of the Widow, the Orphan, and the Sojourner." *Int* 41/4. (October 1987): 341–53.

Graves-Brown, Carolyn. *Dancing for Hathor: Women in Ancient Egypt*. London: Continuum, 2010.

Gray, John. *1 and 2 Kings: A Commentary*. 2nd ed. Philadelphia: Westminster Press, 1971.

______. *Joshua, Judges, Ruth*. New Century Bible Commentary. Grand Rapids: Eerdmans Publishing Company, 1986.

Green, Ronald M. "The Korah Episode: A Rationalistic Reappraisal of Rabbinic Anti-Rationalism." *ASCE*, (1981): 97–120.

Greenberg, Blu. "Marriage in the Jewish Tradition." *JES* 22/1 (1985): 3–20.

Greengus, Samuel. "Sisterhood Adoption at Nuzi and the 'Wife-Sister' in Genesis." *HUCA* 46 (1975): 5–31.

Greifenhagen, F. V. *Egypt on the Pentateuch's Ideological Map: Constructing Biblical Israel's Identity*. JSOT. London: Sheffield Academic Press, 2002.

Grisanti, Michael A. "שׂדה." *NIDOTTE*. Vol. 3. Edited by Willem A. VanGemeren et al. Cumbria: Paternoster Press, 1997, 1217–9.

______. "נתן." *NIDOTTE*. Vol. 3. Edited by Willem A. VanGemeren et al. Cumbria: Paternoster Publishing, 1997, 205–11.

Grossman, Yonatan. "Divine Command and Human Initiative: A Literary View on Numbers 25–31." *BibInt* 15/1 (2007): 54–79.

Gunkel, Hermann, William R. Scott, and John J. Scullion. *The Stories of Genesis*. Trans. John J. Scullion. Vallejo: D & F Scott Publication Inclusive, 1994.

Habel, Norman C. *The Book of Job: A Commentary*. Old Testament Library. Philadelphia: The Westminster Press, 1985.

______. *The Land Is Mine: Six Biblical Land Ideologies*. Minneapolis: Fortress Press, 1995.

Hackett, Jo Ann. "Violence and Women's Lives in the Book of Judges." *Int* 58/4, (October 2004): 356–64.

Hallo, William W., and K Lawson Younger Jr. *The Context of Scripture*. Vol. 1, *Canonical Compositions from the Biblical World*. Leiden: E J Brill, 1997.

Hamilton, Victor P. "Marriage." *ABD*.Vol. 4 K–N. Edited by David Noel Freedman et al. New York, Doubleday: AB, 1992,559–69.

Harland, Philip A. "Congregation." *NIDP* (A–C) Vol. 1. Edited by Katharine Doob Sakenfeld et al. Nashville: Abingdon Press, 2006, 717–9.

Harrelson, W.J. "Law in the Old Testament." *The Interpreter's Dictionary of the Bible: Illustrated Encyclopedia Identifying and Explaining all Proper names and Significant Terms*, (K–P). Vol. 4. Edited by George Arthur Buttrick et al. Nashville: Abingdon Press, 1962, 77–89.

Harris, Gregory H. "Did God Fulfill Every Good Promise?: Toward a Biblical Understanding of Joshua 21:43–45 Part 2." *The MSJ* 24/1 (2013): 69–96.

Harris, R. Laird. "The Book of Job and its Doctrine of God." *Presbyterion* 7/1–2 (March 1, 1981): 5–33.

Harris, Tim et al. eds. *Ancient Egypt and the Near East: An Illustrated History*. New York: Marshall Cavendish Reference, 2011.

Harrison, R.K. *Introduction to the Old Testament*. Grand Rapids: William B. Eerdmans Publishing Company, 1969.

______. *Old Testament Times*. Michigan: William B. Eerdmans Publishing Company, 1974. Hartley, John E. "זמם."*NIDOTTE*. Vol. 1.Edited by Willem A. VanGemeren, et al. Cumbria: Paternoster Press, 1997, 1112–4.

______. "Leviticus." *WBC*. Vol. 4. Edited by David A. Hubbard, et al. Dallas: Word Books Publishers, 1992.

______. *The Book of Job. New International Commentary on the Old Testament.* Edited by R.K. Harrison et al. Grand Rapids: Williams B. Eerdmans Publishing Company, 1988.

Hauser, Alan J., David J. A. Clines, and David M. Gunn, eds. *Art and Meaning: Rhetoric in Biblical Literature*. 1 edition. JSOTSup Series 19. Sheffield: JSOT Press, 1982.

Havea, Jione. *Elusions of Control: Biblical Law on the Words of Women*. Semeia Studies. Atlanta: SBL, 2003.

Hawk L. Daniel. "Allotment of Land." *NIDP* (A–C) Vol. 1. Edited by Katharine Doob Sakenfeld et at. Nashville: Abingdon Press, 2006, 103–105.

Heinemann, Joseph, and Shmuel Werses. *Studies in Hebrew Narrative Art throughout the Ages*. Scripta Hierosolymitana. Jerusalem: Magnes Press, 1978.

Hill, Andrew E., and John H. Walton. *A Survey of the Old Testament*. 2 nd ed. Grand Rapids, Michigan: Zondervan, 2000.

Hnuni, R.L. *Vision for Women in India: Perspectives from the Bible, Church and Society*. Bangalore: Asian Trading Corporation, 2009.

Holter, Knut, and Louis C. Jonker, eds. *Global Hermeneutics? Reflections and Consequences*. International Voices in Biblical Studies. Atlanta: SBL, 2010.

Hubbard (Jr), Robert L.*The Book of Ruth: The New International Commentary on the Old Testament*. Edited by R.K. Harrison et al. Michigan: William B. Eerdmans Publishing Company, 1988.

I., Cornelius. "xa." *NIDOTTE*. Vol. 1. Edited by Willem A. VanGemeren, et al. Cumbria: Paternoster Press, 1997, 345–9.

Ilan, Tal. *Jewish Women in Greco-Roman Palestine: An Inquiry into Image and Status*. Massachusetts: Hendrickson Publishers, 1996.

Imchen, Narola. "Women in the History of Christianity." Jorhat, Assam: Tribal Development and Communication Centre, 2014.

Imsong, Mar. *God-Land-People: An Ethnic Naga Identity*. Dimapur: Heritage Publishing house, 2011.

Jackson, Bernard S. *Studies in the Semiotics of Biblical Law*. Sheffield: Sheffield University Press, 2000.

Jagersma, Abraham Hendrik. *A Descriptive Grammar of Sumerian*. Germany: LOT, 2010.Jacobson, Diane. "Redefining Family in the Book of Ruth." *W&W* 33/1 (Winter 2013): 5–11.

Jacobsen, Thorkild. *The Treasures of Darkness: A History of Mesopotamian Religion*. New Haven: Yale University Press, 1976.

Jamir, Imchen M. "Role of the Ao Women in Church and Society." *IJT* 37 (1995): 45–57.

Janzen, W. "Land." *ABD*.Vol. 4. Edited by David Noel Freedman et al.New York: Doubleday, 1992, 143–154.

Johns, C. H. W. *Babylonian and Assyrian Laws, Contracts and Letter*. Edinburgh: T. and T. Clark, 1904.

Joy, C.I. David and P. Mohan Larbeer (eds). *Journeys into the Deep: Hermeneutical Pattern of M.M. Thomas*. Bangalore: BTESSC, 2016: 53–73.

Kaiser (Jr), Walter C. "Exodus." *The Expositor's Bible Commentary*. Abr. edition:Old Testament.Vol. 1. Edited by Kenneth L. Barker, and John R. Kohlenberger III, Grand Rapids, Michigan: Zondervan, 1994, 64–125.

______. *Toward an Old Testament Theology*. Grand Rapids: Zondervan Publishing House, 1991.

Kaufman, Michael. *The Woman in Jewish Law and Tradition*. New Jersey: Jason Aronson Inc., 1993.

Khala, Khatoli. *Women and Agriculture in Nagaland: A Gender Study of Sumi Customary Law and Custom*. Kohima: N.V. Press, 2012.

Kilchor, Benjamin. "Levirate Marriage in Deuteronomy 25:5–10 and its Precursors in Leviticus and Numbers: A Test Case for the Relationship between P/H and D." *CBQ* 77/3 (July 2015): 429–40.

Killebrew, Ann E. *Biblical Peoples and Ethnicity: An Archaeological Study of Egyptians, Canaanites, Philistines, and Early Israel*. Atlanta: SBL, 2005.

King, Philip J., and Lawrence E. Stager. *Life in Biblical Israel*. Library of Ancient Israel. Louisville: Westminster John Knox, 2002.

Kirk-Duggan, Cheryl A. and Tina Pippin, eds. *Mother Goose, Mother Jones, Mommie Dearest: Biblical Mothers and Their Children*. Atlanta: SBL, 2009.

Kislev, Itamar. "Numbers 36:1–12: Innovation and Interpretation." *ZAW* 122/2 (January 1, 2010): 249–59.

Knauth, R.J.D. "Israelite." *DOTP*. Edited by Desmond Alexander, and David W. Baker. Illinois: IVP Academic, 2003, 452–8.

Koehler, L., and Walter Baumgartner. *The Hebrew and Aramaic Lexicon of the Old Testament*. Vol. 4. Leiden: Brill Academic Publication, 1999.

Konkel, A.H. "אחז." *NIDOTTE*. Vol 1. Edited by Willem A. VanGemeren, et al. Cumbria: Paternoster Press, 1997, 354–8.

Koopmans, William T. "אחזה."*NIDOTTE* . Vol. 1. Edited by Willem A. VanGemeren, et al. Cumbria: Paternoster Press, 1997, 358–60.

Kuhlewein, J. "קרב."*Theological Lexicon of the Old Testament*. Vol. 3. Edited by Ernst Jenni, and Claus Westermann. Trans. Mark E. Biddle. Peabody, Massachusset: Hendrickson Publishers, 1997, 1164–1169.

Kugler, Robert, and Patrick Hartin. *An Introduction to the Bible*. Grand Rapids: William B. Eerdmans Publishing Company, 2009.

Kumar, B.B. *Society and Culture in a Corner of Nagaland*. Meerut: Pragati Prakashan, 1998.

LaCoque, Andre. *Ruth: A Continental Commentary* Trans. K.C. Hanson. Minneapolis: Fortress Press, 2004.

Lambdin, Thomas O. "Egyptian Loan Words in the Old Testament." *JAOS* 73/3 (July–September, 1953): 145–55.

Lang, Bernhard. "Women's Work, Household and Property in two Mediterranean Societies: A Comparative Essay on Proverbs Xxxi 10–31." *VT* 54/2. 2004: 188–207.

Lee, Kyung Sook. "1 and 2 Kings,"*Global Bible Commentary*. Edited by Daniel Patte et al. Nashville: Abingdon Press, 2004, 105–18.

Leeb, Carolyn S. *Away from the Father's House: The Social Location of Na'ar and Na'arah in Ancient Israel*. Sheffield: Sheffield Academic Press Limited, 2000.

Leeuwen Corneluis Van. "אלמנה." *NIDOTTE*.Vol. 1. Edited by Willem A. VanGemeren, et al. Cumbria: Paternoster Press, 1997, 413–5.

Leggett, Donald A. *Levirate and Goel Institutions in the Old Testament with Special Attention to the Book of Ruth*. Cherry Hill, New Jersey: Mack, 1974.

Lemche, Niels Peter. *Biblical Studies and the Failure of History: Changing Perspectives 3*. Edited by Thomas L. Thompson. Copenhagen International Seminar. Sheffield, England: Equinox Publishing Limited, 2013.

LeMon, Joel M, and Kent Richards, eds. *Method Matters: Essays on the Interpretation of the Hebrew Bible in Honor of David L. Petersen*. Atlanta: SBL, 2009.

Leuchter, Mark. "The Ambiguous Details in the Blasphemer Narrative: Sources and Redaction in Leviticus 24:10–23." *JBL* 130/3 (September 2011): 431–50.

Leveen, Adriane. *Memory and Tradition in the Book of Numbers*. Cambridge: Cambridge University Press, 2008.

Levine, Baruch A. *Numbers 1–20: A New Translation with Introduction and Commentary.* Vol. 4A. New York: AB Doubleday, 1993.

______. *Numbers 21–36: A New Translation with Introduction and Commentary.* AB. New York: Doubleday, 2000.

Levy, D., J. Milgrom,"עֵדָה." *TDOT.*Vol. X. Edited by G. Johannes Botterweck, et al. Trans. D.W. Stott. Grand Rapids, Michigan: William B. Eerdmans Publishing Company, 2006, 468–81.

Liedke, G."חקק." *Theological Lexicon of the Old Testament.*Vol. 2. Edited by Ernst Jenni and Claus Westermann. Trans. Mark E. Briddle. Peabody, Massachusetts: Hendrickson Publishers, 1997, 468–72.

Lipinski, E. "נָתַן." *Theological Dictionary* vol. X, eds. Botterweck et al. Trans. D.W. Stott, 90–1.

Litke, John D. "The Daughters of Zelophehad." *CTM* 29/3 (June 2002): 207–18.

Livingston, George Herbert. *The Pentateuch in Its Cultural Environment.* Grand Rapids: Baker Book House, 1974.

Long, Burke O. "Framing Repetitions in Biblical Historiography." *JBL* 106 (1987): 385–7.

Long, Gary Alan."אהל." *NIDOTTE.* Vol. 1. Edited by Willem A. VanGemeren, et al. Cumbria: Paternoster Press, 1997, 300–2.

Longchar, A.Wati, and Yangkahao Vashum, eds. *The Tribal World view and Ecology.* Tribal Studies. Jorhat: *TSC*, 1998.

Longkumer, Limatula. *Women in Theological Education: Pedagogical Issues.* Bangalore: BTESSC, 2012.

Longkumer, Limatula, and Talijungla Longkumer, eds. *Side by Side: Naga Women Doing Theology in Search of Justice and Partnership.* Kolkata: CCA–EGY Unit & Naga Women Theological Forum, 2013.

Lopez, Garcia. "תורה." *TDOT.*Vol. XV. Edited by G. Johannes Botterweck, Helmer Ringgren, and Heinz-Josef Fabry. Trans. David E. Green. Grand Rapids, Michigan: William B. Eerdmans Publishing Company, 2006, 609–46.

Lubitch, Rivkah. *Creative Feminist Midrash.* Women in Judaism, No. 11. Ramat Gan: Bar-Ilan University, 2000.

Mace, David R. *Hebrew Marriage: A Sociological Study.* New York: Philosophical Library, 1953.

Maidman, Maynard Paul. *Nuzi Texts and their uses as Historical Evidence.* Atlanta: SBL, 2010.

Manohar, Christina ed. *Women's Issues and Reflections.* Delhi: ISPCK, 2012.

Manser, Martin H. *Critical Companion to the Bible: A Literary Reference.* New York: Facts on File, 2009.

Marlow, Hilary. "Law and the Ruining of the Land: Deuteronomy and Jeremiah in Dialogue." *PT* 14/5 (2013): 650–60.

Marsh, John. "Numbers: Introduction." *The Interpreter's Bible Leviticus-1&2 Samuel.* Edited by George Arthur Buttrick et al. Vol. 11. New York: Abingdon Press, 1953, 135–308.

Marshall, J.W. "Decalogue." *DOTP*. Edited by T. Desmond Alexander and David W. Baker, 2003, 171–82.

Marsman, Hennie J. *Women in Ugarit and Israel: Their Social and Religious Position in the Context of the Ancient Near East.* Boston: BRILL, 2003.

Martens, Elmer A."עמר." *NIDOTTE.* Vol. 3. Edited by Willem A. VanGemeren et al. Cumbria: Paternoster Press, 1997, 432–4.

Matthews, Victor H. "Family Relationship." *DOTP*. Edited by T. Desmond Alexander, and David W. Baker. Illinois: InterVarsity Press, 2003, 291–9.

______. *Manners and Customs in the Bible: An Illustrated Guide to Daily Life in Bible Times*. Peabody, Mass: Hendrickson, 2006.

______. *Studying the Ancient Israelite: A Guide to Source and Method.* Michigan: Baker Academic, 2007.

Matthews, Victor H., Bernard M. Levinson, and Tikva Simone Frymer-Kensky, eds. *Gender and Law in the Hebrew Bible and the Ancient Near East.* New York: T&T Clark International, 1998.

Matthews, Victor H., Don C. Benjamin, and Claudia Camp, eds. *Honor and Shame in the World of the Bible.* SEMEIA 68. Atlanta: Scholars Press, 1996.

Matthews, Victor H, and James C. Moyer. *The Old Testament: Text and Context.* Grand Rapids, Michigan: Baker Academic, 2012.

McConville, J. Gordon. *Law and Theology in Deuteronomy*. Sheffield: JSOT Press, 1984.

McDonald, Burton. *East of the Jordan: Territories and Sites of the Hebrew Scriptures.* USA: American Schools of Oriental Research, 2000.

McKeown, J. "Land, Fertility, Famine." *DOTP*. Edited by T. Desmond Alexander, and David W. Baker. Illinois: InterVarsity Press, 2003, 487–91.

Mendelsohn, Isaac. "The Family in the Ancient Near East." *BA* 11/2 (May 1, 1948): 24–40.

Mendenhall, George E. "Hebrew Conquest of Palestine." *BA* 25/2, (September 1962): 66–87.

Menezes, Rui De. *The Cultural Context of the Old Testament.* Bangalore: PTI, 2005.

Merrill, Eugene H. *Everlasting Dominion: A Theology of the Old Testament.* Tennessee: B&H Publishing Group, 2006.

Merry, Sally Engle. "Gender Justice and CEDAW: The Convention on the Elimination of All Forms of Discrimination against Women." *Hawwa* 9/1–2 (2011): 49–75.

Meyers, Carol L. *Discovering Eve: Ancient Israelite Women in Context*. New York: Oxford University Press, 1988.

______. *Rediscovering Eve: Ancient Israelite Women in Context*. New York: Oxford University Press, 2013.

______. "Anthropology: Old Testament Cultural." *NIDP* (A–C) Vol. 1. Edited by Katharine Doob Sakenfeld et.at. Nashville: Abingdon Press, December 2006, 170–1.

______. "Everyday Life: Women in the Period of the Hebrew Bible." *WBC*. Expanded edition with Apocrypha. Edited by Carol A. Newsom, and Sharon H. Ringe. Louisville: Westminster John Knox Press, 1998, 251–9.

______. "The Roots of Restriction: Women in Early Israel." *BA* 41/3 (September 1, 1978): 91–103.

______. "Was Ancient Israel a Patriarchal Society?" *JBL* 133/1 (2014): 8–27.

______. "Having their Space and Eating there too: Bread Production and Female Power in Ancient Israelite Households." *Nashim: JJWS & GI*, no. 5 (October 1, 2002): 14–44.

Meyers, Carol L. Toni Craven, and Ross Shepard Kraemer, eds. *Women in Scripture: A Dictionary of Named and Unnamed Women in the Hebrew Bible, the Apocryphal/Deuterocanonical Books, and the New Testament*. Michigan: William. B. Eerdmans Publishing Company, 2001.

Milgrom, Jacob. *Leviticus 1–16: A New Translation with Introduction and Commentary*. Vol. 3. AB. New York: Doubleday, 1992.

______. *Leviticus 17–22: A New Translation with Introduction and Commentary*. Vol. 3A. AB. New Delhi: Doubleday, 2000.

______. *Leviticus 23–27: A New Translation with Introduction and Commentary*. Vol. 3 AB. New Haven: Yale University Press, 2001.

Millard, Alan. "חקה." *NIDOTTE*. Vol. 2. Edited by Willem A. VanGemeren, et al. Grand Rapids: Zondervan, 1997, 251–3.

______. "The Ostracon from the Days of David Found at Khirbet Qeiyafa." *TB* 62/1 (2011): 1–13.

Miller, J. Maxwell, and John H. Hayes. *A History of Ancient Israel and Judah*. 2nd ed. Louisville: Westminster John Knox Press, 2006.

Miller, Patrick D., Paul D. Hanson, and S. Dean McBride, eds. *Ancient Israelite Religion: Essays in Honor of Frank Moore Cross*. Philadelphia: Fortress Press, 1987.

Morrison, Martha A. "Nuzi." *ABD*.Vol. 4. Edited by David Noel Freedman et al.New York: Doubleday, 1992, 1156–62.

______. "A Continuing Adventure: Cyrus Gordon and Mesopotamia." *BA*, 59/1 (March 1, 1996): 31–5.

Mosca, Paul G. "Who Seduced Whom: A Note on Joshua 15:18; Judges 1:14." *CBQ* 46/1, (January 1984): 18–22.

Muilenburg, James. "Form Criticism and Beyond." *JBL* 88/1 (March 1969): 1–18.

Murphy, Roland E., and O. Carm. *Wisdom Literature: Job, Proverbs, Ruth, Canticles, Ecclesiastes, Esther*. Grand Rapids, Michigan: William B. Eerdmans Publishing Company, 1981.

Nakhai, Beth Alpert. "Daily Life in the Ancient Near East: New Thoughts on an Old Topic." *RSR* 31/3–4 (July 2005): 147–53.

Newsom, Carol A. *The Book of Job a Contest of Moral Imaginations*. Oxford: Oxford University Press, 2009.

Niehr, H. "ayfin"." *TDOT*. Vol. X. Edited by G. Johannes Botterweck, and Helmer Ringgren. Trans. Douglas W. Stott, Heinz-Josef. Grand Rapids: William B. Eerdmans Publishing Company, 1999, 44–53.

Nixon, R.E. "Inheritance." *New Bible Dictionary* 3rd edition. Edited by I. Howard Marshall, et al. Secunderabad: OM-Authentic Books, 2007, 505–6.

Noonan, Benjamin J. "Zion's Foundation: The Meaning of !hb in Isaiah 28:16." *ZAW* 125/2 (2013): 314–9.

Noordtzij, A. "Numbers." *Bible Students Commentary*. Grand Rapids, Michigan: Zondervan Publishing House, 1983.

Noth, Martin. *Numbers*. Old Testament Library. Translated by James D. Martin. London: SCM Press, 1968.

______.*A History of Pentateuchal Traditions*. Translated by Bernhard W. Anderson. Eaglewood Cliffs, New Jersey: Prenice Hall, 1972.

O'Callaghan, Roger T. "Historical Parallels to Partriarchal Social Custom." *CBQ* 6/4 (October 1944): 391–405.

Ollenburger, Ben C., Elmer A. Martens, and Gerhard F. Hasel, eds. *The Flowering of Old Testament Theology: A Reader in the Twentieth Century Old Testament Theology, 1930-1990*. Indiana: Eisenbrauns, 1992.

Olson, Dennis T. *The Death of the Old and the Birth of the New: The Framework of the Book of Numbers and the Pentateuch*. Brown Judaic Studies. Chicago, California: Scholars Press, 1985.

______. "The Book of Numbers." *DOTP*. Edited by Desmond Alexander and David W. Baker. Illinois: InterVarsity Press, 2003, 611–8.

Ottosson. "ארץ." *TDOT*.Vol. 1. Trans. John T. Willis. Edited by G. Johannes Botterweck, and Helmer Ringgren. Grand Rapids, Michigan: William B. Eerdmans Publishing Company, 1977, 388–405.

Otwell, John H. *And Sarah Laughed: The Status of Women in the Old Testament.* Westminster Press, 1977.

Pahrii, Z.K. "Naga Women Vegetable Vendors in Nagaland." *Sandeshbharika: Women and Environment.* (2015): 21–5.

Patrick, Dale. "Casuistic Law Governing Primary Rights and Duties." *JBL* 92/2 (1973): 180–4.

Peacore, Linda, "Feminist Theologies." *Global Dictionary of Theology: A Resource for the Worldwide Church.* Eds. William A. Dyrness, et al. Downers Grove: InterVarsity Press, 2008, 317–22.

Pentiuc, E.j. "Judges." *DOTP*. Edited by T. Desmond Alexander and David W. Baker. Illinois: InterVarsity Press, 2003, 484–6.

Perdue, Leo G., et al. *Families in Ancient Israel.* Kentucky: Westminster John Knox Press, 1997.

______. *Reconstructing Old Testament Theology: After the Collapse of History.* Minneapolis: Augsburg Fortress Press, 2005.

______., ed. *The Blackwell Companion to the Hebrew Bible.* Oxford: Blackwell Publishers Limited, 2001.

______. *The Sword and the Stylus: An Introduction to Wisdom in the Age of Empires.* Grand Rapids, Michigan: Eerdmans, 2008.

Pestman, P. W. *Marriage and Matrimonial Property in Ancient Egypt: A Contribution to Establishing the Legal Position of the Woman.* Leiden: E. J. Brill, 1961.

Phillips, Anthony. *Essays on Biblical Law.* London: T & T Clark International, 2004.

Pilch, John J., and Bruce J. Malina, eds. *Handbook of Biblical Social Values.* Peabody, Mass: Hendrickson Publishers, 2000.

Pitkanen, Pekka. "Ethnicity, Assimilation and the Israelite Settlement." *TB* 55/2 (2004): 161–82.

Plate, S Brent, and Edna M. Rodriguez Mangual. "The Gift That Stops Giving: Heline Cixous's 'Gift' and the Shunammite Woman." *BibInt* 7/2. (April 1999): 113–2.

Plaskow, Judith. *Standing Again at Sinai: Judaism from a Feminist Perspective.* New York: HarperCollins, 1991.

Pongener, Mar. *Morung Speaks: Cultural Values and Elements for the Enrichment of Naga Christian Community.* Mokokchung: CTC and the TDCC, 2011.

Pradeep, Panda et al. *Property Ownership & Inheritance Rights of Women for Social Protection: The South Asia Experience.* Edited by New Delhi: International Centre for Research on Women, 2006.

Pritchard, James B, ed. *Ancient Near Eastern Texts Relating to the Old Testament.* 3rd edition with Supplement. Princeton, New Jersey: Princeton University Press, 1969.

Pulikottil, Paulson. *Transmission of Biblical Texts in Qumran: The Case of the Larger Isaiah Scroll 1QIsa*[a]. JSPSup 34. Sheffield: Sheffield Academic Press, 2001.

______. "Isaiah." *South Asia Bible Commentary: A One-Volume Commentary on the Whole Bible*. Edited by Brian Wintle et al. Rajasthan, India: Open Door Publications, 2015, 833–924.

Rad, Gerhard von. *The Problem of the Hexateuch and Other Essays*. Translated by E. W. Trueman Dicken. Edinburgh: Oliver & Boyd, 1966.

Rajkumar, Evangeline Anderson. "Practicing Gender Justice as a Faith Mandate in India." *SWC* 13/1 (January 1, 2007): 33–52.

Razu, Indukuri John Mohan. *Interweaving Methodology and Praxis: Exploring Disciplinary Options in Today's World*. Bangalore: BTESSC/SATHRI, 2007.

Reeder, Caryn A. "Wives and Daughters: Women, Sex, and Violence in Biblical Tradition." *Ex Auditu* 28 (2012): 122–41.

Reiterer, Fabry. V. "שֵׁם." *TDOT*.Vol. XV. Edited by G.Johannes Botterweck, Helmer Ringgren, and Heinz-Josef Fabry.Translated by David E. Green. Grand Rapids, Michigan: William B. Eerdmans Publishing Company, 2006, 128–76.

Reviv, Hanoch. *The Society in the Kingdoms of Israel and Judah*. Biblical Encyclopaedia Library. Jerusalem: Mosad Bialik, 1993.

Richter, Sandra L. "Environmental Law: Wisdom from the Ancients." *BBR* 24/3 (2014): 307–29.

Ringgren, Helmer. "גֹּרַע." *TDOT*.Vol. III. Edited by G.Johannes Botterweck and Helmer Ringgren.Trans. John T. Willis and Geoffrey W. Brommiley. Grand Rapids, Michigan: William B. Eerdmans Publishing Company, 2006, 66–7.

Robins, Gay. *Women in Ancient Egypt*. Cambridge: Harvard University Press, 1993.

Roland, Boer, ed. *Postcolonialism and the Hebrew Bible: The Next Step*. Atlanta: SBL, 2013.

Ron, Zvi. "The Daughters of Zelophehad." *JBQ* 25/4, December 1998, 260–2.

Rooke, Deborah W. "Patriarchy/Kyriarchy." *The Oxford Encyclopedia of the Bible and Gender Studies:* Vol. 2 (PAT–WOM). Edited by Julia M. O'Brien. Oxford: Oxford University Press, 2014, 1–9.

Ross, Allen P. "שֵׁם." *NIDOTTE*. Vol. 4. Edited by Willem A. VanGemeren et al. Cumbria: Paternoster Publishing, 1997, 147–51.

Roth, Cecil. *House of Nasi: Dona Gracia*. Philadelphia: Jewish Publication Society of America, 1947.

Roth, Martha Tobi. *Law Collections from Mesopotamia and Asia Minor*. Edited by Piotr Michalowski. 2nd ed. Vol. 6. Writings from the Ancient World, SBL. Atlanta, Georgia: Scholars Press, 1997.

Rowell, Gillian M. "Ruth." *WBC.* Expanded Edition with Apocrypha. Edited by Catherine Clark Kroeger and Mary J. Evans. Illinois: InterVarsity Press, 2002.

Roy, Aphuno Chase. *Women in Transition: Angami Naga Women from 1878 to the Present*. Kohima:ACLS, 2004.

Ruiten, Jacques van, and J. Cornelis de Vos, eds. *The Land of Israel in Bible, History, and Theology*. Vol. 124. Leiden: BRILL, 2009.

Russell, Stephen C. "The Hierarchy of Estates in Land and Naboth's Vineyard." *JSOT* 38/4 (June 2014): 453–69.

Ryken, Leland, James C. Wilhoit, and Tremper Longman III, eds. *Dictionary of Biblical Imagery. An Encyclopedic Exploration of the Images, Symbols, Motifs, Metaphors, Figures of Speech and Literary Pattern of the Bible*. Secunderabad: OM–Authentic Books, 1998.

Sadie, Yolande. "Women's Rights in the Islamic World: An Overview of Twenty-Six Countries." *JIS* No. 20 (2000): 63–98.

Sakenfeld, Katharine Doob. "Feminist Biblical Interpretation." *TT* 46/2 (July 1989): 154–68.

______. "In the Wilderness, Awaiting the Land : The Daughters of Zelophehad and Feminist Interpretation." *PSB* 9/3 (1988): 179–96.

______. "Zelophehad's Daughters," *PRS* 15/4 (Winter 1988): 37–47.

Salisbury, Joyce. *Encyclopedia of Women in the Ancient World.* California: ABC–CLIO, 2001.

Sandoval, Timothy J., and Carleen Mandolfo, eds. *Relating to the Text: Interdisciplinary and Form-Critical Insights on the Bible*. London: T&T Clark International, 2003.

Sasson, Jack M. "The Issue of *Ge'ullāh* in Ruth." *JSOT* 5, January 197:8 52–68.

Sassoon, John. *Ancient Laws and Modern Problems: The Balance Between Justice and a Legal System*. Bristol: Intellect Books, 2005.

Satterthwaite, Philip E. "The Elisha Narratives and the Coherence of 2 Kings 2–8." *TB* 49/1 (May 1998): 1–28.

Satterthwaite, Philip E., and J. Gordon McConville. *Exploring the Old Testament: A Guide to the Historical Books.* Vol. 2. Illinois: InterVarsity Press, 2007.

Sawyer, John F. A., ed. *The Blackwell Companion to the Bible and Culture*. Blackwell Companions to Religion. Oxford: Blackwell, 2006.

Saxena, Samuel Richmond. "Tribal's and Ecology: A Theological Response." *ATJ*, 4 (2014): 15–26.

Schenker, Adrian. "The Biblical Legislation on the Release of Slaves: The Road from Exodus to Leviticus." *JSOT* 78 (June 1998): 23–41.

Schmid, H.H. "ירשׁ." *Theological Lexicon of the Old Testament,* vol. 2. Edited by Ernst Jenni and Claus Westermann. Trans. Mark E. Biddle. Peabody, Massachusetts: Hendrickson Publishers, 1997, 578–81.

Schroer, Silvia, and Sophia Bietenhard, eds. *Feminist Interpretation of the Bible and the Hermeneutics of Liberation.* Vol. 374. JSOTSup Series. London: Sheffield Academic Press, 2003.

Sean P. Kealy. *The Wisdom Books of the Bible–Proverbs, Job, Ecclesiastes, Ben Sira, Wisdom of Solomon:* A Survey of the History of their Interpretation. UK: The Edwin Mellen Press, 2012.

Seebass, Horst. "'Holy' land in the Old Testament: Numbers and Joshua." *VT* 56/1 (2006): 92–104.

Selman, M.J. "Law." *DOTP.* Edited by Desmond Alexander, and David W. Baker. Illinois: IVP Academic, 2003, 497–515.

Sema, Hokishe. *Emergence of Nagaland: Socio-Economic and Political Transformation and the Future.* Delhi: Vikas Publishing House Private Limited, 1986.

Sema, Piketo. *British Policy and Administration in Nagaland: 1881–1947.* Delhi: Scholar Publishing House, 1992.

Sered, Susan Starr. *Women as Ritual Experts: The Religious Lives of Elderly Jewish Women in Jerusalem.* New York: Oxford University Press, 1992.

Shead, Andrew G. "An Old Testament Theology of the Sabbath Year and Jubilee." *RTR* 61/1 (April 2002): 19–33.

Sjoberg, Mikael. "Jephthah's Daughter as Object of Desire or Feminist Icon." *BibInt* 5/4–5 (2007): 377–94

Ska, Jean Louis. "Old and New in the Book of Numbers." *Biblica* 95/1 (January 2014): 102–16.

Shemesh, Yael. "A Gender Perspective on the Daughters of Zelophehad: Bible, Talmudic Midrash, and Modern Feminist Midrash." *BibInt* 15/1 (2007): 80–109.

Shields, Mary E. "Subverting a Man of God, Elevating a Woman: Role and Power Reversals in 2 Kings 4." *JSOT* 58, (June 1993): 59–69.

Singh, Rakesh K., and Renuka Ramanujam, eds. "Women's Link." Women, Work and Economy, *SAT* Vol. 20 (December 2014): 1–58.

Snaith, Norman Henry. "The Daughters of Zelophehad." *VT* 16/1 (January 1966): 124–7.

Snell, Daniel C., ed. *A Companion to the Ancient Near East.* Oxford: Blackwell Publishing, 2005.

Soggin, J. Alberto. *An Introduction to the History of Israel and Judah.* Translated by John Bowdon. 3rd ed. London: SCM Press, 1999.

Sprinkle, J.M. "Law." *DOTHB*. Edited by Bill T. Arnold and H. G. M. Williamson. Downers Grove: InterVarsity Press USA, 2005, 643–50.

Steinberg, Naomi. "Kinship and Gender in Genesis." *BR* 39 (1994): 46–56.

Sterring, Ankie. "The Will of the Daughters." *Feminist Companion to Exodus and Deuteronomy*. Sheffield: Sheffield Academic Press, 1994.

Stichele, Caroline Vander, and Todd Penner, eds. *Her Master's Tools?: Feminist And Postcolonial Engagements of Historical-Critical Discourse*. Atlanta: SBL, 2005.

Szlos, M. Beth. "A Portrait of Power: A Literary-Critical Study of the Depiction of the Woman in Proverbs 31:10–31." USQR 54/1–2 (2000): 97–103.

Taggar-Cohen, Ada. "Law and Family in the Book of Numbers: The Levites and the Tidennutu Documents from Nuzi." *VT* 48/1 (January 1998): 74–94.

Thomas, Heath. "Building House to House (Isaiah 5:8): Theological Reflection on Land Development and Creation Care." *BBR* 21/2 (2011): 189–212.

Thomas, M. M. *Nagas Towards A.D. 2000, and other Selected Addresses and Writings*. Madras: Centre for Research on New International Economic Order, 1992.

Thompson, J.A. *Handbook of Life in Bible Times*. Downers Grove: Inter-Varsity Press, 1986.

Thompson, Thomas L. *Early History of the Israelite People from the Written and Archaeological Sources*. New York: BRILL, 1992.

Tokunboh Adeyamo, Solomon Andria, Issiaka Coulibaly, and Tewoldemedhin Habtu, eds. *Africa Bible Commentary*. Nairobi, Kenya: WordAlive Publishers Zondervan, 2006.

Trible, Phyllis. "Depatriarchalizing in Biblical Interpretation." *JAAR* 41/1 (March 1973): 30–48.

______. *Rhetorical Criticism: Context Method and the Book of Jonah*. Minneapolis: Augsburg Fortress Press, 1994.

Ulrich, Dean R. "The Framing Function of the Narratives about Zelophehad's Daughters." *JETS* 41/4 (December 1998): 529–38.

Vaux, Roland de. *Ancient Israel: Its Life and Institutions*. Trans. John McHugh. London: Darton, Longman & Todd, 1961.

Venuh, Neivetsi. *Naga Society: Continuity and Change*. Delhi: Shirpa Publications, 2004.

Vitso, Adino. *Customary Law and Women: The Chakhesang Nagas*. New Delhi: Regency Publications, 2003.

Volschenk, G.J. "The Land: Primary Category of Faith." *HTS* 60/1 (2004): 625–38.

Wafawanaka, Robert. "Is the Biblical Perspective on Poverty that 'There shall be no Poor among You' or 'You will always have the Poor with You'?" *R&E* 111/2 (May 2014): 107–20.

Waite, Jerry. "The Census of Israelite Men after their Exodus from Egypt." *VT* 60/3 (2010): 487–9.

Wakely, Robin. "חיל." *NIDOTTE*. Vol. 2. Edited by Willem A. VanGemeren, et al. Grand Rapids: Zondervan, 1997, 116–26.

Waltke, Bruce K., and Charles Yu. *An Old Testament Theology: An Exegetical, Canonical, and Thematic Approach*. Grand Rapids, Michigan: Zondervan, 2007.

Walton, John H. *Ancient Near Eastern Thought and the Old Testament: Introducing the Conceptual World of the Hebrew Bible*. Grand Rapids: Baker Academic, 2006.

Warren, Nathanael. "Adoption-Alienation in Ezra 47:22–23 and in the Ancient Near East." *ZAW* 126/3 (2014): 421–4.

Watson, Duane F. and Alan J. Hauser. *Rhetorical Criticism of the Bible: A Comprehensive Bibliography with notes on History and Method*. Vol. 4. Leiden, New York: E. J. Brill, 1994.

Watts, James W. *Reading Law: The Rhetorical Shaping of the Pentateuch*. Sheffield: Sheffield Academic Press, 1999.

Weinfeld, Moshe. "Origin of the Apodictic Law: An Overlooked Source." *VT* 23/1 (January 1973): 63–75.

Weingreen, Jacob. "Case of the Daughters of Zelophehad." *VT* 16/4, (October 1966): 518–22.

Wenham, Gordon J. *Numbers. An Introduction and Commentary*. Tyndale Old Testament Commentaries. Leicester: Inter-Varsity Press, 1981.

______. "Law." *New Bible Dictionary*. Edited by I. Howard Marshall et al. 3rd edition. Secunderabad: OM-Authentic Books, 2007, 672–5.

West, Gerald O., ed. *Reading Other–Wise: Socilly Engaged Biblical Scholars Reading with their Local Communities*. No. 62. Atlanta: SBL, 2007.

Westbrook, Raymond. *A History of Ancient Near Eastern Law*. Handbook of Oriental Studies. Leiden: Brill, 2003.

______. *Property and the Family in Biblical Law*. JSOTSup. No. 113. Sheffield: JSOT Press, 1991.

Wiley, Tatha. "Canon and Conscience: A Feminist Perspective." *W&W* 29/4 (fall 2009): 357–66.

Wilson, Ian. *Out of the Midst of the Fire: Divine Presence in Deuteronomy*. SBL Dissertation Series 151. Edited by Michael Fox (OT). Atlanta, Georgia: Scholars Press, 1995.

Wood, Beulah, ed. *Side by Side: Gender from a Christian Perspective*. Bangalore: SAIACS Press, 2007.

Woude, A.S. Vann Der."שׁם." *Theological Lexicon of the Old Testament.* Vol. 3. Edited by Ernst Jenni and Claus Westermann. Trans. Mark E. Biddle. Peabody, Massachusetts: Hendrickson Publishers, 1997, 1348–67.

Wright, C.J.H. "Family." *ABD*. Vol. 2 D–G. Edited by David Noel Freedman et al. New York, Doubleday: Doubleday, 1992, 761–9.

______. "אב." *NIDOTTE*.Vol. 1. Edited by Willem A. VanGemeren, et al. Cumbria: Paternoster Press, 1997, 219–23.

______. "Year of Jubilee." *ABD,* Vol. 3. Edited by David Noel Freedman. et al. New York: Doubleday, 1992, 1025–30.

______. "ארץ." *NIDOTTE.* Vol.1. Edited by Willem A. VanGemeren, et al. Cumbria: Paternoster Press, 1997, 518–24.

______. "ירשׁ." *NIDOTTE*.Vol. 2. Edited by Willem A. VanGemeren, et al. Grand Rapids: Zondervan, 1997, 547–9.

______. "נחל." *NIDOTTE*.Vol. 3. Edited by Willem A. VanGemeren et al. Cumbria: Paternoster Press, 1997, 77–81.

______. *The Mission of God: Unlocking the Bible's Grand Narrative.* Downers Grove: IVP Academic, 2006.

______. *Old Testament Ethics for the People of God.* Leicester: Inter-Varsity Press, 2004.

Wright, David P. *Inventing God's Law: How the Covenant Code of the Bible used and Revised the Laws of Hammurabi.* New York: Oxford University Press, 2009.

Yanthan, Zuchamo et al., eds. *Nagas Today: Indigeneous Discourse.* New Delhi: Naga Students' Union, Delhi Publication, 2010.

Yee, Gale A. ed. *Judges and Method: New Approaches in Biblical Studies* 2nd ed. Minneapolis: Fortress Press, 2007.

Yeo, Khiok-Khng. "Cultural Hermeneutics." *NIDP*(A–C) Vol. 1. Edited by Katharine Doob Sakenfeld et al. Nashville: Abingdon Press, December 2006, 808–9.

Yoder, Christine Roy. "The Woman of Substance (אשת־חיל): A Socioeconomic Reading of Proverbs 31:10–31." *JBL* 122/3 (September 2003): 427–47.

Zakovitch, Yair. "מכרא לירא" *A Biblical Commentary for Israel,* (רות). Magnes: The Hebrew University Magnes Press, 1990.

Zehol, Lucy. *Women in Naga Society.* New Delhi: Regency Publications, 1998.

Zevit, Ziony. "Dating Ruth: Legal, Linguistic and Historical Observations." *Zeitschrift Für Die Alttestamentliche Wissenschaft* 117, no. 4 (2005): 574–600.

Online Article and others

Agarwal, Bina. *A Field of One's Own Gender and Land Rights in South Asia.* Cambridge: Cambridge University Press, 1994. https://www.google.co.in/ (5 July 2016).

Castle, Stephen. "Church of England Votes to accept Women as Bishops." *The New York Times* 14/14, http://www.nytimes.com/2014/07/15/world/ europe (14 July 2014).

Chara, Elijah. "Justice for Naga Women and the Patriarchy." *Nagaland Post* 9/15, http://www.nagalandpost.com/PostMortem/ (9th March 2015).

Jamir, M. Sashi. "The Impact of Modernization on the Nagas: Anthropological Analysis and Theological Response, 8." https://sashi2jamir.files.wordpress. com/2012/07 (15 July, 2014).

Jamir, Toshimenla. "Engendering Public Space in Naga Society: Tradition and Modernity." *Indian Folklife* 33, July 2009:http://www.indianfolklore.org/ journals/index.php/IFL/article/view/108. (11 November 2014).

Steinberg, Naomi. *Romancing the Widow: The Economic Distinctions between The almana, The issa–almana and the eset-Hammet.* 2004. In https://www. google.co.in/ Pdf.

Tuni, Sao. "Is there Gender Inequality in Nagaland." ***The Morung Express*** 10/15. http://morungexpress.com. Editorial column 10 December 2015, (14 December 2015).

Venugopal, Vasudha. "CSI appoints woman as bishop." *The Hindu* 28/13*http:// www.thehindu.com/news* (28 September 2013).

"Brief Industrial Profile of Tuensang District, Nagaland State." http://dcmsme. gov.in/dips/DIPR-Tuensang-Final.pdf (9 October 2013).

"Census 2011: Government of India."

http://www.census2011.co.in/census/state/districtlist/nagaland.html.

(9 October 2013).

"Merneptah Stele" *wikipedia.org*http://en.wikipedia.org/wiki/Merneptah_Stele (2 February 2013).

"Naknyulum; conquest of 'darkness by light.'" *Nagaland Post,* Article issued by Chang Khulei Setshang. http://www.nagalandpost.com/PostMortem (24 July2014).

"Tuensang District Map," *Maps of India.Com* http://www.mapsofindia.com/ maps/nagaland/districts/tuensang.html (30 August 2016).

"20 years since the Beijing Declaration, where do we stand?" *The Morung Express* 11/15 http://www.morungexpress.com/express_review/129283.html. (11 December 2015).

"Nagaland ranks 25th in population in India." *The Shillong Times* 11/12 http:// www.theshillongtimes.com (11 July 2012).

"NSCW Organizes Seminar on Legal Rights of Women in Wokha." *Nagaland Post*http://www.nagalandpost.com (26 February 2014).

"Women's Equal Property and Land Rights hold key to reversing toll of poverty and HIV/AIDS in Swaziland: A Human Rights Report and Proposed Legislation." https://www.law.georgetown.edu/academics/law-journals/gjil/upload/1-WomensEqualProperty.pdf.

Work force Participation Rate in Nagaland: A Female situation http://www.questjournals.org/jrhss/papers/vol3-issue5/E352837.pdf (24 December 2015).

Ao, Akala. "Land and Tribal Women: A Cry for Gender Just Society." Paper presented at the Seminar on Significance of Land and its Resources Vis-a-vis Tribal Identity. Clark Centre for Peace Research and Action, Aolijen, Mokokchung, November 13–14, 2014.

Newspaper Article

Times of India, 1June, 2016.

Thesis unpublished

Nyimangyang. "A Comparative Studies of the Feasts and Festivals of Chang Naga and Israelites." BD Thesis. Senate of Serampore College/University, 2000.

Interview

1. Ms. Achila Associate pastor, Tuensang Town Baptist Church, 17 May 2014.
2. Ms. Akhala from Bhumpak Village, 9 May 2014.
3. Mr. A. Koma, Tuensang Town, 3 May 2014.
4. Ms. Alepla, Assistant Teacher, Litim Village, 4 May 2014.
5. Ms. Ayang, Nakshou Village, 9 May 2014.
6. Mr. H. Sao, Kejok Village, 15 June 2015.
7. L. Chaba Chingmei, Assistant Teacher, 30 October 2015.
8. L. Ongmang, former Executive secretary, CBLT, 10 January 2016.
9. Mr. Limba from Noksen Town, 26 October 2015.
10. Mr. M.B. Kelap, Senior Citizen, Tuensang Village, 9 May 2014.
11. Mr. M.Y. Chusa, Tuensang Town, 11 May 2014.
12. Mr. Nokching, Tuensang Village, 24 May 2014.
13. Mr. K.N. Somba, Tuensang Village, 25 October 2015.
14. Mr. Nokchingsomba, Sipongsang Village, 25 May 2014.
15. Chenyang Senti, Helipong Village, 14 May 2014.
16. Mr. Sipong, Chingmei Village, 30 April 2014.
17. Y. Akala, Tuensang Town, 29, October 2015.
18. Ms. Yongching, Tuensang village, 10 May 2014.

19. Ms. Yimtsusangla Chang, Advocate, Tuensang District, 12 May 2014.
20. Disinherited woman from Tuensang Town (Name withheld for privacy reason), 4 June 2014.